Bobby Fischer vs. the Rest of the World

Bobby Fischer vs. the Rest of the World

BRAD DARRACH

STEIN AND DAY/*Publishers*/New York

First published in the United States of America
Copyright © 1974 by Brad Darrach
Library of Congress Catalog Card No. 73-81322
All rights reserved
Designed by David Miller
Printed in the United States of America
Stein and Day/*Publishers*/Scarborough House, Briarcliff Manor, N.Y. 10510
ISBN 0-8128-1618-8

For Suzanne

Contents

I am my acts.

—J. P. SARTRE

1

Bobby Fischer in Weird City

Bobby Fischer was struggling to get back to sleep when he heard a knock at the door. It was shortly after 10 A.M., Thursday, June 29, 1972 —three days before his match with Boris Spassky for the world chess championship. Only his lawyer and a few friends were supposed to know he was at the Yale Club in New York City, yet just now a man had phoned and asked for Mr. Fischer. Bobby hung up without a word and went back to bed. He had slept twenty of the last thirty-six hours; even so, he kept slipping deeper into exhaustion.

The match was to begin on Sunday morning. Bobby couldn't fly to Iceland on his Sabbath, which began at sundown on Friday. That left Thursday night and Saturday night. But if he flew up Saturday night he would arrive bone-tired only six hours before the game began. So it was tonight or never. But Bobby didn't want to think about that right now. He wanted to rest up.

The knock was repeated.

"Who's there?"

"Package for Mr. Fischer."

Bobby is careful about opening doors to strangers, but since a husky friend named Jackie Beers had dropped by to see him he decided to take a chance. He rolled out of bed and stumbled toward the door in his jockey shorts. Room 1003 was tiny and dingy. No TV, no air conditioning, not even AC current. "It was the worst room in the Yale Club," Bobby's lawyer, Andrew Davis, admitted later. "I didn't want Bobby to feel like lingering."

Bobby opened the door, expecting to see a Yale Club employee. Instead, a short, heavyset man in street clothes blocked the door with his foot.

"Excuse me, Mr. Fischer," he began, "but I wonder if—"

"Who are you?" Bobby asked in alarm.

The intruder said he was a British journalist and wanted an interview. A journalist! The match hadn't even begun and already the press was hounding him! Bobby ordered him to leave. The reporter insisted. Beers strode across the room and with one shove sent the reporter reeling. Bobby slammed the door and rushed to the phone. Five minutes later he got through to Davis.

"Don't leave the room," Davis told him. "Someone will come to you as quickly as possible." Later Davis said, "Bobby was scared. At a moment when he couldn't stand the slightest shock, he got a bad one."

Boris Spassky was in Reykjavik, Iceland, when the crisis broke. So were 150 newspaper, magazine and television reporters from at least thirty-two countries, all waiting for Bobby to fly up for the match. Many had arrived eight days before and were red-eyed from rolling out of bed to meet the 5 A.M. plane from New York. Not seeing Bobby walk off that DC-8 was getting to be an unpleasant habit.

Why was Bobby dragging his heels? Most reporters assumed the answer was greed. They figured that by lingering in California and New York, Bobby was hinting to Gudmundur Thorarinsson, head of the Icelandic Chess Federation, that he might not come at all if Iceland didn't fatten the kitty. Lawyer Davis was of course using the delay to do just that. Phrases like "greedy little bastard" and "spoiled brat" began to be muttered.

When Bobby didn't come and didn't come, some reporters made other assumptions. "Is it really possible," a British correspondent asked, "that this yahoo is going to stand us all up? Either he's the smartest little Sammy who ever came out of Brooklyn or he's some sort of nut. I just can't *believe* what's happening!"

Nobody could. And nobody could believe that an intellectual sport about as popular as differential calculus was making front-page headlines day after day; that people all over the world were waiting for two grown men to sit down on a solitary butt of lava in the North Atlantic and push wooden soldiers across a miniature make-believe battlefield. The pundits explained that there was more to this match than chess. It was a war in effigy between the U.S. and the USSR. It was a chance to watch Russia lose the championship for the first time in twenty-four years—in fact, the title had been held by Russian-born grandmasters for forty-one of the last forty-five years—and to watch America win it for the first time in history. It was Boris against Bobby, a handsome and easygoing Russsky against a demonic genius at the most demonic moment in his career. But what more than anything else had gripped us all were the weird personality and approximately superhuman achievements of Bobby Fischer.

In chess circles, Bobby had been a celebrity for fifteen years, ever since he won the U.S. championship at the incredible age of fourteen, but only in the last fourteen months had the nonchess-playing public become really aware of him. In May 1971 he had ridden an eight-game winning streak into the first of three prechampionship matches and defeated grandmaster Mark Taimanov of the Soviet Union, 6–0, the first shutout in fifty years of recorded grandmaster play. He repeated the shutout against a more dangerous opponent, grandmaster Bent Larsen of Denmark. Then in Buenos Aires in November 1971, Bobby gave a 6½–2½ thrashing to the Soviet Union's Tigran Petrosian, a former world champion, extending his winning streak to twenty-one games—the longest in chess history. The media decided they had better take a good look at what they had here.

What the press decided it had was a comic-strip monster. Bobby was presented as a monomaniac who was terrified of girls and Russian spies but worshiped money and Spiro Agnew, as a high school drop-out who combined the general culture of a hard-rock deejay with a genius for spatial thinking that made him quite possibly the greatest chess player of all time. The monster was in some ways a caricature of Bobby, but he made terrific copy.

Obligingly, he made terrific copy for four months before the world championship was scheduled to begin. First he refused to play Spassky where the Fédération Internationale des Echecs (F.I.D.E.) told him to play—half the match in Yugoslavia, half in Iceland. Finally the whole match was ceded to Iceland. But at that point Bobby boggled at "burying" the contest in such a "primitive" country and complained about the financial terms—even though the $125,000 prize was ten times any purse ever put up for a chess match. When the Icelanders, after a public outcry against the "arrogant Fischer," swallowed their pride and met his demands, Bobby made new demands. When the Icelanders rejected his new demands, Bobby disappeared.

On June 8, only twenty-five days before the match was scheduled to begin, Bobby took off from a resort near San Diego, where he had played in a tennis tournament for sports stars. For the next twelve days not even his lawyer knew where he was. Iceland decided to go ahead and spend up to $75,000 on a match that was not even sure to come off, but by June 23 the Icelandic Chess Federation (I.C.F.) was, as one of its officers admitted, "shitting blood."

Bobby meanwhile was living in Santa Monica with a couple he knew, sleeping late, soaking up sun, eating lots of fruit, and as usual staying up all night, a rock station garbling in his ear, to pore over chess periodicals and play through the latest grandmaster games. "He's like a kid on vacation," a friend said. "When somebody mentions the Spassky match he smiles this happy little evil smile and then covers it up, as though he had a juicy secret. I think the secret is that Bobby is *not* going to play."

"I'm absolutely certain Bobby will play," Davis insisted on Saturday, June 24, one day before Bobby was originally scheduled to arrive in Iceland. But in the next breath Davis said Bobby "probably" wouldn't fly to Iceland the next day. Instead, Bobby had asked Fred Cramer, a former president of the U.S. Chess Federation (U.S.C.F.), to hop up to Reykjavik and check out the conditions.

Monday, June 26, I called Bobby myself.

"Hi, Brad! How ya doin'?" The words were Bobby but the voice was startlingly confident. I had expected what I usually heard when Bobby picked up the phone, a faint suspicious *uuuuh?* that might mean hello or might just be electric clutter on the line. But this voice rolled out of the receiver like an orange bulging with California sunshine. I thought: "He's coming. He feels great. God help Spassky."

Bobby wanted to know everything about Reykjavik. Did I like the playing hall? What was the chess table like? How about the weather? "Sixty degrees! Wow! That's coooold! But the air's great, huh?" Then he wanted to know how Spassky looked. "Nervous," I told him, and he guffawed. "And Geller—" I intended to say something about Yefim Geller, Spassky's second.

"Geller," Bobby cut in, "is *stupid!*"

Then it happened. "Geller," we both heard the voice of a young woman (I assumed she was an operator) say in an Icelandic attempt to mimic Bobby's Brooklyn accent, "is *stupid!*"

Bobby gasped. "They're listening in on my calls!" he yelled. "I knew it! They got spies on the line!" His voice, so full a second before, jangled like an alarm clock. "That rotten little country! Call the head of the telephone company, Brad! I want that person *found and fired!*"

I called the supervisor, who said she would look into the matter. Then I called Bobby again. He was still furious. "Imagine that! Listening in on *my* phone calls! It could be the Russians, y'know? They'll do anything to find out what I'm thinking!"

As he nudged the episode into the familiar context of his long battle with the Russians, the warmth came back into his voice. Soon we were chatting away almost as happily as before. I was careful not to ask if he was coming to Iceland—I knew that question was taboo. But just before hanging up he said, "Don't call me at this number any more. I'll be leaving soon."

Anthony Saidy looks like a mad scientist in a comic book. His head is wide at the temples, dished in at the back, and covered with blue-black hair. His nose is an angry hook and his eyes, the color of black coffee, bulge and glitter. He is an M.D., a strong chess player (he once won the U.S. Open Championship) and the author of a first-rate book on chess strategy. Yet the minute he begins to talk, he reveals an anxious need to please. "Tony has a victim instinct," a grandmaster told me. "He needs to lose." Like many of Bobby's friends, Saidy can't quite manage to be himself in Bobby's company. He has hitched his wagon to a star and seems afraid he might miss the ride. To keep the friendship, he agrees with almost everything Bobby says.

Saidy is a New Yorker—he met Bobby when he was eighteen and Bobby was twelve—but was working in Los Angeles when Bobby showed up in Santa Monica. Saidy began visiting him every couple of days. As the date of the match drew near, he was appalled to see Bobby making no moves in the direction of Iceland. So on Sunday, June 25, the day Bobby was scheduled to arrive in Reykjavik, Saidy called and said casually that he would be flying east on Tuesday to see his father, and wouldn't Bobby maybe like to come along? "Lemme think it over," Bobby answered. When Saidy called back an hour later he said, "Yeah, might as well. Be nice to have company on the plane." Saidy said he had "a strange feeling that if I hadn't called, Bobby would still be there."

The tanned and vigorous young man who boarded the plane at Los Angeles would stand out in any gathering. Bobby is tall and broad-shouldered; his face is clean-cut, masculine, attractive. But on second glance this impression dislocates into a number of odd parts.

His head, for instance. That amazing brain is lodged in a small oval skull that doesn't reach very far above the ears. His low forehead makes his jaw look large, at certain angles almost Neanderthal. When he feels weak or uncertain he resembles the dopey kid Jerry Lewis used to portray. Yet there is a sense of danger about Bobby. When he is angry or confident his face is alert but unthinking, the face of a big wild animal that hunts for a living. His eyes are like a tiger's, with the same yellow-green serenity and frightening emptiness. When he laughs, his wide, full-lipped mouth opens into a happy cave filled with white teeth. Most of his facial expressions are rudimentary displays of fear, hunger, anger, pleasure, pain, suspicion, interest—all the emotions a man or animal can have without feeling close to any other man or animal. I have rarely seen him register sympathy, invitation, acknowledgment, humor, tenderness, playfulness. And never love.

Bobby wears a business suit about as naturally as a python wears a necktie. He stands six one, weighs close to 190, and a padded jacket makes his shoulders seem so wide his head looks "like a pea sitting on a ruler," somebody said. His torso is flaccid, his arms girlishly soft. But his hips and thighs are powerful and his movements vigorous. Sometimes they are comically awkward. Bobby walks twice as fast as the average hiker, but he walks the way a hen runs—and this hen fills a doorway. He comes on head forward, feet wide apart and toes turned in, shoulders lurching side to side, elbows stuck out, fingers flipping. Fastening his eyes on a point about four miles distant and slightly above everybody else's head, he charges toward it through the densest crowds.

Bobby functions like Frankenstein's creature, a man made of fragments connected by wires and animated by a monstrous will. When the will collapses or the wires cross, Bobby cannot execute the simplest acts. When he loses interest in a line of thought, his legs may simply give out, and he will shuffle off to bed like an old man. Once, when I asked him a question while he was eating, his circuits got so befuddled that he jabbed his fork into his cheek.

Bobby seems to keep only one thought in his mind at once, and a simple thought at that. He talks in simple sentences that lead him where he is going like steppingstones, and his voice is flat, monotonous, the color of asphalt—the voice of man pretending to be a machine so people won't be able to hurt him. But Bobby is too vital to play dead successfully. Energy again and again escapes in a binge of anger. Every night, all night, it escapes into chess. When he sits at the board, a big dangerous cat slips into his skin. His chest swells, his green eyes glow. All the life in his body flows and he looks wild and beautiful. Sprawled with lazy power, eyes half closed, he listens to the imaginary rustle of moving pieces as a tiger lies and listens to the murmur of moving reeds.

Bobby's nerves tightened several notches at the Los Angeles airport. But the return ticket, paid for by the U.S. Chess Federation, soothed him. At Kennedy Airport Bobby and Saidy separated, agreeing to meet the next day—Wednesday, June 28. Bobby seemed pleased when he ran into a British TV executive he had met on David Frost's program, and was offered a free ride to the Yale Club in the executive's limousine. He might have been less pleased if he had foreseen the sequel. Frost's man told somebody where Bobby was staying, and the news eventually reached that short, heavyset British reporter who pulled the plug that started Thursday down the drain.

Slips like that were what Davis feared most. To prevent them he had prepared the kind of script they used to write for "Mission: Impossible." The plan was to abduct a man for his own good and do it so sneakily that the victim wouldn't know what was happening to him. It was a job for a genie, but Davis didn't have one in his address book. So he asked Tony Saidy to keep Bobby out of trouble by taking him on a shopping trip, and rounded up two friends and a professional chauffeur to help. None of the five had ever abducted anything trickier than a cookie.

Herb Hochstetter and Morris Dubinsky turned up at the Yale Club at 8:30 Wednesday morning. They sat in Dubinsky's limousine for four and a half hours, waiting for Bobby to wake up. Hochstetter, a well-known marketing consultant and an old friend of Davis's, is a stocky, energetic man of fifty-five with a hard mouth and pale amused eyes almost concealed by folds of skin that hang from his eyebrows like worn portieres. About twelve years ago, Hochstetter hired Bobby to promote a gimcrack called the Mandarin Chess Set, and Bobby worked so earnestly on the hopeless project that Hochstetter conceived a deep respect for him. When Davis called, he scrapped a busy schedule and agreed to spend two days bear-leading Bobby around Manhattan.

Dubinsky is an ex-butcher from the Bronx and as independent as a rubber chicken. When the supermarkets took over the meat business he closed his shop and, rather than work for anybody else, sold his house and bought a taxi. Two years later he traded it in for a Cadillac limousine. Not long ago he bought six limousines, all shiny-new, and paid cash—$81,000 plus tax. "I don't owe nobody," Dubinsky told me. "That way nobody's gonna lean on Morris." At fifty-four, Dubinsky is built (as he is the first to admit) "like an ox." He stands five ten, weighs 183 and has muscles in his hair. When Dubinsky doesn't like something, he lets you hear about it—and you don't need an ear trumpet.

By one o'clock Wednesday afternoon, Hochstetter and Dubinsky were getting antsy. Saidy arrived, went upstairs, and by 2 P.M. had dug Bobby out. Though the day was pretty well shot, Bobby was in no mood to hurry. While they drove across town, he lolled on the expensive upholstery and called some friends on the radiophone. After fifty minutes at the bank, they moved down the street to the Stage Delicatessen, where Bobby had some soup, a sandwich and several glasses of fresh orange juice.

By now it was 3:30. In the next hour and a half, Bobby managed a couple of minor errands, and then it was time to head back to the Yale Club for a meeting with Davis. In theory he was getting ready to go to Iceland; in fact he moved like a man struggling out of deep sleep and knowing he wasn't going to like what he saw when he opened his eyes.

Andrew Davis is a slim man of middle height with quick dark eyes behind professorial specs, a small head penciled with careful hair and a crashing Teddy Roosevelt smile. He is forty-three and has the crinkles to prove it, but he also has a squirrely brightness and a windbag-popping sense of fun. A pipe-and-elbow-patches sort of fellow, Davis likes to think of himself, I suspect, as something between an English master at Choate, a hard-haggling garment jobber and a dwindled Disraeli. He reads widely, but his intellectual side subordinates without regret to the zestful practical man.

Davis is shrewd, precise and so ethical that friends call him St. Andrew. He shares with his father a law practice that provides a comfortable living but will never make him rich. He certainly won't get rich off Bobby. In twelve years Davis has logged hundreds of hours of work for him without charging a dime. Why not? "Traditional Jewish awe of intellect," a friend of Davis's explained. "Andy sees Bobby as a sort of holy idiot, a frail vessel into which the pure Logos has been poured. He will never abandon him."

For several weeks, Davis had been wishing he could. Bobby took

time and energy that other clients needed. But Davis hung in there
—there was nobody to take his place. Like everybody who cared about
Bobby, Davis saw black days ahead if he backed out of the match. The
media, already annoyed, would gut him. The public, denied a spectacle it was panting after, would remember him with contempt. The
chess world would write him off as a second Paul Morphy, a genius too
morbid to realize his talent. Organizers of major matches would
hesitate to sign a man who might not even show up to play.

But what worried Davis most was the potential effect of such mass
rejection on Bobby himself. "Being the best chess player in the world
is Bobby's only way of relating to the world," he once told me. "If he
doesn't play this match, we could see a serious breakdown there." He
looked me in the eye. "Maybe suicide."

Davis respected Bobby. "I think of him as a courageous person," he once said, "who happens to be physically timid. I often have
to appear weak with him so he won't be scared away."

Davis also respected Bobby's reasons for not wanting to play in
Iceland. In March, Bobby had said Iceland was too small and primitive, "a stupid place for the match." The hall was inadequate and he
was sure the problems of lighting a championship match were beyond
the skills of the local technicians. As for hotels, he said there was only
one on the island fit to live in, and he was convinced he would have to
share it with Russians and the press. "No privacy. And another
thing—there's no way for me to relax between games. The TV is dull,
the movies are three years old, there's no good restaurants hardly. Not
one tennis court on the whole island, not even a bowling alley. Things
like that might hurt my playing."

Bobby was disturbed also by Iceland's isolation and the problems
of media coverage. A few reporters might fly in for the start and finish
of the match, but the games could not be telecast to North America
and Europe—no Intelsat equipment. "And this match ought to be
televised. If it is, I predict that chess will become a major sport in the
United States practically overnight."

Isolation made financial problems too. Bobby was sure that gate
receipts would be disastrous because there just weren't enough
Icelanders to fill the seats—and who could afford to travel all the way
to Iceland and stay there for two months to watch a chess match? He
considered himself a superstar, and when it came to money he wanted
what superstars like Joe Frazier and Muhammad Ali were offered.

I.C.F. had already met two of his three conditions: a guarantee of

$78,125 to the winner and $46,875 to the loser, plus a thick slice of the film and television profits—30 per cent to Boris, 30 per cent to Bobby. But when Bobby demanded 30 per cent of the gate, I.C.F. had stonewalled. "If we give Bobby 30 per cent, we must give Boris 30 per cent," said Thorarinsson. "But if we do that, how will we raise the prize money? No, the prize money is Bobby's share of the gate."

At that point, Bobby had stonewalled too. "If I don't get the gate," he told Davis, "I don't go."

Even before discussion with I.C.F. began, Bobby had been flirting with the idea of blowing up the match. He had been suspicious of Iceland because it was Spassky's first choice as a site, and his suspicions had been aggravated when he was told that Thorarinsson had said he was "arrogant" and should forfeit the match. Brooding in his room at Grossinger's Hotel in the Catskills, where he had set up his "training camp," Bobby found enemies everywhere. He described Dr. Max Euwe, the president of F.I.D.E., as "a tool of the Russians." He said Ed Edmondson of the United States Chess Federation, who had spent two years of his life and about $50,000 of the U.S.C.F.'s money to nurse Bobby through the challenge rounds, had "betrayed" him to the Russians. And he was sure that Lothar Schmid, the German grandmaster selected by Edmondson as chief arbiter (referee) for the match, was part of the plot. By the time he left for California, Bobby had decided that the U.S. government was against him, too. Edmondson and Euwe, he figured, had been persuaded by Washington to sidetrack the match to Reykjavik, where a Fischer victory would be so effectively entombed that it would not disturb the developing *détente* between the U.S. and the Soviet Union.

By the time Bobby returned to New York from California, these speculations had overgrown his mind like vines. He was gripped by the idea that Euwe must be "punished" and Thorarinsson "destroyed." He told Davis to make sure that the deal they made would prevent the Icelanders from earning a krona on the match and if possible leave them with a loss. Even on those terms, he wasn't sure he would go. He shrugged off the money he would be giving up and seemed unconcerned that the title would lapse by default to his lifelong enemies, the Russians. As for his career, he had no fears. "Everybody knows I'm the best, so why bother to play?"

It was clear to Davis on Wednesday that these ideas still had the run of his client's head. It was also clear that reasonable discourse would hardly drive them out in a day. A Gordian stroke was called for, and a little after 6 P.M. Davis delivered it.

He walked Bobby into the Yale Club bar for a meeting with Chester Fox and Richard Stein. Fox was the almost unknown director I.C.F. had signed to make a documentary movie of the match, a thirty-seven-year-old cherub with an acute case of freckles and a halo of fuzzy orange hair. Stein was his backer, a stocky wheeler-dealer who had made millions in athletic apparel and then started a second career in the law. From what he'd heard of Bobby, he figured he was in for some heavy haggling, and that suited him just fine.

They had come, Stein announced, to offer Bobby a deal. Bobby's contract with I.C.F. guaranteed him 30 per cent of all profits from the films of the match. In addition to that, Stein offered him a percentage (Fox later said it was 12.5 per cent) of the profits of Chester Fox Inc. According to Stein, all Bobby had to do in return was go to Iceland and play chess—and maybe read some comments accompanying the film Fox intended to make of the match. Stein ran through the deal on roller skates—residuals, syndications, costs above and below the line —and skidded to a stop in front of Bobby like a performer signaling for applause.

Bobby sat twisting and mashing a paper cup. Suddenly, eyes narrow with suspicion, he said what he was thinking.

"Yeah, but how much am I gonna *make?*"

Stein blinked. "I realized then," he told me later, "that deals to Bobby were like chess to me. He hadn't understood a word I'd said."

Patiently, Stein explained that the profits of a complicated venture are hard to predict. "But I wouldn't be involved if I didn't think it would make money. And whatever it makes, you get a share."

Bobby's eyes narrowed again. "Are you gonna make more money than me?"

Stein explained to Bobby that in the American way of doing business, the people who risk the money are entitled to most of the profit. Bobby knew that, but Stein gathered that he wasn't sure that the principle applied when *he* was involved.

"Well," Stein asked finally, "have we got a deal or haven't we?"

Bobby wouldn't say yes, but he didn't say no. Turning to Fox, he said, "You better hurry up or you'll miss that plane to Iceland."

Davis almost laughed out loud. Bobby telling Fox to get on a plane to Iceland without a nailed-down deal was like Gaston at the guillotine saying, "After you, Alfonse." But if Bobby wanted Fox in Iceland, did that mean he expected to be there too? Had Stein's offer made the match seem more desirable?

Not for long. Ten minutes after they left, Bobby was bad-mouthing the Icelanders again. The Gordian stroke had missed its mark.

Robert Haydock Hallowell III goes bounding through life like a St. Bernard through a blizzard. His eyes are bright, his voice is clear, his grin is large and welcoming. He stands six feet two, weighs 250 pounds and at thirty-four has the same hard-hitting energy that made him a third-string tackle on the worst Harvard team since World War II. He is a successful executive—"director of new ventures" for the Franklin Mint—with an education in the classics and a fine salty turn of phrase. Hallowell met Bobby in 1965, when he supervised production for the Xerox Corporation of a paperback, *Bobby Fischer Teaches Chess.* He met Andrew Davis at the same time and became his friend and client.

When Hallowell showed up at the Yale Club that crucial Thursday morning, he ran head on into a crisis. The story of the Tussle in the Doorway was on the wires by 11 A.M. and in a few hours half the newsmen in New York would be there. Bobby had to be yanked out fast. But that British reporter and a photographer were patrolling the lobby like bloodhounds with a panther up a tree. Hallowell, Saidy, and Hochstetter worked up a scheme. Then Hallowell took the elevator up to 1003.

Bobby opened the door suspiciously. His face was puffy with sleep and he was wearing jockey shorts.

"Oh, hi, Bob! Come in!"

Still indignant about the attempt to break into his room, Bobby was delighted at the idea of escape. "Yeah," he said with a big toothy smile. "Good idea!" He promised to get ready, but two hours later Hallowell and Saidy found him still stumbling around in his shorts. While Bobby dawdled through his preparations like a nine-year-old on a school morning, Hallowell, Saidy and Beers sat in the tiny room feeling like sixteen clowns in a phone booth. At last, at about 2 P.M., the plan of escape was run off.

Saidy took the front elevator to the lobby. The reporter had left, but the photographer was still there. Principally for his benefit, Saidy informed Hochstetter in a loud voice, "He's not going out. Let's take off." And off they went. The photographer, smelling a rat, ran to check the freight entrance. He arrived just in time to see the back door swing open and Bobby, Hallowell and Beers walk out.

The photographer had met Bobby a few weeks before, so when Hallowell told him to buzz off, he turned to his subject with a pleading look. "Bobby, do you want me to go?"

Bobby said nothing. The photographer left, heading east on Forty-fourth Street. Bobby headed west. Suddenly reversing direction, the photographer ran ahead of Bobby and began snapping shots.

"This is what I get," Bobby told him angrily, "for what I did for you at Grossinger's!"

"I'm sorry, Bobby," the young man answered. "I've *got* to."

With that, Hallowell recalls, "Bobby wheeled around and took off in the opposite direction like a big-assed bird." He turned at the corner and ran south for two blocks at top speed, dodging cars, startling pedestrians. After him, knees high, came Hallowell and Beers.

At Forty-second Street, they all stopped. Hallowell and Beers were gasping. Bobby had plenty of wind left. They looked back. No photographer. A smile spread across Bobby's face. "Really showed *him,* huh? Ha! Ha!"

Hallowell laughed with him. He had no way of knowing that in the incident there had emerged a theme of flight that for the next twelve hours would follow their enterprise like a cold wind.

The next problem was Dubinsky. After one afternoon in Bobby's company, he had decided that his chief passenger had "a hernia in his head." He was also appalled by the behavior of Bobby's friends. "They treated him like some idiot king. I'm tellin' ya, it was disgusting the way these educated people crept up his behind." When Bobby and his entourage stopped for brunch at a Horn & Hardart Automat on Sixth Avenue, Dubinsky took the opportunity to go off and grab an untroubled sandwich.

Bobby seemed happy at H.&H.—he usually is when he's eating—but Unbelievable Syms was a downer. Dubinsky had recommended the store as a great place to buy a suit ("Two hundred dollars is ninety dollars there"). After about ten minutes Bobby walked out. "They don't have a big enough selection," he said.

Dubinsky was suspicious. On the way to Barney's, a clothing store at Seventh Avenue and Seventeenth Street, he sizzled Hallowell for dropping a cigarette ash on his carpet. Then he called the salesman at Syms and satisfied himself that Bobby had walked out because he thought Dubinsky was getting a kickback. "And that," as Hochstetter put it, "really started the pissing match."

Bobby bought three expensive ready-made suits at Barney's and then asked to be driven farther uptown to buy a Sony TV and a digital clock. Smoldering, Dubinsky complied. Meanwhile, Bobby's mood had been steadily souring. He told Saidy he definitely didn't want to go to Iceland—the deals weren't right and besides, there was too much to do first.

Saidy's reaction was to make understanding noises. "Saidy figured it was better to ride along with Bobby on the downswings," Hallowell told me, "and then try to carry him over the top on the upswings. But he often came off sounding mealymouthed." Hallowell and Hochstetter hit Bobby with pep talks about Iceland. In reply Bobby made a sound that could have been "mm" or "nn."

Everyone in the car felt a sense of emergency. Hochstetter cut out on a brief errand and made a wild call to his brother, the film lobby's man in Washington, asking him to persuade Vice-president Agnew, Bobby's favorite politician, to send a telegram wishing Bobby godspeed. His brother tried, Hochstetter said, but Agnew couldn't be reached.

A little later, Hallowell went to the Yale Club to pick up Bobby's baggage and check him out. Bobby lives out of enormous plastic suitcases that look like toasted piano crates, and hefting one around gave Hallowell his second unexpected workout of the day. Dubinsky drove Bobby, Saidy and Hochstetter to the Upper West Side, where Bobby had left some clothes with a friend. Bobby came out carrying a suitcase with a handle that wouldn't stay on. "And now," said Hochstetter, "the Mack Sennett stuff started."

Basically a sociable man, Dubinsky saw his chance to make up. "I'll fix it," he said, coming forward.

"You can't fix it," Bobby told him irritably.

"I can fix anything!" Dubinsky answered—and proceeded to. When the handle was reattached, he stood back and gestured confidently at his handiwork.

Bobby picked the suitcase up. The handle came off. "See?" Bobby sneered.

That was the last time that day Dubinsky had kind words for anybody.

Shortly after 6:30 P.M., while Davis was reading over the agreement with Stein and persuading him to sign it even though Bobby might refuse, he got an anguished phone call from someone in Bobby's party: "Get here fast. We don't know how long we can hold him."

"Take him to my place right away," Davis answered calmly. "I'll meet you there."

In Reykjavik meanwhile it was about 10:30 P.M. The president of the Icelandic Chess Federation took the elevator to the eighth floor of the Hotel Esja. At thirty-two, Gudmundur Thorarinsson was what one journalist called "a striking Viking"—ash-blond, square-jawed, fierce-eyed. Six feet even and weighing 190 pounds, he had heavy muscles under his tweed jacket. Slap him on the back and you could bruise your hand.

Thorarinsson looked like a jock and came on like a country boy. He smacked his lips when he ate, and he walked as if he had grown up in wooden shoes. When he stood, his legs were like fenceposts planted in concrete. *Seigur* is the Icelandic word for him. Tough. "A man like that," an Icelander told me, "if there isn't a gate, he walks through the wall." But there was sweetness in his mouth and in his blue-gray eyes sometimes a twinkle of irony. He was a natural leader, daring and usually right.

Thorarinsson had grown up poor in a family his father had abandoned. His brother was given away but nobody would take Gudmundur, a surly little cuss who beat up every kid on the street and was never there when you wanted him. He was raised in Reykjavik by his grandmother, and at twelve he was apprenticed to a mason. "I was an animal," Thorarinsson told me, "but he saw possibilities." The mason forced him to finish high school and take a course in business law. At the university, Thorarinsson switched to engineering. "In those days I just wanted to be strong and rich. I was cunning and before I was through college I had put together enough money to buy three apartments."

What changed Thorarinsson from a heavy to a hero was the discovery that he could sway people with words. In 1970, his name as a construction engineer established, he ran for office on the moderately socialistic Progressive ticket and became the youngest member of Reykjavik's city council. "I am very ambitious," he told me one day with a kind of shy defiance. "I intend to be prime minister of Iceland someday."

Right from the start, Thorarinsson saw the chess match as a political opportunity. Chess had been his hobby since he was twelve and he had been president of I.C.F. for two years when his brother Johann, "a lazy fellow with brilliant ideas," put the bug in his ear: Why not get the Spassky-Fischer match for Iceland? Thorarinsson laughed him off. But the bug kept buzzing. Thorarinsson put the question to Iceland's prime minister, a close friend. After weeks of arguing, he won the government's promise to back the match with $60,000. Thorarinsson's first idea was to offer a $25,000 prize, but a week before the bidding closed he read a false report in a German chess magazine that Iceland had made a bid of $100,000. Assuming other bidders would try to beat that, he set Iceland's offer at $125,000.

Belgrade, Yugoslavia, posted the high bid ($152,000), but because Spassky did not want to play in the heat of a southern summer, the match was divided—first twelve games to Belgrade, second twelve to Reykjavik. "Euwe made a Solomonic decision," Edmondson remarked with a sour smile. "He sawed the baby in half." The arrangement depressed Thorarinsson too. If one player took a runaway lead over the other, the match might be over before Iceland got its turn.

Thorarinsson therefore decided to steal the first half of the match from Belgrade. Meanwhile the Belgrade organizers had decided to steal the second half of the match from Iceland. But with *Sitzfleisch* and resolute bluffing Thorarinsson won the poker game. Iceland got the whole match.

This was the man Bobby and his lawyers were bargaining with. Practical, forceful, shrewd, on the whole the strongest individual involved with the match. But he was also proud, ambitious, moralistic, fanatical, stubborn—so much like Bobby it was scary. And in a few minutes he would grapple with Bobby in what might well be their last attempt to negotiate.

The elevator in the Hotel Esja reached the eighth floor, and Thorarinsson started down the hall to room 822, where he had arranged to take a phone call from Davis and reply to Bobby's ultimatum: "If I don't get thirty per cent of the gate, I don't go."

The Davis apartment is a pleasant straggle of fairly large rooms in a good unswanky building in the West Seventies. Bobby arrived there looking like a grenade about to go off. "The atmosphere was so tense it was unreal," Hallowell told me later, and Davis agreed. "He was obviously at the point of refusing to take the plane. I felt like a psychiatrist trying to cool out a patient hanging on a ledge."

Davis played the occasion as a casual evening with old friends. Hallowell, Saidy and Hochstetter sank into some solid chairs and a fat sofa grouped around a glass coffee table. Davis's wife Jessie, a gentle dark-haired woman who has made her own career as a pediatrician, brought them drinks. Bobby took a chair in the darkest corner and sat there with his face stony. But he brightened a little when he saw a consoling furball, the Davises' cat.

Jessie brought the cat over and Bobby began to stroke it firmly and rapidly. "That cat usually likes to be petted," Hallowell told me. "But for some reason, whenever Bobby touched it, the creature would wriggle free and run away. Jessie brought it back several times, but it still wouldn't settle down. Finally Bobby gave up and just sat there looking peeved." He perked up again when Jessie brought him a big roast-beef sandwich and a glass of milk, but when the others tried to include him in the conversation he looked away.

Davis was in his bedroom, packing and dressing for the trip. Takeoff was scheduled for 9:30 P.M. and Kennedy Airport was an hour away. There was a second 9:30 flight that usually took off a little later, then a final flight scheduled for 10:30, but Davis wanted to keep them as emergency reserves. Eight o'clock, he figured, was about as late as they could leave.

At 7:30 Davis slipped into a baggy tweed jacket, strolled into the living room, and inquired, "Well, shall we go?"

The others rolled out of their chairs and moved toward the door, but Bobby looked startled. "Huh? I haven't agreed to go! What's the deal? What about those open points?"

"Why don't you guys go on down and wait in the car," Davis continued calmly. "Bobby and I have some business to do." Then he turned to Bobby. "Okay, why don't I call Thorarinsson and see what I can work out? I'll call from the bedroom—want to come in?"

"No, I'll stay out here. You handle it." As long as he stayed in the living room, he could repudiate any deal Davis might make—even a deal for 30 per cent of the gate.

"Fine," said Davis. But he knew the situation was anything but fine. As he saw it, Bobby was in the grip of a suicidal impulse, and what scared him most was that Bobby didn't seem aware of the impulse. All his sensible reasons for not going had congealed into one big one:

Thorarinsson. Davis feared that if Bobby could not go to Reykjavik clutching a victory over Thorarinsson, he would not go at all.

Somehow Davis had to reach across 2600 miles of cultural separation and three months of adversary procedure to make Thorarinsson realize that the best way, maybe the only way, to get what he wanted most, the match, was to give up something he wanted a little less, a certain amount of money.

Davis reached for the phone.

I was sitting about four feet from the man Davis was calling. Thorarinsson was visiting grandmaster Lothar Schmid, the chief arbiter of the match, in his room in the Esja Hotel. Thorarinsson, standing at the window, squinted into a sun that even at thirty minutes to midnight stood ten degrees above the horizon.

Fred Cramer, acting as Bobby's representative, was making a vehement pitch to Schmid. "Bobby is concerned that there should not be the slightest possibility of anyone drugging or poisoning the food provided for the players backstage. The area *must be guarded* at all times by known and trustworthy people."

Cramer stood five feet five with a little help from his shoemaker and looked like any of the seven Disney dwarves, depending on his mood. He was fifty-nine and his bald head was fringed with white. His glasses, held in place by a strip of black elastic that circled his head, made his pink scalp look like a ham in mourning. His legs were short but when he walked he kicked them out importantly. When he talked to somebody he stood toe to toe, then leaned back from his waist and bellowed in a bass voice that waffled upward like an elk fart in a well shaft.

Recently retired from the lighting-fixture business in Milwaukee, Cramer was a self-made millionaire and past president of the U.S. Chess Federation. He registered as a simple, likable Huckleberry Babbitt, but his har-har heartiness concealed a quick mind and energies excited by dreams of fame. Cramer was Reykjavik's leading lobby orator. "I have been authorized to inform you," he announced to a circle of newsmen, "that Mr. Fischer is on his way to Iceland. He is being brought by submarine from Greenland and will come ashore in a kayak after a rendezvous at sea with the Icelandic Navy. Har! Har!"

To men whose editors were screaming for headlines three times a day, the witsnappers seemed less than witty. They privately called

Cramer "Bubblehead," "Mr. Magoo" and "the Milwaukee talkie." One reporter remarked that "he's too short for the urinals in Reykjavik, so he's pissing all over us."

When the food-poisoning question had been settled, Cramer and Schmid took up the Sunset Problem.

"Now Lothar, as you know," Cramer said, "Bobby's Sabbath begins at sunset on Friday and runs till sunset on Saturday. During this time no games may be scheduled. But if an adjourned game is played off on Friday we will have to know the exact moment of sunset so that the game may be adjourned again, if necessary, before Bobby's Sabbath begins ... But in that case, Lothar, we will face a peculiar problem. In Iceland at this time of the year—*there is no sunset!* Har! Har!"

We all laughed with him, realizing suddenly that we were just as silly to humor Bobby's demands as he was to make them.

We were still laughing when the phone rang. It was 11:40.

"Hello? Mr. Davis? Thorarinsson. And how are things there?"

We followed every shading in his voice.

Thorarinsson began to pace, then stopped. "If I understand you correctly, Mr. Davis, in addition to the many concessions and advantages we have given him, Mr. Fischer is now demanding thirty per cent of the gate receipts ... I am sorry, but we cannot do it. We have gone as far as we can. There is nothing more that we have to give ... I understand. But *you* nust understand that we have made concession after concession. We have begun to wonder if it is *possible* to satisfy Mr. Fischer. Icelanders are generous people, Mr. Davis, but we are also proud. We will be freely generous but we will not be forced to be generous."

Thorarinsson stood tall, eyes shining, like an orator addressing a crowd.

"However, let me say this to Mr. Fischer. Trust me. Come to Iceland. Play the match. I guarantee that when the receipts are added up, the Icelandic Chess Federation will be generous to the players."

This was an offer? With the house burning down, Thorarinsson had stood there, hose at the ready, and said sorry, we just can't spare the water. If Bobby did the same—and such a refusal would strongly tempt him to—the match would go up in flames.

"I am sorry," Thorarinsson was saying, "I can do no more. I hope that Mr. Fischer will come. Thank you. Goodbye."

He turned and saw our shocked faces. "Believe me, if I gave in to this demand there would be another. And another. And after I have given in to all his demands, he will not come. Yes, gentlemen," he finished gravely, "unless there is a miracle, the match will not take place."

Davis walked into the living room briskly, like a man who had just accomplished something. It was 7:55. Explaining what had happened, Davis suggested that Thorarinsson might take a different stand if he could be sure that this was Bobby's last demand. "I think I can make a deal," he concluded. "So why don't we go to the airport now? On the way we can talk the deal over. I can call Thorarinsson from the airport. We can keep the limousine. If we have to come back, we'll come back."

Bobby very hesitantly said okay. Davis asked Jessie to call Loftleidir (Icelandic Airlines) at Kennedy Airport and ask the manager to hold the 9:30 plane. Jessie and the children wished Bobby good luck and kissed him goodbye. Embarrassed but pleased, Bobby hurried out to the elevator.

Outside, a light rain was falling—along with some debris from Dubinsky's latest explosion. While waiting, Hallowell and Hochstetter had run over to Gitlitz's Deli. They came back with three corned-beef sandwiches—one for Saidy too—and opened the back door of the Cadillac.

"Just one minute, gentlemen," Dubinsky announced. "Not in *my* car you don't eat sandwiches."

"But Morris, it's raining out here and we don't have raincoats."

"I don't care if it's a blizzard out there. I been through all this before. Ketchup smears on the upholstery, coffee puddles on the rug. I'm sorry, gentlemen. No eating in this car."

Hochstetter, Hallowell and Saidy crossed the street, sat on somebody's steps, and ate in the rain.

Damp but still game, they hurried back to the limousine when Bobby and Davis came down. Dubinsky opened the door of the limousine and waited for Bobby to get in. But he didn't. He just stood there, head down and glaring, like a steer at the gate of the butcher's van.

"I mean, what's the deal?" He whirled on Davis. "Why should I go if I don't have a deal?"

"All right," Davis said calmly. "Let's walk around the block and talk." Bobby had no raincoat and was carrying his chess magazines, but Davis was afraid that if they went back to the apartment they would never get out again.

"What I have in mind," Davis began, flashing his wickedest paw-in-cookie-jar grin, "is a deal that gives the players *everything* and doesn't give the Icelanders *anything.*"

Bobby's eyes lit up. Davis went on winging it, flinging it, building a dream castle of a deal that made Bobby feel like a king and shut Thorarinsson in a financial dungeon that in fact had no walls at all.

"Well," Davis wound up firmly, "shall I try it on him?" Startled, pleased, suspecting a trick but unable to see it, Bobby said ye-e-es. Davis got him back upstairs before he had time to change his mind. When Jessie saw Bobby walk in, her smile was less than sincere, and the cat hid.

A flicker of triumph lit Thorarinsson's face as Schmid handed him the phone and said, "New York." We had been sure it was all over. But Thorarinsson had obviously *expected* Davis to call back!

For five minutes the conversation was numbers. Twenty-four games, fifteen hundred people, five dollars a head, etc. After hanging up, Thorarinsson explained Davis's offer. "The players will take all of the gate receipts above $250,000."

Fifteen hundred people paying five dollars apiece to attend twenty games equaled—$150,000!

"But you can't lose!" Cramer burst out. "You could feature naked usherettes and you'd never take more than $200,000! My God, it's brilliant! Andy's saved the match!"

Thorarinsson looked dubious.

Schmid said, "If the concession costs you nothing, and there is a chance it will save the match, why not make it?"

Thorarinsson frowned. "But you know, an agreement with him is not really an agreement. He will sign nothing. And what is to prevent him from demanding further concessions?"

"Time," Cramer suggested.

"Pah! He can put off the flight until Saturday night."

"To arrive on Sunday morning and play Spassky on Sunday after-noon?" Schmid shook his head.

"If Bobby agreed to the deal Andy described," I said, "he's ready to come. All he's asking for is something to save his face. Is that so much to give?"

Thorarinsson lifted his chin. "Bobby Fischer's face," he said, "is not the only face that must be saved. People in Iceland feel that he has insulted our country. They feel that we have already made too many concessions."

"Are you trying to please the voters or stage the match?" Cramer cut in. "Anyway, in the long run the voters'll be more pleased by a chess match that puts Iceland on the map than by a strong stand that puts Bobby Fischer in his place."

"Yes, *if* we get the match," said Thorarinsson. "Bobby is only *half* the problem, you know."

Was Thorarinsson afraid that if he gave Bobby too much, the Russians would holler foul and maybe even back out? I felt a cold flash. If Thorarinsson really believed that Bobby had decided not to come, why not make sure that Bobby came off as the hideous American dragon and Thorarinsson as the brave defender of Iceland's virtue? And the best way to do that would be to stand firm now and let Bobby have his head. Whatever Bobby decided, Thorarinsson would be a hero.

We pressed him hard, and he seemed to be coming around. The phone rang.

"Yes, Mr. Davis," said Thorarinsson, "I have spoken with one of my colleagues of the Icelandic Chess Federation. I am sorry but we cannot accept. We have gone as far as we can. This is our final decision . . ."

We had expected something short of outright acceptance but certainly more than flat rejection. I felt tricked; we all did. And yet, when Thorarinsson put the phone down, his face was so gray I wondered if he was ill.

"Well, Gudmundur," Cramer burst out, "I don't know how to say this, but—you blew it!"

With a sad smile Thorarinsson sat back slowly on the edge of Schmid's bureau. "Gentlemen, for weeks I have been expecting such a last-minute offer. Mr. Davis was sincere when he made it, but if I had accepted the offer Mr. Fischer would not have come. Nobody speaks for Mr. Fischer except Mr. Fischer."

He was trying hard to restore our confidence in him. Would he care what we thought if he didn't expect the match to come off? I took a stab in the dark.

"Then you *do* expect Bobby to come!"

He grinned. "Yes, I do. I expect Mr. Fischer to come and I expect him to come tonight. I said that only a miracle could save the match, but I believe—I *know* that miracle will happen! I have always known! Gentlemen!"

Leaning forward, he went on in a voice rich with mystery. "I must tell you that Iceland in some ways is a very strange and special island. The people here—it is very common among us—have ... *certain powers!* I have had prophetic dreams in which I was assured that the match would take place here and would be a success. I also consulted a person with spiritual gifts and I was assured of the same thing!"

We stared at him. Was he putting us on? If he wasn't—and the burning look in his eye said he wasn't—then a man would have to squint very hard to see any significant difference in degree of irrationality between the chess freak from Brooklyn and the sober councilman of Reykjavik.

At 1:40 A.M. the discussion at the Esja was wandering like something lost in the woods. It was 9:40 in New York. If the plane had taken off on time, we should soon hear from Loftleidir that Bobby was—or was not—on board.

"Why don't I call Andy's home?" I suggested. "Maybe Jessie will know what's happening."

Three minutes later Jessie was on the line. "No, they left for the airport—oh, almost an hour ago."

"They left for the airport?"

When I said that, Cramer exploded out of his chair and yelled "Wow!"

"Did they expect to take the plane?" I asked Jessie.

"I suppose so. It seems silly to go all the way out there if they didn't intend to, don't you think?"

When I finished repeating what Jessie had said, Thorarinsson was grinning, Schmid was laughing out loud, and Cramer was practically doing cartwheels. "By Jesus, Gudmundur, maybe you were right! We're still in the ball game!"

Thorarinsson's reply gave Davis nothing to work with, but somehow he persuaded Bobby there was a chance of getting the deal he wanted. The limousine pulled away from Davis's apartment at about 8:45—forty-five minutes before takeoff. Traffic being normal, they would be about fifteen minutes late. For that long, Loftleidir would delay the plane.

But traffic was not normal. Three minutes from home they were caught in a jam. Dubinsky made a dogleg and broke free—into another jam. It was raining harder now. Dubinsky began to snort and mutter.

Bobby was in a foul mood too. The minute he sat in the back seat and felt all those big shoulders hemming him in, he began to shallow-breathe and dart his eyes around. Saidy force-fed him reassurance. "Man, think of the fantastic deals you've got! The prize money alone is ten times anything there's ever been in chess."

"Yeah," Bobby said, "if I *get* it."

"You'll get it," Saidy insisted. "It's in trust for you. In trust means it's *there* for you. And on top of that there's your cut of the film and television sales, the fee you're getting from TelePrompTer for letting them use your name, not to mention the house, the car, a staff of three. And when you're champion they'll be beating a path to your door with endorsements and TV and film offers."

Saidy meant well, but when you're dealing with Bobby casting bread upon the waters often brings up a crocodile.

"Yeah, that reminds me," Bobby said, turning to Davis. "What about that $125,000 Paul Marshall said he'd get me from Chester Fox?"

"What $125,000?"

Horror filled Bobby's face. "You mean you okayed the deal with Fox and it didn't include that?"

"I don't know anything about it."

"Oh!" Bobby groaned, looking almost ill. "How could you *do* that!"

Davis began to feel like the captain of a peapod in a hurricane. "Okay," he said, picking up the radiophone. "Let's call Paul Marshall and get the facts."

Marshall was one of David Frost's New York attorneys, a brilliant negotiator who had worked with Bobby until midspring, when Bobby repudiated a general agreement that Marshall had patiently teased out of the Icelanders. At that point, Marshall had resigned, but he was still friendly to Bobby's interests in a distant way.

As the phone rang, Davis noted that the limousine was still on the Manhattan side of the Fifty-ninth Street Bridge. There was almost an hour to go before they reached Kennedy, an hour in which Bobby could dream up all sorts of mind-pretzeling problems.

Marshall sounded depressingly relaxed. "Not on the plane yet? I thought you were already up there."

"We're on our way," Davis answered.

"Yeah," Marshall said drily, "but you're not there yet. Well, what can I do for you?"

Davis told him and Marshall quickly laid out the terms of an agreement he had worked out some weeks before with Fox. As it turned out, the terms were similar to the terms Davis and Stein had arrived at a few hours earlier. Marshall's agreement was a little better for Bobby, but there was no problem, Marshall and Davis agreed. The text could be altered and Fox could sign it in Reykjavik.

"No! No! I'm not going!" Bobby yelled. "Not under those conditions!"

Davis handed him the phone.

"Look," Marshall said, "Fox is nothing without you. He's got to go along. As for the Icelanders, what are you worried about? Not even Ali gets that kind of contract with a percentage guarantee."

Bobby muttered some more but, as always happened when Marshall began to speak, the tightness and suspicion in his face relaxed. It was clear that Marshall still had magic for Bobby. Davis sensed it, and wondered: was Bobby at that moment wishing that Marshall and not Davis were at his side? Back in January and February Marshall had fired up Bobby's passions for glamour and power. Had he resparked those passions in him now? tempted him to capture fame and fortune in Reykjavik? or inclined him instead to hold out for more money?

By the time Dubinsky reached the other end of the bridge it was 9:15, Kennedy was still almost an hour away and Davis had chewed his lips to a fringe. Dubinsky struck out through back streets that hadn't seen a Cadillac since the asphalt went down.

As the car picked up speed, Bobby seemed to relax a little.

2

A Night at the Airport

It was 9:50 P.M. when the limousine reached the Loftleidir passenger terminal. "Press up the ass," Hallowell told me. "Looked like thirty, maybe forty newspaper and television people, on the sidewalk or inside the glass doors." They were all looking sharp at the cars that pulled up.

The limousine eased to a stop about thirty yards beyond Loftleidir. Davis left the car and slipped through the crowd. Soon he was in close conversation with two young men.

Both were slim, alert, bright-eyed, blond. Tedd Hope, the manager of Loftleidir's Kennedy operation, looked like Tab Hunter ten years ago. Hans Indridason, head of the reservations department and a troubleshooter for the U.S. branch of the company, had a narrow bright ice ax of a face. Good friends on the job and off, both Hope and Indridason had the kind of energy that gets things done under pressure, and both had been vigorously informed by their superiors that getting Bobby to Iceland was a matter of national concern. The Loftleidir staff stood ready to move Bobby north by any means short of a Viking raid on Dubinsky's limousine.

Davis gave a quick fill-in on the situation ("very touchy"). Hope said the first of the 9:30 flights was already loaded, but the second was still open and there was the 10:30 flight too.

The three of them put together a simple plan to ease Bobby on the 9:30 plane in the next ten minutes. The problem, as they saw it, was to elude the media—and the crowds. It was June 29, the start of the July Fourth weekend and the height of the summer rush to Europe. Cars, buses and stretch limousines, honking and darting, exploded brightly colored passengers and luggage. People were kissing and laughing and running around with blank airport faces. On top of everything, it was raining cantaloupes.

The plan was to keep Bobby in the limousine until he could be slipped into a Loftleidir station wagon and driven to the plane. Hope hurried off, and a few minutes later double-parked a white station wagon beside Dubinsky's Cadillac. A cop banged on his fender. "Move along, mister." Hope explained the baggage transfer. "Make it quick," the officer ruled.

Hope ran to his tailgate and opened it. Dubinsky emerged into the rain and opened the trunk. Bobby's luggage was placed in the station wagon. Davis checked the bags to make sure they were all there.

"It's 10:15," Hope said. "This plane is already forty-five minutes late. If you want to make it, we have to move now."

Hallowell opened the back door of the limousine on the curb side and stuck his head in. "Bobby—" He stopped. The limousine was empty.

Hallowell spun around. "Where is he?"

"I don't know," Hochstetter answered. "He said he wanted a digital clock. Tony said he'd get it, but Bobby jumped out and went after him. That's the last I saw of either of them."

Davis turned white. "Can you hold it ten minutes?" he asked Indridason, who nodded. "All right, God damn it, let's find him before those reporters do!"

Davis, Hallowell and Indridason ran toward the main lobby. Hochstetter waited briefly at the limousine, then decided to join the hunt. Hope jumped into the station wagon and, in line with Davis's instructions, drove the baggage out to the plane.

Dubinsky flung his arms in the air. "What *is* all this horseshit?" he inquired of nobody in particular.

Bobby and Saidy came back just as Dubinsky, pressed by the cop, was drifting his limousine toward the east arcade, an area that includes a taxi stand and a secluded courtyard.

When they arrived at the limousine, Bobby asked Dubinsky to open the trunk so he could stow the clock he had just bought in one of his suitcases. Dubinsky stepped out and explained that the suitcases were no longer in the trunk. "We moved them into an airline station wagon."

"What!" Bobby gasped. "You moved my baggage without my permission?" He turned to Saidy. "That's not right!"

Nervously, Saidy agreed—at the moment, it was difficult to do anything else.

"How dare you!" Bobby whirled on Dubinsky. "How dare you take my baggage without my permission!"

Dubinsky tried to explain the situation calmly, but Bobby would not listen. In a fury, he chewed Dubinsky out.

"Listen, mister," Dubinsky announced in a voice warm with promises of strangulation, "you better keep your mouth shut. If you don't, I'll shut it for you, and if you don't think I can do it, keep talking!"

Saidy was in a panic—if Dubinsky hit Bobby, he might knock him all the way back to California.

"And I'll tell you something else," Dubinsky went on, "you may be a genius at chess, but in everything else *you're a big jerk!*"

Bobby's fury began to collapse. He had pictured himself as the boss raising hell with an employee, but suddenly the boot was on the other foot. "Aaaaaa!" he said, edging toward the safety of the limousine.

"Me," Dubinsky yelled after him, "I'm a genius at *everything*. What I did with your baggage I did right, and I did it on the instructions of the man who is paying me, which you are not!"

Dubinsky was still letting him have it when Bobby ducked back into the limo. "That man's dangerous!" he told Saidy. "Who is he? He looks like some kind of foreigner."

Saidy, who looks approximately like Abdul the Bulbul Ameer, replied soothingly, "Yeah, we don't need any foreigners around here."

When Davis, Hallowell and Indridason arrived at the limousine, they found Bobby and Saidy sitting very quietly in the back seat and Dubinsky standing grim-faced under a canopy nearby.

"What happened?" Bobby asked.

Davis said they'd all been looking for him everywhere, because the plane was already an hour late.

"Oh," Bobby said coldly, "is there a decision from Iceland?"

Davis said no.

"So why go?" Bobby asked.

"Bobby," Davis began, "I think—"

"I mean," Bobby cut him off, "stop trying to hustle me, right?"

It was time to back off.

"And how about my baggage?" Bobby's eyes were hard.

"It's in the plane," Indridason said.

Bobby was staggered. "What? In the *plane!* I never said I'd go. I'm sitting right here—I'm not getting out of this car until my baggage is returned! Do you understand? *I want my baggage!*" His voice was high, his hands trembling, his eyes wide.

Davis hesitated, still hoping to turn the moment around, but Saidy jumped in to support Bobby. "You shouldn't have done that," Saidy said, tears for some reason welling in his eyes. "Putting a man's baggage on a plane without his permission! That's really terrible!"

"That's right!" Bobby rushed on. "I never said I'd go. What are you trying to do, shanghai me?" With Saidy's support, he rapidly propagated an awkward moment into a nightmare of shadowy motives and sinister potentials.

Davis and Hallowell explained that the bags had been moved with the best intentions. "In fact, we thought you were sitting in the car and watching us move them." But Bobby refused to listen. Taking Indridason aside, Davis said, tight-lipped, "All right, bring the fucking bags back!"

Bobby seemed to blame Davis for the baggage incident. Something had to be done to soften his mood.

"Hey, I'm hungry," Saidy said. "How about you, Bobby? Why don't we go upstairs and get something to eat?"

The restaurant was a risk. Reporters and photographers were everywhere. But letting Bobby brood in the Cadillac seemed a much greater risk. Food was to Bobby what air was to a tire, and it was clear he needed some reinflation. Besides, Saidy was gung-ho to talk to Bobby alone and—who could tell? A firm hand hadn't worked. Maybe a soft voice would.

"Good idea," Davis said.

In Reykjavik, an hour and a half had passed since Jessie had told us Bobby was on the way to the airport. About 2:45, Thorarinsson made a phone call in Icelandic and ten minutes later he got one. *"Já . . . já já . . . Takk fyrir!"* He turned to us. "New York says the Fischer party is in the airport and is preparing to board the plane!"

He was coming! We stood up and congratulated Thorarinsson, then solemnly shook hands all around.

"The flight takes five hours," Cramer said. "If we go to bed now we can get at least three hours before we meet the plane." But we decided to wait up for Loftleidir to confirm Bobby's departure even though it seemed now that the call would be just a formality.

Cursing, Hope drove the bags a winding mile from the plane to a service port near the main lobby. Then Indridason, Hope and an assistant hand-hauled Bobby's and Davis's luggage—four or five suitcases and packages—through the rain to a corner of the lobby.

Davis, Hochstetter and Hallowell had meanwhile stepped upstairs to the bar next to the coffee shop where Bobby and Saidy were talking. After a decent interval, Davis crossed over to join them.

Soaked to the skin and mad as wet hens but determined to be polite, Hope and Indridason arrived in the coffee shop. Bobby and Saidy were sitting with Davis in a booth near the entrance. Indridason explained courteously that the bags were now about two hundred steps from the coffee shop. Hope went to the heart of the matter. "The plane is now almost two hours late," he told Davis. "You or somebody will have to make up his mind right now."

"Give me a couple minutes," Davis answered.

"We've been giving you a couple minutes all night," Hope said, and left.

Five minutes later, Davis came down to check the baggage. It was rain-spattered. Somebody ran off to get paper towels, but Bobby arrived first. He went straight to the first bag he saw and picked it up. The handle came off. "I'll—uh," Davis said with a gulp, and snatched the handle away from Bobby.

Then Bobby noticed the carton containing his new Sony television set. "It's wet!" he gasped.

"What do you expect," Hope answered, "coming in out of the rain?"

Bobby was appalled. "You mean this has been standing in the rain? Oh, no! What kind of place *is* this?"

For the first time that night Davis groped for an answer and drew a blank. He found himself feebly wiping the Sony carton with the suitcase handle.

When paper towels arrived, everybody began "blotting like crazy," as Hallowell put it, "all assholes and elbows."

Hope asked again if anybody wanted to make this plane.

"No," Bobby said, "I gotta talk about it some more with Tony."

Hope left, glowering. The 9:30 plane moved off the ramp at 11:29 P.M.

When the bags were as dry as five hardworking high-income executives could make them, Bobby stood over his possessions with what one observer described as "the wary look of a gorilla guarding a pile of bananas." "Okay," he announced, "from now on *nobody* touches my bags, understand? I want this baggage in lockers. And *I* want the keys!"

Indridason, deadpan, pointed out the nearest lockers, about ninety feet away. Bobby insisted on carrying most of the bags himself. Hallowell showed Bobby how to put coins in the slots so the keys would come out of the locks. With a smirk, Bobby then pocketed all the keys.

Turning to Saidy, Bobby invited him back up to the restaurant. Then he marched off, stone-faced, leaving Davis and the others standing there like untipped porters.

At 3:50 A.M., Loftleidir Reykjavik called Thorarinsson and said they had just received a routine Telex from Loftleidir New York reporting that the 9:30 plane had taken off at 11:35 P.M., New York time. No word about Bobby but we were virtually certain he was on board. If he didn't intend to come, why had he stayed at the airport so long?

By 11 P.M., most of the media people were tipped that Bobby was somewhere at Kennedy. For a full hour dozens of story-starved reporters, photographers and cameramen ran a dragnet through the airport. Only a few feet off the corridor but somehow too obvious to be seen, Bobby sat in the coffee shop gobbling eggs and toast and talking with Saidy.

The conversation was going well, Saidy said later. He had no idea what old terrors were slithering through Bobby's mind, but he felt he had finally persuaded him to take the plane.

Then the chutney hit the propeller.

"There was this little blond kid," Hochstetter said. "He'd been cruising the corridor with the newspaper photographers and the TV news crews. You could tell this was the big moment of his life."

Worried at seeing so many people passing so close to Bobby, Hochstetter "stayed in the hallway between the bar and the coffee shop, where I could keep track of things. This kid came along, just sniffing around by himself, and I saw him duck into the coffee shop where Bobby was eating. A minute later he came running out and went tearing down the corridor to where most of the press was waiting.

"I dashed into the coffee shop. 'Go across to the bar!' I told Bobby and Saidy. 'Way at the back! They'll never suspect you stayed so close!' So they did. Well, the whole megillah came thundering up, at least twenty of them. Nikons, TV cameras, strobes. They charged into the coffee shop and then out again. 'You looking for Bobby Fischer?' I said. 'He went down there!' And I pointed to the stairway that goes down to the ground floor. So they all ran down there and I figured that's the end of that."

Two minutes later they all came charging back up again. "And then that damn kid fooled me. He snooped around in the bar and came running out hollering, 'He's in there! He's in there!' So then they all rushed in."

Hallowell was ready for them. When they hit the end of the bar, the 250-pound former third-string tackle threw the greatest block of his career. For about thirty seconds Hallowell had twenty men piled up in front of him. "I'm sorry, gentlemen," he announced, making like the manager, "but the bar is closed."

"I'm from NBC!" a reporter informed him.

"No shit," Hallowell answered.

That blew his cover. Suddenly they all broke through—only to meet Bobby charging out. For a moment his narrow head waved above the crowd like a hatchet. Shoulders twisting, he pushed through. There were shouts, flashes, shoving, cries of "Bobby! Bobby!"

Just ahead lay the corridor. As Bobby hit it, he turned left. Hallowell was not far behind, and after him came a TV cameraman, an assistant carrying a battery pack and a rack of lights, and the twelve-year-old who had started it all. The lights were blazing, the camera was whining, and the boy was squealing, "Mr. Fischer! Mr. Fischer!" as they all turned left too.

At that moment a large hand covered the TV camera's lens. The hand belonged to Herb Hochstetter, who had been waiting in the corridor for just such an opportunity. "It was like putting pepper in a Turkish wrestler's jock strap," Hochstetter explained. "The cameraman let out a scream. The lighting man screamed too. Finally they pushed me out of the way but as the cameraman went past I gave him a good swift kick—right in the crack. He yelled and started after me."

Bobby ran down the stairs, Hallowell about twenty feet behind. After them came the yelping newshounds.

Thanks to Hochstetter's holding action, Davis and Saidy reached the stairs ahead of the press and raced for the bottom, where they turned to make a stand. For about five seconds they body-checked the horde. Somebody threw a punch at Saidy. Davis gave way slowly and as the TV cameraman rushed past him he stepped—accidentally, he insists—on the cord that connected the camera to the battery pack. The camera went dead. The cameraman stared in disbelief. Screeching incoherently, he pushed a floppy punch at Davis's head.

By the time the press broke out of the stairwell, Bobby and Hallowell were out of sight.

Yelling and cursing, the newsmen closed on Davis, Saidy, and Hochstetter. A Port Authority policeman hurried over. "What's going on here?" he demanded.

The cameraman began, "We're here to photograph Bobby Fischer, and—"

"Who's he?"

Everybody explained at once and then the cameraman indignantly described the first assault on his person. Another cop grabbed Hochstetter by the arm. He denied the charge. The cameraman then accused Davis of punching *him*. Davis drew himself up and declared, "You, sir, are a liar and a worm."

The cops knew a lawyer when they heard one. "Break it up," one of them said. "Move along."

Davis, Saidy and Hochstetter stared at what was left of one another. Hochstetter had been up since eight that morning and had eaten almost nothing all day. Saidy was pale with shock. Davis looked battered, but there was still plenty of fight in him.

"Shee-it!" he said. Then he went on briskly. "Okay. Anybody see which way he went?"

Nobody had.

Davis was really scared now. Hour by hour Bobby's string had been tightening—had it snapped? Suddenly the order of priorities shifted. Putting Bobby on the plane was the second thing now. The first thing was to make sure he was emotionally fit to go.

Davis turned to Indridason. "How long can you hold the plane?"

"We'll hold it."

Davis turned to Hochstetter. "He won't leave the airport without his baggage. Go watch that locker."

Saidy rushed off with Hope to the terminal services supervisor's office. Two minutes later his voice boomed out of dozens of loudspeakers. "Mr. Fischer, Mr. Fischer. Please call Dr. Saidy at 656-4476."

For fifteen minutes, Saidy paced back and forth, praying for a call. But the only result of the announcement was a media stampede to the Loftleidir ticket office.

Meanwhile, for the second time that night, Davis was organizing a manhunt, and this time the job looked hopeless—Kennedy was the size of Galveston, Texas. The best chance, Davis decided, was to spot-search the restaurants and men's rooms. Their ace in the hole was Hallowell. If he was still with Bobby (and if he wasn't, why wasn't he there with the rest of them?) sooner or later he would get to a phone and tell them where Bobby was. In the meantime, Davis and Saidy rushed from bars to coffee shops to men's rooms. Trying hard not to look like voyeurs, they checked urinals and hurried along rows of stalls, peering nonchalantly under each door, hoping for a glimpse of Bobby's shoes.

About 12:45, Davis came full circle to the Loftleidir terminal. Sagging but unstoppable, he proposed plan B. "Let's call every hotel and motel in the airport area." Loftleidir came up with a list, and Davis and Saidy called from phone booths, leaving the Loftleidir lines open for Hallowell.

One by one the hotels answered. Bobby was registered at none of them. It was one o'clock in the morning, a full hour since Bobby had bolted. The last plane to Reykjavik was now two and a half hours late. It looked as if Bobby had blown it.

Bobby had run down the steps two and three at a time. In the main lobby he raced for the nearest door, hitting it with both palms just as the photoelectric cell popped it open.

He turned left and began to sprint. Hallowell came pounding after him. "Are they still behind us?" Bobby hollered as he ran. Hallowell glanced back. "No!" Bobby picked up his knees and really poured it on.

Hallowell was in no shape for this. On weekends he swam and played a little tennis but five days a week for the past five years that big body had done nothing more strenuous than push his chair away from his desk. Remembering his morning workout on the sidewalks of New York, he wondered how long he could keep it up. He was sagging after fourteen hours of nervous tension, and as he watched Bobby blast off he had a sinking sensation that he was chasing a man so charged up he might run for an hour. He set his will hard. As long as he held on, there was a chance he could talk Bobby back to the plane.

Bobby was running in a blind burst of emotion. His feet hit the pavement like blows struck in anger and his legs leaped as if shackles had just been struck off. Hallowell saw in horror that he was running straight toward the Loftleidir terminal, where the media poeple had been headquartered all night. The sidewalk was empty now—could they zip by without being seen? They made it halfway. Then Hallowell heard a scurry of running feet.

"Bobby! Wait!" a newsman shouted. *"Please!* I've been here all week!"

Inexplicably, Bobby apologized for escaping. "I'm sorry!" he yelled—but kept on running.

Veering, he crossed the airport's two-lane circular highway. Puffing, Hallowell raced after him into the enormous airport parking lot.

At the third or fourth step, Hallowell landed splat in a deep puddle. Water splashed up, drenching his knees, and gushed through a hole in one shoe.

"Bobby!" he pleaded. "Slow down!"

Throwing a frightened look over his shoulder, Bobby asked, "Is anybody still there?"

"We've lost them," Hallowell assured him.

Bobby kept on running. "Stick with me!" he shouted. "Believe me, I know what I'm doing."

Behind them, the roar of traffic died to a murmur. Now they heard only the slap of their own feet and the wheeze of their own breathing.

Hallowell's chest was collapsing, his legs were unliftable. "Bobby, wait!" he gasped. "I got an idea!"

Bobby trotted to a stop.

Catching his breath in spasms, Hallowell explained. "American Airlines . . . V.I.P. Lounge . . . I'm a member . . . No press people . . ."

"No! I want to get out of this airport, y' unnastan'?" Bobby remembered a restaurant several miles from the airport. "We'll get a cab. Nobody'll find me there."

"Anywhere you say, Bobby. But let's get there fast!"

In the cab, Bobby was still quivering. Hallowell made small talk, giving him time to wind down. Suddenly the driver remembered that the restaurant had been wiped out by a cloverleaf. Hallowell groaned —more time wasted.

"Where shall we go?" Bobby asked.

Hallowell suggested a Howard Johnson's motel and restaurant they had passed. The driver jumped the island in the middle of Southern State Parkway and drove back.

Bobby looked around suspiciously. "We far enough away from the airport?" Hallowell reassured him.

There was $6.60 on the meter. Bobby paid, thanked the driver, and threw in a quarter tip. Inside, they were told that the restaurant was closed but the bar was still open. Bobby said he wanted food, so they ran about a hundred yards through the rain to the Hilton Motel next door. At the Hilton, both the bar and the restaurant were closed. So they ran back to Howard Johnson's. When they finally got settled in a dark corner of the cocktail lounge, it was close to 1 A.M.

Bobby seldom drinks liquor, but he asked for a whiskey sour and started talking about the press with concentrated hatred. Not a word about Iceland or catching the plane. Hallowell *had* to get to a phone, but if Bobby suspected a call was being made he might not be there when Hallowell got back. Taking his chances, Hallowell eased away to the men's room.

From a pay phone he called information. The phone rang interminably. Then the operator said there was no number for Loftleidir at Kennedy. Hallowell called the main number in Manhattan.

"I'm sorry, sir," a young woman told him, "we have no tie line to Kennedy."

Hallowell almost jumped into the mouthpiece. Any minute now, Bobby might come looking for him. Shaken up, the girl agreed to call Kennedy and tell somebody there to call Hallowell.

Minutes later, Hallowell's phone rang.

"Andy! I'm with Bobby."

"Thank God! Where *are* you?"

Hallowell explained.

"We'll be right over. And for Christ's sake, don't let him out of your sight!"

A Loftleidir station wagon roared up to Howard Johnson's. Davis, Saidy, Hope and Indridason jumped out. Moments later, Hochstetter arrived in the Cadillac with Dubinsky, who at last resolved his conflict between hate and duty.

"Look," Dubinsky told Hochstetter, "I find this Fischer a very depressing person and I no longer wish to have him in my car. I am sure you will have no trouble getting home. I will send you a bill on the first of the month. Good night."

While the others stood in the lobby and watched, Bobby, Saidy, and Davis paced back and forth under a sign that said RUM KEG ROOM. "For the first time that night," Hope said later, "Bobby was really opening up. He was waving his arms and talking. We thought, 'Okay. Somebody finally got through to him. Now he'll go.' "

In fact, Bobby was telling Davis emphatically that he would not go to Iceland until the deal was right. He wanted Davis to go instead and see if he could make it right. "Here are my demands," he said in a cold voice. "One, I want a nonplaying referee. Lothar Schmid has to go. Two, I want a better TV deal signed by Chester Fox. Three, I want the loser's share of the prize money *in my hand* when I get off the plane in Iceland. Four, I want 30 per cent of the gate. When I've got those things, I'll *think* about going."

Davis looked at Bobby's eyes. They were hard and opaque and didn't look back. Four people pushing for two full days with all their might had failed to budge Bobby an inch. And now they had run out of time.

"Okay, Bobby," Davis said. "Suppose I go. Suppose I get a reasonable betterment of the deal. Will you come?"

"I'll think about it."

"Come on, I don't want to go up there on a wild goose chase."

Bobby's eyes were scared. "All right, I'll go, but—I want Tony there, too."

Davis looked at Saidy. Saidy nodded. Davis held out his hand. "On that basis," he said, "I'll go."

As the Loftleidir station wagon pulled away, a little grin tugged at Bobby's mouth. Saidy was so exhausted he could hardly speak, and Hallowell and Hochstetter were not much better off. They figured they had just watched Bobby destroy his career. But Bobby spoke and moved like a man who had just had a major success.

Wearily, Hallowell called for two limousines—one for himself, one for Bobby and the others. When his Cadillac came, Bobby jumped in eagerly. He was going to stay at Saidy's father's house in Douglaston and he liked Saidy's mother's Lebanese cooking.

"Well, anyway," Hochstetter thought, "it's over for now. No more problems tonight."

"Where to, sir?" the driver asked.

"Queens," Hochstetter said.

The driver's face was blank. "Where's Queens?"

Somehow they made it to Tony's house. Before he got out of the limousine Bobby shook Hochstetter's hand and said respectfully, "Thank you very much, Mr. Hochstetter."

Bobby and Saidy raided the refrigerator and put away several platefuls of Lebanese leftovers. Then Saidy took him to the third floor, where there were three bedrooms and a bathroom. "Nobody else up here," Saidy told him. "You've got it all to yourself." Bobby nodded happily and seemed impatient to be alone. Saidy had the impression he wanted to play chess.

About the same time Bobby arrived in Douglaston, the group in Schmid's room at the Esja Hotel was happily batting the breeze. When Schmid looked at his watch it was 6:00!

Thorarinsson stretched. "Well, I've got to be going. I've got to get some sleep before I meet Bobby's plane."

The phone rang. Thorarinsson listened, then hung up with a stunned expression. "Bobby's not coming," he said. "But Andy's on the plane!"

We stared at each other out of the kind of eyes they close in morgues.

Thorarinsson was the first to speak. "Well, my friends," he said, "I am sorry. I should have accepted Mr. Davis's offer."

Nobody could think of a reply. Finally Cramer said, "As long as Andy's coming, there must be some hope."

We nodded uncertainly, then shook hands with Schmid and stood silent in the elevator as it dropped us toward the lobby. It had been a very long Thursday. We crinkled our eyes against the morning glare and then shuddered as the chill hit us. Thorarinsson turned. "I am thinking of Mr. Fischer," he said softly. "I fear there is a very great tragedy in the making."

3

A Dollar's Worth of Destiny

The stars at Bobby's birth foretold a special and powerful existence. Seen from Chicago on March 9, 1943, at 2:39 P.M., Mars, Mercury, Saturn, Uranus and Neptune were arranged at the apices of an equilateral triangle, a formation known as a Grand Trine and often considered to portend either supreme fortune or utter disaster—or both. A Grand Trine occurs in the horoscopes of Rembrandt, Goethe and Leonardo da Vinci—as well as in those of most major earthquakes.

Bobby's mother, Dr. Regina Wender Fischer Pustan, was scarcely less astonishing than Bobby himself. Daughter of a Jewish dress cutter, she was born in Switzerland in 1914 and transplanted to St. Louis as a small child. At nineteen, riding the radical surge of the depression years, she entered medical school in Moscow. In 1938, medical studies still incomplete, she married German biophysicist Gerhardt Fischer and moved back to the States with him. Their first child was a gentle brown-eyed beauty named Joan; their second child, born six years later, was Bobby.

When Bobby was two, Regina and Gerhardt were divorced and his father dropped out of his life. Bobby likes to say he didn't need a father; friends say he has made only one visit to the elder Fischer, who lived for many years in Chile.

Regina was a powerhouse with the energy to be father and mother both. One acquaintance has called her "a wise and devoted mother . . . a gifted woman with a strong social conscience." Another remembers her as "ugly, short, with a big nose. The kind of woman who telephoned you at 1 A.M. to tell you things that could have waited till the next day. A woman who thought only of what she wanted and had to have it right away."

Regina worked like a mule to keep her little family going. By turns a stenographer, a welder and a teacher, she moved her family from Portland, Oregon, to a small town near Phoenix, Arizona, and finally to Brooklyn, where they settled in a four-room apartment a few blocks from Ebbetts Field. In the middle forties, Regina took her master's degree in nursing education with the highest marks ever handed out by the N.Y.U. School of Nursing. Then she started working double shifts at a hospital—a schedule that left her little time for the children.

From the time she was seven, sister Joan baby-sat brother Bobby. No father, an absentee mother, an overprotective sister, hardly any children his own age to play with—it was a peculiar life, and Bobby became a peculiar little boy. He lived in fantasies, estranged from the world outside his four walls. "Not exactly disturbed," says a family acquaintance, "but definitely odd."

One of Bobby's oddities was a passion for games and puzzles. Joan discovered that a set of Japanese rings or a Parcheesi board would keep him amused for hours. He also showed fantastic speed in re-arranging the numbered squares in a game called Fifteen and is now considered the unofficial world champion.

One day when Bobby was six, Joan came back from the candy store with a dollar's worth of destiny—a game called chess. Reading the instructions on the box, the children taught themselves to play. As usual, Bobby was so quick to learn that Joan got discouraged. For a while Bobby almost gave up chess because he had nobody to play with. But when he was seven he found a collection of chess puzzles in a summer cottage, and from that day the game was his obsession.

Bobby played chess from the instant he woke up till the instant he fell asleep. He played at breakfast, lunch, dinner; in bed, in the bathroom, at school. When he wasn't playing he was reading chess books or staring at the chessboard he had painted on his bedroom ceiling. His mother became alarmed. Before chess took over, Bobby had sometimes played stickball with other boys; now he thought other children were boring unless they were chess nuts—and hardly anybody his age had even heard of the game. Regina tried to interest Bobby in being a doctor or a lawyer. Nothing doing.

Finally she tried to scare up some other little boys who played chess by placing a want ad in the Brooklyn Eagle. The Eagle's chess editor suggested that Bobby play against a former champion of Scotland who was about to give a simultaneous exhibition in Brooklyn.

In his first public performance, Bobby lost in about fifteen minutes —and cried. His fervor was noted by Carmine Nigro, the president of the Brooklyn Chess Club, who became Bobby's first teacher.

Bobby was not a chess prodigy like Capablanca and Reshevsky, who were beating rated adults when they were only five years old. Bobby was just a chess-crazy kid who played thirty games a day. When his mother took him shopping he would rush up to perfect strangers and say, "I'm Bobby Fischer! Someday I'm going to be chess champion of the world!"

The moment came when all the longing and reading and playing paid off. "When I was eleven, I just got good." At twelve, Bobby won the U.S. Junior Championship. At thirteen, he won a game so brilliant it is still known as the Game of the Century. At fourteen, he staggered the chess world by winning the U.S. Championship. At fifteen, he became the youngest grandmaster in history. "And Bobby did all this," his sister proudly points out, "in a country almost totally without a chess culture. It was as if an Eskimo had cleared a tennis court in the snow, taught himself the game and gone on to win the championship."

Catapulted into world fame at an age when most boys were still busting their brains over long division, Bobby was totally unable to handle his success. In social development, "Baby" Fischer was hardly out of rompers. At thirteen, while he was giving a chess exhibition, he announced that he had to go to the bathroom. According to an eyewitness, his mother took him by the hand, led him to the men's room, waited until he was through, then led him back to the chess table. Absurdly innocent, he was a prize sucker. Somebody once persuaded him to peel a raw egg. Time and again other kids stole one of his rooks in the middle of a game and were always rewarded with genius-size tantrums.

Bobby covered his fear and loneliness with arrogance. He showed up for prestigious tournaments in sneakers and a sweater. He sneered at players four times his age. Half Jewish himself, he assumed a pose of anti-Semitism in a New York chess community that was better than four-fifths Jewish. "Jews," he told a reporter, "have taken the class out of chess." Worst of all, a chess official told me, "Every other word out of his mouth was 'fuck'—he was an extremely vulgar and unpleasant boy." The sedate Marshall Chess Club at first refused to admit him. "We have no room," said the widow of grandmaster Frank Marshall, "for a brat who wipes his nose on his sleeve." But she finally gave in.

People always did. They forgave Bobby everything because he was a genius, and Bobby kept inventing new ways to test his power. In San Francisco for the Junior Championship, he ordered six large pizza pies for dinner. After taking one bite out of each pie, he left the rest for garbage. In New Jersey, summoned to a stage to receive first prize, a handsome piece of luggage, Bobby took one look at it and snorted, "I don't need *that!*"

Regina made a no less calamitous impression in the chess world. Once she was sure that chess was Bobby's destiny, she got behind him like an avalanche. When the American Chess Foundation refused to give Bobby a grant, she launched a public campaign against them and demanded an I.R.S. audit of their books. When the U.S. Department of State refused to give a student chess team permission to play in East Germany, Regina picketed the White House and won a reversal of the decision. When she needed cash to finance Bobby's career, she tried to set up a wholesale business in Bobby Fischer chess wallets.

Bobby blocked that one. He hated Regina's "interference" in his affairs and accused her of trying to "exploit" him. In public, Bobby made faces behind her back. In private, there were shouting arguments. "They were so much alike," says a man who watched their struggle, "all drive and no give. Life in the Fischer household was trench warfare." But beneath Bobby's hatred there was respect. When complimented on his capacity for work he sometimes says, "You should see my mother."

When Bobby was twelve, he met Jack Collins, a talented spastic-paralytic who may be the greatest chess teacher of all time. In the last twenty years, Collins has developed three grandmasters (Bobby Fischer, Robert Byrne, William Lombardy) and two international masters. Jack became the father Bobby never had, and Jack's warmhearted sister Ethel supplied the soothing qualities that were missing in Regina's character. For five years, Bobby spent more time at the Collinses' than he did at home. He gobbled up Jack's knowledge, gobbled up Ethel's hearty meals, gobbled up the love they both gave him. "It was the only real home Bobby ever had," says a friend of Jack's, "and it gave him what little trust he has in the human race."

When Bobby was fifteen, his childhood abruptly ended. He broke decisively with his mother, who left the country to make a peace march to Moscow. During the march she met an Anglo-Polish professor of English literature named Pustan. They married and settled eventually in England, where Regina completed her medical education in the summer of 1972—at the age of fifty-eight. The same year Bobby's mother left, his sister got married and moved to California.

Bobby said he was glad his mother was gone—"I got rid of her," he liked to brag. In fact, her departure was a major shock. She sent him money, but he lived on alone in the Brooklyn apartment, a very odd boy indeed. Almost a total recluse, he kept the blinds drawn, slept most of the day, sat awake most of the night pursuing his obsession. Left back a grade because chess tournaments had made him miss too many sessions, Bobby hated Erasmus High School and showed up just often enough to keep the truant officer off his neck. Solitude, said grandmaster Robert Byrne, became his "luscious vice." He rarely had a visitor, left the apartment only to play chess or to take on some junk food at a neighborhood luncheonette.

"The apartment looked like an indoor dump," said a shocked visitor. "Newspapers and pieces of clothing all over the floor. Chess books and chess sets everywhere. The bathtub drain got clogged up and Bobby never bothered to get it fixed. The only way he could take a bath was to visit somebody. Finally the toilet got clogged up too." The kitchen was unbelievable. "There were bags of rubbish on the floor and the sink was full of dirty dishes with mold growing on them. When you went in the roaches ran in all directions and about thirty flies roared around and settled down again."

At fifteen, Bobby got another big shock. It was the dream of his life to visit the Soviet Union—he worshiped everything Russian, especially the great Russian chess players—and suddenly the dream came true. Financed by a TV show, Bobby and his sister took a trip to Moscow, where Bobby eagerly expected to meet the top Soviet masters and show his mettle. The Russians had other ideas. Fearful that their masters might be humiliated by a child, the Soviet chess bosses ordered their top players to keep out of his way.

Bobby was hurt and rightly insulted—as U.S. champion, he was entitled to better treatment. For two weeks he made hash of second-level Soviet masters. Finally, Tigran Petrosian, a thirty-one-year-old future world champion, was ordered to put the upstart in his place. Petrosian edged him in an informal blitz match, but not by much.

Bobby was not appeased. When he left for home, his hatred of the Russians was growing like the wild bean—and it was the Russians themselves who had planted the seed.

At seventeen, Bobby dropped out of high school with two years still to go, and that was the end of his formal education. His ignorance was almost as amazing as his talent. Grandmaster Bent Larsen tells how he once sat up half the night with Bobby, who was down with a bad cold, reading aloud to the young genius from a Tarzan book. Another time, when a less kindly chess master informed Bobby that Goethe was one of the Russian astronauts, Bobby replied, "Oh, yeah, that's right. Yeah." Perhaps in compensation for his ignorance, Bobby developed delusions of cultural grandeur. "I speak all languages," he once told a friend in dead earnest.

When he was seventeen, Bobby set out to bootstrap into respectability. He stopped swearing and stepped into European tailor-made suits. "I'm gonna have seventy-five suits," he promised a friend. "I'm gonna be the best-dressed chess player in the world." To another friend he confided, "If I wasn't so great at chess, I'd be a famous rock singer." He also claimed to have royal blood and assumed a divine right to special treatment at all times. In Yugoslavia, for instance, while driving with a journalist and his wife, Bobby insisted on switching places with the wife—he rode in the back seat, she rode next to the driver. "If we had an accident," he explained, "the world would lose its best chess player."

Behind the barricade of pretensions a small boy still crouched in terror. Food poisoning was one of his main phobias—he still has deathly fear of maraschino cherries—and to guard against it he became a nature food fanatic. He was also terrified of homosexuals. "Once when we were eating in a Greenwich Village restaurant," says an actress who met him in those days, "somebody told him that the owners were gay and that they put something in the food to turn their customers gay. Bobby stopped eating and couldn't wait to get out of there." Most of all, Bobby was afraid of women. "He was absolutely dying for an experience," says the actress, "but he was afraid that he might be physically injured in the sex act."

Nevertheless, Bobby tried. In South America he once visited a house of convenience and said he enjoyed the experience—"but chess is better." Another time he spent more than ninety minutes with an attractive *fille de joie*. When asked afterward how he had managed to last so long, he answered, "Oh, I just thought about chess openings." But his erotic career came to a dismaying climax during a 1960 tournament in Buenos Aires. When he entertained a young woman in his hotel room, his chess suffered severely—he finished fourteenth in a field of twenty. "That settled that," says a grandmaster who knows him well. "If it was sex or chess, sex had to go." Bobby dated a few girls in the sixties, but friends say the dates were purely platonic.

In 1962, all Bobby's problems converged. At Stockholm, early in the year, he had won the first of two elimination tournaments with such ease that he seemed sure to win the second and meet Botvinnik for the world championship at the unheard-of age of nineteen. But at Curaçao all sorts of things unaccountably went wrong. At the halfway point, Bobby stood fifth in a field of eight and was almost inside out with frenzy. One night he quarreled another U.S. grandmaster, Pal Benko, but backed down after throwing one punch and taking two. One day he was seen roaming the tidal basins looking for lobsters and smashing them with big stones. A night or two later his second found him catching moths in a water glass and setting them on fire. The fire spread to a chair and Bobby had to pay the hotel an upholstery charge.

Bobby wound up fourth in the tournament and lost his crack at the title. Heartsick, he dictated an article for *Sports Illustrated* accusing four of the five Russians in the tournament of conspiring to keep the title in Russia by playing to win against Fischer, playing for draws with each other, and throwing games to the men they wanted to win. The Russians angrily denied the charges and put out the usual rap about Bobby being a bum sport and an ill-mannered high school dropout besides. Unhappily, most American chess players thought the Russians were right. In fact, Bobby was right. Ex-world champion Mikhail Tal, who fell ill during the tournament, later admitted to friends that the Russians had played as a team against Bobby and had even thrown games to make sure a Russian won.

Bobby's blast was a powerful move on the big board of chess politics. At one stroke he broke the Soviet stranglehold on the title. Soon after Curaçao, F.I.D.E. reformed its procedures to prevent Russian domination of the elimination rounds. The path to the throne was now open, but during the next two F.I.D.E. cycles Bobby seemed less interested in capturing the title than in winning points of pride.

In the 1963–66 cycle, Bobby boycotted all international chess meets. In the 1966–69 cycle, he dropped out of the interzonal tournament (which he was leading) after a quarrel over playing conditions that was cunningly escalated by Moscow. "I'm leaving all those patzers," he announced, and went to Los Angeles, where he claimed to be "plotting my revenge." In fact, he was fighting off nervous collapse. For months at a time, afraid to live alone, he mooched on indulgent friends. Finally he rented a one-room flat and furnished it with a bottle of milk and a chessboard. There he stayed for more than a year, a lonely old man of twenty-five, sleeping all day, hunching half the night in fluorescent eateries, dreaming of glories his genius could win if only his devils would give it a chance.

Religion was his consolation. In the early sixties, Bobby had tuned in on a couple of electronic evangelists named Herbert and Garner Ted Armstrong, a father and son who spoke for a fundamentalist sect called the Worldwide Church of God. The church has some odd beliefs, among them the doctrine that the populations of the United States and Northern Europe are descended from the Ten Lost Tribes of Israel, and friends say that Bobby at first considered Garner Ted the "cornball of all time," listening just for laughs.

Then he got hooked and began to practice what the Armstrongs preached—mainly the strict observance of the Old Testament regulations about diet and the Sabbath. No pork, no shellfish. Complete avoidance of pleasure from sundown Friday to sundown Saturday. There were also prohibitions against smoking, divorce and dancing cheek to cheek. Necking, as a matter of fact, was called fornication, and was rated a "capital sin," on a par with murder.

For several years Bobby lived in Puritanical ecstasy. He carried a Bible wherever he went and claimed he could recite every word of it from memory. One friend reports that Bobby told him, "Religion helps me play better chess, that's all I care about." Most friends say his faith is deeply held and point out that the old-time religion imposed a patriarchal order on Bobby's existence that he had longed for all his life.

The sunny climate and sweet life in Southern California were also good for Bobby. By 1969, he was ready to resume his push to the top, but once again his "principles" got in the way. By refusing to play for the U.S. Championship—he said the tournament was too short—Bobby disqualified himself as a contender for Boris Spassky's title in the cycle ending in 1972. Three more years wasted. When a reporter asked him how soon he would become world champion, Bobby sighed and said, "I don't know, but I'm getting *awful* tired of waiting."

In one conversation Ed Edmondson turned Bobby's life around. As boss of the U.S. Chess Federation, he offered to pay all Bobby's expenses for more than two years and throw in "honorariums" averaging about $1000 a month if Bobby would take a crack at the title. In addition, he promised to act as Bobby's manager and man Friday until the title was won. After long and suspicious study of the proposal, Bobby agreed. But how could he play in an interzonal tournament for which he had not qualified? Edmondson had a foxy answer.

Tall, trim, soft-spoken and whip-smart, Edmondson was a retired Air Force colonel who at forty-five was the ablest executive and smoothest politician in F.I.D.E. Calling in a mass of political debts, he persuaded F.I.D.E. to let Bobby replace one of the American entries in the interzonal *if* one of the entries happened to withdraw. One did—after the U.S. Chess Federation gave him a consolation payment of $2000.

Edmondson spent almost $75,000 during the challenge rounds to make sure that Bobby got the best possible prizes and playing conditions. For almost a year, Bobby idolized the older man. Unfortunately, Edmondson did his job so well that reporters began to tell the public he deserved some of the credit for Bobby's successes in the elimination rounds. Bobby became restive. In Buenos Aires, after his victory over Petrosian, he threw a screaming tantrum and accused Edmondson of mismanaging his affairs. Outraged, Edmondson shouted back that Bobby was an "ungrateful shit." Bobby simmered down and they patched things up, but the romance was over.

Back in New York, Bobby began to look for somebody to take Edmondson's place. By the end of March, three months before the match was to start, he had found Paul Marshall, the most aggressive force to enter his life since his mother left it. Forty-three and running to midriff, Marshall had a smattering of ugliness that he used, like a character actor, to grab attention. Pale bulging eyes looked out of scruffy gray skin that blotched pink when he got excited. When he talked he kept licking his lips, and his voice scraped and roared like a concrete mixer. He walked with explosions of eagerness that usually put him a step ahead of everybody else, and his mind worked the same way. His talk was packed with wit and images and on any given day he had more schemes in his head than a snake has wriggles. He was a born manipulator and in negotiation was known as a man who could speed-read between the lies and write an agreement in the other fellow's blood. He also had the common faults of brilliance. Easily bored with routine and with people less clever than Paul Marshall, he liked quick successes and sometimes lost a battle because he had unwisely won a skirmish. He liked to talk up a storm and then stand at the center of it while the world swirled around him in admiration.

From the moment they met, Marshall played Svengali to Bobby's Trilby. He blew Bobby's head full of extravagant though not in fact exaggerated notions of his potential in the marketplace. After a couple of meetings with Marshall, Edmondson seemed pale porridge indeed—"a small-timer," Bobby called him—and all his arrangements for the Spassky match too petty for the superstar Bobby now perceived himself to be. But how to get rid of him? Bobby lacked the courage to come right out and say what was on his mind. In direct discussions with Edmondson he was sweet as pie; behind Edmondson's back he conjured up the conspiracy theory. One night toward the end of March, Edmondson was staggered when Bobby telephoned to tell him he was fired and all arrangements he had made were canceled.

Marshall took over negotiations with Thorarinsson, but Bobby was bound that Marshall would not become another Edmondson. From now on, he meant to run his own show. After more than a month of haggling, Marshall came up with a somewhat more advantageous set of deals. But Bobby told him, "I want 30 per cent of the gate too." Disgusted, Marshall quit. Bobby accused him of "disloyalty" and decided he could do without him. Without anybody. Without the match.

4

The Achilles of Cedar Street

Davis arrived in Iceland looking like a tomcat somebody had forced to take a bath. "Where's Cramer?" he snarled. Rushed to his hotel, he took a room across from Bobby's suite and made phone calls to Fox, Thorarinsson and the U.S. embassy. Fox ducked his calls all day—he figured there was contract trouble and wanted to postpone it as long as he could. Thorarinsson did not call back for several hours and then showed no eagerness to discuss. He was busy at the playing hall, where curtains were still going up and rugs going down; besides, he had heard from Loftleidir-Kennedy that Bobby was crazy and Davis had no real authority to speak for him. The U.S. chargé d'affaires gave Davis an appointment for 3 P.M. "Now that," Davis said, "is a man I *really* want to see!"

Unshaven and haggard, Tony Saidy came scuffing into the kitchen a little before 10 A.M. Friday. He felt like a horror-show hero taped to a time bomb. The last plane that could possibly take Bobby to the match in time would leave at 9 o'clock Saturday night. Somehow in the next thirty-four hours, somebody had to "pull Bobby's head out of his ass," as Indridason put it. On Thursday the job had proved too big for seven men. Now it was all up to Tony Saidy.

What's more, Bobby was only the second most harrowing problem on Tony's hands. Fred Saidy, Tony's father, a well-known broadway librettist who wrote the books for *Jamaica, Bloomer Girl,* and *Finian's Rainbow,* was on the verge of kidney failure. He refused to go to a hospital, and it was up to Tony to beat down his resistance and put him in an ambulance—fast.

"Breakfast?" Tony's mother asked. Marie Saidy was a vigorous full-bodied woman with large hazel eyes that usually sparkled but now were dull with worry and exhaustion. She was a talented cook, and an offer of breakfast was not to be taken lightly. But Tony didn't need breakfast. He needed help. Who could he recruit on such short notice? Edmondson, Lombardy, Marshall? Sooner or later they might all be useful, but right now Tony needed somebody to give Bobby a big hello when he came downstairs, watch Lawrence Welk with him, squeeze him a quart of fresh orange juice two or three times a day.

Tony needed his family. Both as a son and as a doctor he wanted his family's attention to be centered on Fred Saidy—but where else could Bobby go? Put him up at a motel and he might take the next plane back to California. Feeling guilty, Tony asked his mother how she would feel if Bobby stayed till Saturday night.

"Not good," Mrs. Saidy said. "How important is it?"

Tony told her what had happened at the airport the night before.

"Let's see how things go," Mrs. Saidy said.

That morning, before his guest got up, Dr. Saidy gave the family a prescription for handling Bobby Fischer. Screen his phone calls if he gets any. Keep the newspapers away from him—they would probably be full of anti-Fischer tirades. Don't tell anyone, especially not the media, that he's here. And above all don't argue with him. Just be friendly. Let him calm down. At the right moment he might listen to reason. "He's *got* to," Tony said. "He's *got* to make that plane to-morrow night."

Theodore Tremblay, the U.S. chargé d'affaires in Reykjavik, was a sallow medium-sized man in his late forties. He wore three-button suits, narrow ties and the sober expression of a doorman at an expensive apartment hotel. He said all the right things but he said them without expression, as though someone were moving his jaws by pulling a string. But he knew his job and did it well.

Tremblay's P.R. man was Robert Garrity, who ran the Reykjavik branch of the U.S. Information Agency. Like Tremblay, he kept his nose clean and used it whenever possible to smell a rat. They both smelled a big one in Bobby Fischer.

"We've had an uphill fight here," Garrity told me. "During World War II there were a lot of G.I. babies and the air base is regarded as a national insult. The Icelanders fought more than four hundred years for their independence, and they're pretty touchy about it. But we've been keeping a low profile and quietly winning friends. Then comes this—this ill-mannered person making public announcements that Iceland is primitive and backward. You should have seen the headlines here. Bobby Fischer has set back America's position in Iceland at least ten years!"

This was the situation that faced Andrew Davis when he and Fred Cramer walked into Tremblay's office at 3 P.M. on Friday, June 30. After reminding the diplomats "how important this match is, both to the United States and to Iceland," Davis assured Tremblay and Garrity there was "a very serious possibility" that it would not take place because I.C.F. could not improve its offer. "If that happens, Bobby Fischer will become the most hated man in Iceland, and a great deal of that hatred will spill over into the United States."

Tremblay nodded cautiously.

The Icelandic Chess Federation, Davis went on, would be out of pocket approximately $50,000. But since I.C.F. was backed by the Icelandic government, it was Icelandic taxpayers who would therefore be doubly incensed at Bobby—and at the U.S.

"Under these circumstances," he concluded, "I would think it almost certain—wouldn't you?—that the United States would pay that fifty thousand dollars to Iceland."

Tremblay's eyes jumped with surprise.

"Consider the alternative," Davis went on. "What would happen to the U.S. image in Iceland *if the Russians paid it first?*"

There was total silence in the room. Very quietly Tremblay asked, "What do you suggest?"

"Since the United States is going to spend the money anyway, why spend it *after* most of the damage has been done? Why not spend it first and *prevent* the damage? Why not offer the Icelanders fifty thousand dollars *now?*" With an extra $50,000 in hand, Davis added, I.C.F. could meet Bobby's demands for a share of the gate. Bobby would agree to play—and would almost certainly win. "The Icelanders would be grateful. The Americans would be popular. The Russians would take a beating. Isn't that a pretty good return," Davis asked, "on a investment of fifty thousand dollars?"

Tremblay and Garrity were dumbfounded. In effect, Davis was proposing to blackmail the U.S. government! What's more, Davis seemed to be inviting Tremblay to become his accomplice in the scheme!

Still partly in shock, Tremblay replied, "I'm afraid I must tell you, Mr. Davis, that we are a very small mission in a very small country and we conduct our affairs on a very small budget. We cannot buy a paper clip without an appropriation from the U.S. Senate. It would therefore be impossible for us to spend fifty thousand dollars or even fifty dollars in the way you suggest."

"Is there any way," Davis asked, "that you can *get* the authority and the money?"

Tremblay shook his head. "No way at all. I'm sorry."

Davis rose, his face flushed. As he left the embassy, he muttered, "Fucking idiot! I'll fix his ass!"

A deep rumble jarred the Saidy residence. Big truck in the neighborhood? It came again. Tony and his mother looked at each other.

Bobby was up.

Tony glanced at the time—not quite twelve. Bobby in motion before noon? Practically unheard of. Was he ill?

Ten minutes later Bobby was downstairs, smirking nervously. Tony and Mrs. Saidy were all smiles as they said good morning.

"Did you sleep well?" Mrs. Saidy asked, giving him a motherly once-over. He looked pale and strung out, and his eyes were jumpy.

"Yeah, yeah," he answered. "Hungry, though."

Hungry? After that 3 A.M. orgy?

Ten minutes later, while the Saidys looked on in awe, Bobby was shoveling away a stevedore's dream of a breakfast that he probably considered skimpy. First came two large glasses of orange juice, then four poached eggs on toast, six or eight slices of bacon, four pieces of buttered toast, and two large glasses of milk.

Mrs. Saidy brought him another glass of orange juice and he put it down in three gulps. "Good, good," Bobby said. His relationship with Mrs. Saidy was beginning to be reestablished. "It was the same relationship we had when he was thirteen," she told me. "I was maternal, he was puerile."

Mrs. Saidy opened the door of the automatic dishwasher and stacked dishes inside.

"Hey, what's that?" Bobby wanted to know.

Mrs. Saidy said it was a dishwasher.

"Hey, wow! I heard of those." He looked suspicious. "It really gets 'em clean?"

Mrs. Saidy showed him how it worked.

"Very simple, very practical," he said. "Tremendous convenience, I can see that. Wow, yeah. I want one of those when I get my apartment."

Bobby slowly relaxed a little. He seemed especially comfortable with Peter Saidy, Tony's younger brother, who was about Bobby's age. Tall, wiry and immensely likable, Peter was making ends meet by working as a part-time bartender and taxi driver and eating a lot of meals at his parents' home. As a boy, Bobby had felt much more mature than Peter. Now it was Peter who seemed more experienced. But it was hard to resent him for it, even though he was wearing long hair and beads and looking like everything Bobby said he despised. There was no rivalry in Peter and no hidden threat.

Tony asked Bobby if there was anything he wanted to do that afternoon. Bobby said he might like to do a little shopping. So about 3 P.M. Bobby and Peter drove to a shopping center in Fred Saidy's car.

Mrs. Saidy sighed. She had been with Bobby off and on for the better part of three hours and she felt as if she had spent three hours picking her way through a minefield. "I'll make him a big Lebanese dinner tonight," she told Tony, "but tomorrow you're on your own."

On the way to Surrey in his Rolls, James Derrick Slater skimmed the London *Evening Standard*. A quick-moving man in his early forties with a large head, a strong mouth and clear eyes, he was Britain's most gifted financier. In eight years he had converted a £2000 bankroll into a £250 million investment banking company called Slater-Walker. His partner, Peter Walker, was now Secretary of State for Trade and Industry in the British Cabinet.

On an inside page, Slater took note of a small article reporting that grandmaster Robert Fischer had appeared at a New York airport but for reasons unstated had not taken the plane to Reykjavik. Slater looked thoughtful. He had a keen interest in chess. As a boy he had hoped to become a chess professional but decided the financial rewards were too meager. Now he expressed his passion for the game by putting up chess prizes and making cash awards to promising young players. Most of his gifts were given anonymously and without strings. He didn't want glory—just results.

After glancing through the article again, he turned the page.

As they cruised along in Fred Saidy's Charger, Peter talked about his decision to drop out and his crappy but amusing jobs. In Manhasset they went to Abraham & Straus and Bobby bought a pair of dark-red slacks, cut mod. After mousing around the store awhile they cruised back home.

The dark circles under Bobby's eyes were darker when they arrived, and Mrs. Saidy quickly supplied an enormous sandwich to hold him till suppertime. Bobby lifted the top slice of bread and peered in.

"What kind of meat's that?" he asked.

"Tongue," Mrs. Saidy told him.

"Tongue!" He seemed astonished. "You mean the tongue of an animal?"

"A cow's tongue."

"Oh!" He was staring at the meat uneasily. "I never saw that before. How do they make it?"

"They boil it or smoke it. It's very good. Try it."

Carefully, he took a bite and began to chew.

"Mm," he said. "That's *very* good. I never knew you could eat tongue."

The sandwich disappeared in a matter of seconds and Bobby slumped upstairs to "rest up" before supper.

Before dinner the Saidys got together in the living room and had a noisy affectionate Levantine gab, including Bobby as a member of the family. For the first time in days Bobby's eyes began to lose that burned-out-light-bulb look. He told Fred that he had read one of his scripts, something about Czechoslovakia. "You really made the people seem like real Czechs." Fred was pleased.

Mrs. Saidy drew Tony aside and showed him a bottle of cologne in the shape of a chessman. "I got this for *you*," she whispered. "Shall I give it to Bobby?"

"Perfect!" Tony whispered back. "He'll love it!"

She gave it to Bobby and he did, handing it around like a birthday boy for everyone to smell. By the time dinner was ready, Bobby was busting out in huge toothy smiles, almost having a good time.

Dinner completed his undoing. It began with a dish fit for an emir—a platter of grape leaves rolled in tubes the shape of a small cigar, then stuffed with rice and ground lamb and cooked in lamb broth laced with fresh lemon juice and fortified with marrow bones. Bobby rolled his eyes and said, "Good, good."

Then came the main course: a rack of steaming ruffle-edged tartlets the size of a man's palm, each filled with chopped lamb and pine nuts and topped with sour homemade yogurt. Bobby is a yogurt buff, but he had never tasted anything even faintly like this fierce tribal ambrosia. As he finished his fourth tartlet he looked at Mrs. Saidy with something like worship in his eyes and said, "Great, really great!"

"You win the title from those Russians," she said, putting in a good word while his guard was down, "and I'll *really* make you a Lebanese dinner!" Bobby laughed but said nothing.

Bobby began to talk about how horrible reporters were and wound up describing the night before. Talking about the incident seemed to relieve his feelings. His scowl turned to a grin. "I'm gonna get a bumper sticker made up," he announced, "and I'm gonna paste it on my forehead. It's gonna say, *I will not give any interviews.*"

After dinner, incredibly, Bobby was still hungry. Mrs. Saidy brought him a bowl of Jell-O.

"What's *in* Jell-O?" he asked a bit nervously. The Saidys explained.

Changing the subject, somebody asked him about his new clothes. He swarmed up the stairs three at a time and came down wearing his new slacks and a dark-brown reversed-leather jacket. He was also carrying two pairs of shoes and several ties.

"Look at that jacket, isn't that beautiful?" he exclaimed, standing stiffly and turning around. "I got it in Argentina. They got great craftsmen down there. And how about those shoes! Feel the weight of them." He handed each of the Saidys a shoe. "They're light, right? But they're strong. Can you imagine what shoes like that would cost up here? Fifty dollars anyway, right? You know what they cost down there? *Eleven dollars!* Unbelievable, isn't it? And they'll last for years. Now take a look at these ties!"

His voice became almost reverent as he displayed the ties, which were aggressively ordinary. "Look at these designs! We got lousy ties up here, y'know? But down there they got great designers! Look at this one. Beautiful, huh? Now why can't *we* make ties like that?"

After the fashion show, Bobby and Tony played a game of chess in their heads, calling out the moves, first one, then the other. Bobby won. Then Bobby sat shyly with a niece of Mrs. Saidy's who had dropped by, and watched George Jessel on the Merv Griffin show. About 9:30 he trudged upstairs to start his Sabbath retreat.

Ten minutes later Bill Lombardy arrived. Grandmaster Lombardy was a Roman Catholic priest, no doubt the finest ecclesiastical chess player since the sixteenth-century Spaniard Ruy Lopez. "A magnificent talent," Edmondson had often said. "Probably as great as Bobby's." At sixteen, Lombardy fought through to the World Junior Championship, winning eleven games in a row—one of them from a boy named Boris Spassky. The experts foretold a great career, possibly the world championship, but Lombardy chose the church. At thirty-five he was black-haired, rosy-cheeked, six feet tall, and at 240 pounds massive all over, like a sumo wrestler. His movements were quick and powerful, his jaw assertive. As a priest he was liked because he was a "regular fellow" with a rough and ready sense of humor. But this regular fellow was far more martial than the usual Christian soldier.

Being with Lombardy was like being at war; he did everything to win. He stood tall, as if trying to be taller than the people around him. In his steady, dark-blue eyes there was often the sort of look that silences a noisy class. People he didn't like he stared through as if they weren't there. Conversation he didn't like he overrode, pushing his own sentences over another person's like a lawnmower over a patch of weeds. He had a strong mind that could hold only one point of view on a given subject. Lombardy was in fact remarkably like Bobby. Under his hard shell he concealed a childish softness and a total inability to cope with women. Bobby and Lombardy were flint and steel, Edmondson said. In collaboration they would necessarily strike sparks.

Collaboration had been planned. Bobby had asked Lombardy back in April if he would be available as a second in Reykjavik, and Lombardy had said yes. But as usual, Bobby had not made a firm commitment. Lombardy was waiting and wondering. He was also wondering, now that Bobby's amazing victories had pumped chess prizes up to six figures, if he should take a leave of absence from Cardinal Hayes High School in the Bronx, where he taught English, and mount an all-out campaign to win the world championship in 1975.

When Lombardy arrived, Bobby was watching TV in his third-floor bedroom. Lombardy went upstairs and tried to ease the conversation around to topic A, but could hardly make himself heard over the racket of the TV. Finally he asked if Bobby had made up his mind about playing the match. Bobby said he wasn't going unless he got what he wanted.

Lombardy asked how long he planned to stay at the Saidys'.

"Oh, three-four days," Bobby answered.

Lombardy suggested it might be better to stay at a hotel, what with Tony's father being sick and his mother so busy and worried.

"Oh, no," Bobby reassured him. "I don't mind."

Lombardy blinked. Of all possible answers, this was the last he could have imagined.

Tony came up and they both made a major effort to break through to Bobby. Tony went over what he called the "positive arguments" for playing the match: to humiliate the Russians, to bring the title to the U.S., to make chess a popular sport, to reform F.I.D.E., to get rich.

"Ye-eah," Bobby said from time to time.

Coming to "negative arguments," Tony told Bobby he was certain that if he didn't play the match there would be a strong hostile reaction all over the world. The public would be convinced that he was an arrogant, greedy coward who had put himself before his country and run away from the match because he was afraid he couldn't beat Spassky.

"Naa, naa," Bobby said. "Maybe they won't understand right away, but if I don't play I'll be right, y'know? And in the long run I'll be vindicated. Anyway, why should I do anything for the public?" he finished with a sneer. "What has the public ever done for me?"

Patiently, earnestly, Tony and Lombardy went around and around the problem. Bobby was guarded, but now and then he would state his objections to the match. At one point he objected that he couldn't do his setting-up exercises in Iceland because he couldn't get Jack La-Lanne on Icelandic television. His friends heard his objections respectfully and reasoned them down to size. But they were making debating points, not changing Bobby's mind.

"If I go without getting my demands," Bobby told Tony toward the end, "people will think I'm weak."

When Tony and Lombardy left, they felt like men emerging into the real world after wandering in a catacomb. Bobby was still trapped in his intricate delusions.

"Bobby was drifting," Tony said later, "waiting for something to happen that would make the decision for him."

Bobby in fact was doing what he usually did when he found himself in a mess: letting other people worry about it. He had learned at his mother's knee and under his sister's wing that passivity in himself produced activity in others. When a decision became too complex for him—and decisions often did—he would fly into a tantrum and announce something outrageously self-destructive. All sorts of people would then rush to solve his problem. In a way he enjoyed all this; it made him feel important. But in another way it bored him. People bored him, especially when there was chess to play or a TV program to watch. The whole situation was beginning to bore him now and his friends sensed it. They found hope in the fact because they knew that whenever Bobby became bored he went back to chess. But would he go back to chess with Spassky? Everything depended on what happened Saturday.

"I was just checking out the turf today," Andrew Davis told me before he went to bed Friday night. "A lot depends on what I can get tomorrow. I've got to twist some major concessions out of Thorarinsson."

"Suppose you do," I asked. "Will Bobby come?"

"I have no idea," Davis said. Then he grinned. "It's deliciously existential, isn't it?"

5

The Second Reykjavik Expedition

On Saturday, July 1, at 7 A.M., Boris Spassky was playing tennis with his trainer, Iivo Nei, on a concrete court about fifty yards from the Saga Hotel, where the Russians were quartered.

"Good morrrning, Hahrry!" Spassky called out with a wave of his racket. "Please not photographing me—photographing Iivo. He is *so* much better!"

Harry Benson, the other half of *Life*'s Bobby Fischer team, looked like a poet in a daguerreotype, tall and willowy with a romantic shock of black hair and big dark suffering eyes. In fact, the eyes were as efficient as a hawk's and Benson was *Life*'s top general-assignment man. Spassky liked Benson, and so did Bobby. They felt he was one of their kind, a poor boy who had made it from the slums of Glasgow to a major British football team to *Life* magazine.

Spassky played hard, chasing impossibilities and sometimes making an almost miraculous save. "He's a fighter," Benson thought. "He likes it best when the heat's on."

"That's enough!" Nei called out in Russian, and they all started back to the hotel.

"What do you think?" Benson asked Spassky. "Is Bobby coming?"

Spassky looked startled, as if his mind had been read. "No," he said. "I do not think Robert James will come."

Spassky looked like an Italian movie star of the late fifties. He was tanned, muscular, above middle height, and his large head was encased in a mane of rich brown hair. His brow was massive, his jaw strong, his nose long and expressively languid, his mouth sensuous and a little arrogant, but it relaxed into a smile so charming it was almost menacing. His eyes, green and wild, burned like a fire sprinkled with copper salts.

The first time I interviewed Spassky, he came sauntering into the lobby of the Saga Hotel, wearing an orange-gold sport shirt and a green cashmere sweater that flattered his eyes. As he passed the big mirror in the lobby, he checked himself like an actor about to go onstage. He obviously liked what he saw.

So did Benson and I. Spassky was affable, witty, modest. He posed helpfully for photographs on a volcanic moor and spoke with a frankness that seemed almost reckless in a prominent Russian. When I said I hadn't met grandmaster Petrosian, he gave a contemptuous snort and replied, "You haven't missed much!" When I asked if he missed Leningrad, he said, "Oh, yes. But I am not allowed to live there. So! There is no sense to think about it." When I noted that Bobby had never won a game from him, he answered with a sweep of his hand, "Oh, he will do that!"

A few nights later Benson got Spassky a ticket for a Margot Fonteyn ballet and arranged for him to meet the leading lady after the show. Spassky brought a smashing bunch of roses and as he offered them blushed like a country boy. When Benson began shooting pictures, Spassky's blush deepened and he murmured to Dame Margot, "I did not intend—please understand, Harry Benson is very naughty!" But he was flattered to be there, perhaps somewhat smitten. Returning from a short trip some nights later, he hit his fist into his hand when Benson told him he had missed a dinner with Dame Margot. "Damn!" he said with feeling.

On these excursions, Spassky was like a kid let out of school. At all other times, even when he went for a walk on the beach, he moved in a close convoy of assistants. About two blocks behind, there was always a gray English Ford that stopped when they stopped, started when they started up again. "We have reason to believe that Spassky and his people are heavily watched," an Icelandic official told me. "Since the first of June more than seventy Soviet nationals have entered Iceland. In a usual month there are no more than eight or ten. Most of these people claim to be tourists, but they have not toured. They travel only to the Russian embassy."

I saw several of them padding the halls of the Saga, small men in shapeless gray suits who told me the time in heavy Russian accents. Every time Benson and I left Spassky's suite we were followed, and once a man in Russian shoes ran out of the Saga, aimed an eight-millimeter movie camera at us for about thirty seconds, then ran back in. Later I discovered that Spassky and his assistants were convinced their hotel rooms were bugged.

One night Spassky was the personal guest of the local K.G.B. chief, a strutting bully named Viktor Bubnov. Short and thick-chested, he rolled his shoulders powerfully, darted his eyes here and there and jutted his jaw as if to remind himself how dangerous he was. He had a curious non-Communist passion for golf, and he hauled Spassky out for a midnight round at Reykjavik's dismal little nine-hole course, as flat as the sea beside it and liberally spattered with gull droppings. Benson and I went along to take pictures, but as it turned out Spassky had never played the game—and besides, it wasn't much fun trying to hit the ball with your coat pulled over your head to protect it from the feathered bombers. Spassky stayed for more than two hours before making his excuses. "It is important," he explained as we left, "not to offend certain people."

Why all the security? Possibly because of a rumor that Spassky was watching for a chance to defect. He had a long record of disaffection with Soviet policies and there were problems in his second marriage. But the main reasons for the K.G.B.'s concern probably arose from Spassky's moody, dramatic, profoundly Russian character.

Born in Leningrad on January 30, 1937, Spassky was the second of three children—his younger sister, Irina, is women's checkers champion of the USSR—and like Bobby he was born under the powerful aspect of a Grand Trine. Not true that he was half Jewish, as most U.S. journalists assume. His father's father was an Orthodox priest—"Spassky" is related to the Russian word for savior—and his mother's father was a delegate to the Duma. Spassky's father was an engineer and, like Bobby's father, abandoned the family when Spassky was a small boy. Spassky's mother was a grade-school teacher and, like Bobby's mother, strong-willed, stubborn and a political activist—but she was also passionately religious.

When Spassky was four, the family fled to Moscow to escape the German attack on Leningrad. There were many days when the Spasskys had nothing to eat. Spassky's mother injured herself and could not hold a regular job. Friends helped out, but at six Spassky was "the head of my family."

Spassky fell in love with chess when he was nine. After the war, he studied the game at the Leningrad Palace of Pioneers, where he found the first of two fatherly men who shaped his chess success. Coached by

Vladimir Zak, he reached the quarterfinals of the Russian championship tournament when he was fourteen. Considering the level of the competition, his precocity was almost as amazing as Bobby's. "I played, though," Spassky once told Leonard Barden, "like an old man, very positional and solid."

To liven up his game, Spassky studied with an intrepid attacker named Alexander Tolush, and at eighteen he won both the World Junior Championship and the Soviet Championship (tied with Taimanov and Averback). "A genius!" Botvinnik told friends. "In a few years he will be world champion."

Whereupon Spassky went into a seven-year slump. Genius, he discovered, counts for less than character in the making of a champion, and Spassky's character was the despair of his bosses in the Soviet Chess Federation. "Boris is so Russian I want to scream," says a friend. "He is the Brothers Karamazov rolled into one!"

Socially, Spassky was attractive and successful. Along with his charm came tact, humor, appreciativeness—plus a wide natural understanding. When he got moving, he had tremendous drive. Once in Yugoslavia a friend saw him miss a six-foot high jump nine times in a row, but on the tenth try he cleared the bar.

Much of the time, unhappily, Spassky's force was out of control. Like Bobby, he had grown up a spoiled darling of the chess establishment. In his early twenties, as a result, his ruling passion was getting what he wanted and getting it now. "He could not stand the slightest refusal," says an old acquaintance. "He once punched another grandmaster because the man took a cookie that he wanted." He liked travel, cars, sharp clothes, Western gadgets, money. A friend says, "He was a Soviet playboy." In chess politics, he was shrewd and unscrupulous. He dropped his coaches and his patrons with cold indifference whenever he got a better offer.

With women, Spassky was a flamboyant seducer. Once at a banquet where he was guest of honor he spotted a beautiful girl he had been pursuing. Leaping up, he strode from the speaker's table and in full view of the guests made his way to his inamorata. After kissing her hand, he sat beside her and there remained throughout the evening, while the people showing him honor sat and steamed. His affairs were usually brief and broken off in a burst of bad feeling. "In life," says a friend, "his end game is not good."

No part of Spassky's life was good during his seven lean years. At Moscow University, he dropped out of mathematics, his real interest, and took gut courses in journalism. Then he made a bad marriage and "for three years ... my nervous energy was completely destroyed." He began to quarrel with Tolush, a high-strung irritable man who called him "a very stupid boy." Distracted a dozen ways, Spassky lost concentration, lost his will to win, lost the race for the title to Mikhail Tal.

In 1961, Spassky found the right coach: grandmaster Igor Bondarevsky. "Before Bondarevsky," says Spassky, "I was drifting. I did not really understand the game. But he is the finest chess teacher in the world. He formed my fighting spirit." In 1965 Spassky whipped Keres, Geller, and Tal, and in 1966 met Petrosian for the title.

Spassky lost—partly because he hadn't worked hard enough, partly because a woman he loved threw him over in the middle of the match. But three years later, in splendid form, Spassky beat Petrosian 13–10 and at thirty-two became world champion. After twenty-three years of competitive chess and six years of direct assault on the title, Spassky stood at the pinnacle—and he hated it. He hated the speeches, the committees, the public appearances, the lack of privacy, the sense that everybody he played was trying to grab a jewel from his crown. For years he had been weary of chess; now he became sick of it. He stopped playing in tournaments and even in private games. Word went around that he was "the laziest champion since Capablanca."

A general decline set in. He smoked too much, drank too much, put on weight. Always reckless in his political remarks—he had openly criticized Soviet intervention in Czechoslovakia and Cuba—he now began to associate with some very odd types indeed. "It was like nostalgia for filth," says a close friend. "Some of his most frequent companions were pickpockets and housebreakers! We were all terribly worried."

At the same time Spassky's second marriage went from bad to worse. Larisa was the daughter of a high official in Russia's natural gas industry, and Spassky seemed to resent her privileged childhood. Encouraged by Bondarevsky, an Asiatic in his view of women, Spassky made no attempt to hide his love affairs and even discussed other women freely in her presence. Larisa became more and more miserable. By the fall of 1971 they had agreed to divorce. About the same time, Spassky also broke with Bondarevsky.

With the title match less than ten months away, the champion was in total disarray. He was sick of everything, especially himself. He felt that his life was going down the tubes and he wasn't sure it was worth saving. As he began to prepare for the match with Bobby, Spassky was less interested in winning the title than in pulling himself out of the worst emotional hole he had ever been in.

Spassky decided not to find a successor to Bondarevsky—like Bobby, he wanted to become more independent and felt he could do without a mentor. Instead of a father figure, he chose a big brother, a forty-two-year-old Estonian chess trainer named Iivo Nei. Blond, muscular, a good athlete and a first-rate chess theoretician, Nei in most ways was the flat opposite of Bondarevsky. Bondarevsky was earthy, orgiastic, situational in his ethics, something of a wild man in his personal life—all the things Spassky felt he had to stop being. Nei was systematic, controlled, discreet, an old-fashioned man of honor who believed in right and wrong—all the things Spassky felt he had to become. At the same time, Nei was modest and witty, a good companion for the long haul of training. Spassky was sure he had chosen a man on whom he could depend without becoming dependent, and he persisted in this belief even as he loaded Nei with a heavy armful of portfolios: chief of staff, physical trainer, spiritual director, psychoanalyst, friend.

With Nei's help, Spassky selected the rest of his team. Nikolai Krogius, a third-rate grandmaster with frog eyes, dewlaps and a blob of gristle on the back of his neck, was an unworldly fellow who hid his timidity behind strut and sneer. Because he had written a book on chess psychology, Western experts assumed he would be in charge of psychological warfare against Bobby. In fact, Spassky considered Krogius something of a joke. He was taken on to answer phones, buy candy bars, go to meetings and in general act as Spassky's dogsbody.

Selecting an official second was not so easy. Spassky needed a high-level grandmaster with a plus score against Bobby and skills that would complement his own. The obvious choice was grandmaster Yefim Geller, a runty Ukrainian with a chest like a gorilla, a big lolling kewpie-doll head and a jaw that shot in and out like a trundle bed when he was nervous. Geller had won more games from Bobby than any other Russian and his specialty was the opening game, where Bobby was strong and Spassky had some weaknesses. Geller had some disadvantages, though. He tended to flap when the going got tough and he had a reputation for telling tales out of school if so ordered by his superiors in Moscow. Spassky nevertheless decided to go with Geller, and in October 1971 the team began to hold strategy conferences in Moscow.

Spassky's chess condition was obviously bad—he finished sixth in a warm-up tournament—but his physical condition was what worried his team. When training began, Spassky couldn't jog fifty yards without stopping. At Nei's suggestion he quit smoking; on his own hook he stopped drinking. They began to run in a Moscow park and Spassky slowly picked up stamina. Then to his horror Nei discovered that Spassky hadn't been to a dentist in fifteen years and had as many cavities as teeth. In the next few weeks Spassky had six or seven teeth pulled and more than a dozen filled. Geller had almost as much repair work done.

In midwinter, Spassky and his team spent three months in the high Caucasus, where Spassky worked fairly hard at his chess but had a fine vacation too. Nei and Spassky worked out every day and sometimes at night went snowshoeing over mountain trails. Spassky spoke at length about his life and their friendship deepened. Nei came to understand that for Spassky the match was far more than a match; it was a vehicle of salvation. But he also came to understand that for Spassky the way to salvation might detour through all sorts of quixotic aberrations.

One night on a narrow mountain trail, for instance, Spassky and Nei came face to face with a small herd of wild buffalo, four cows and a calf. Ordinarily not aggressive, the cows stood their ground because of the calf. Nei suggested that he and Spassky should move aside and let the animals pass, but Spassky set his jaw stubbornly. "No! *They* must give way," he cried, caught up in an extravagant fantasy of power, "because *I am a grandmaster!*" It was only with difficulty that Nei persuaded him to back down.

After a few weeks in Moscow, the Spassky party finished its work in Sochi, a summer resort on the Black Sea. Spassky came to Reykjavik looking like a million rubles. Theoretically, he was as well prepared for Bobby as eight months of training and the full resources of the Soviet chess establishment could make him. Spassky's team had studied every game of Bobby's that had ever been published. Every important grandmaster in the Soviet Union had contributed an analysis of Bobby's play and made recommendations about how to beat him. Several of the strongest grandmasters had visited Spassky's headquarters and played training matches against him. In none of them had Spassky played especially well.

After all his work, Spassky was not really in the mood for a match, not really in form. He blamed himself, but there were moments when he blamed others too—his team for its shortcomings, his bosses in

Moscow for not letting him meet Bobby to agree on a site for the match, Bobby for unsettling his mood by calling the match off and on and off. The Spassky who was waiting for Bobby to arrive in Reykjavik was physically and technically prepared for the match, but emotionally it could only be said that he seemed better off than Bobby.

Chester Fox had sunk his bottom dollar in the film project and on Saturday morning when he showed up at the playing hall he was worried green. "If that chucklehead don't come," he groaned, "I'm back in Brooklyn eatin' Wonder Bread."

There was something in Fox that was not of this world. With his sweet smile and cherubic ringlets he looked like a dreamy young rabbi in a poor congregation, and he might have been happy as that. Instead, his dumbhead guardian angel had talked him into a business where he had to be a rat to win the rat race.

There he was, jabbing wary glances at his fingernails, at a passing carpenter, up at the rafters, down at his watch—anything to avoid meeting the eyes of the person he was talking to. "Yeah," he kept saying in a tone that guaranteed he wasn't listening. A moment later, though nothing funny had been said, he released an enormous unreal *haw!* Suddenly he was glancing in every direction and cleaning his teeth vigorously with his tongue, like a chimp who had just polished off an orange.

What did all the mugging mean? Perhaps that, early in the Reykjavik project, Fox had found himself in a production situation far beyond his experience. People kept demanding decisions he felt unable to make, but he made them anyway, jutting his jaw to signify leadership. Though Fox's gestures impressed no one else, he began to feel like the force he was pretending to be, and this gave him the confidence to make really big mistakes.

Born in 1935 in a fresh-air ghetto in eastern Poland, Fox came to Brooklyn when he was five. At sixteen he was hired by Mike Todd as a "gopher" and later became a theatrical press agent. In 1969 he directed a short called *First Class* that starred Marcel Marceau and won twenty-three prizes.

Even after *First Class*, Fox was a small-timer, but for Paul Marshall this was an asset. "I didn't give a damn if Fox was any good as a director. The main thing was to have a man I could control, somebody who needed money and would give Bobby everything in order to get the deal."

"Mr. Fox!" somebody called. Fox spun around and peered at a very peculiar object, one of a pair that stood at opposite sides of the stage. About four feet square and fourteen feet high, the object was covered with yards of brown burlap and looked like a two-story outhouse. The eye of a movie camera peered through a hole.

"What do you think, Mr. Fox?" a voice called through the burlap. "Is the camera too noticeable?"

"Hell, no!" Chester answered. "Bobby wants it outa sight but I got my rights too. Screw it, that's plenty good." That settled, Fox slumped. "Two nights no sleep," he told the nearest workman. "Wake me in twenty minutes, huh?" Then he lay flat on his back on the fresh-laid carpet at the back of the stage and in less than a minute was snoring.

While Fox slept, his head cameraman, Gisli Gestsson, had something to say.

"When Chester came here, he said he was a famous American director. I looked him up in *Who's Who in Film* and I couldn't find his name. He also said he had a working capital in excess of two hundred thousand dollars. I have a friend in the bank Chester uses here and he tells me Chester's working capital is three thousand dollars. Not much, when you consider that his weekly nut is at least eight thousand. I'm waiting to see if he meets his first payroll. I supplied the crew, you know, and some of the equipment. If he doesn't pay us, we'll all pull out."

"Does he need all the people he's got?"

"No. He has three cameras and two men to each camera. One man would be plenty. He's wasting money all over the place and he doesn't seem to know it. He arrived much too late and he has only emergency plans that change every fifteen minutes. He made an incredible mess of the lighting. We have had to do it all over a couple of times. And look at those horrible towers! I think Chester's heading for big trouble."

At 11 A.M. Saturday, Davis and Thorarinsson came to grips in a Loftleidir Hotel conference room. Two other I.C.F. board members were there, and so was Cramer.

"I want Bobby to play the match," Davis opened. "I'm assuming that's what you want too. But I warn you my client is prepared to break off the match if his conditions are not met." Davis then made a straight-faced pitch for 30 per cent of the gate.

Thorarinsson repeated what he had said Thursday night. Now it was Davis's turn to enter a strong counterplea. But he didn't! He dropped the subject like a used Kleenex.

"Now I come to a point," Davis was saying, "that is relatively new to our discussions but *very* important to Bobby. He had great difficulty getting his prize money after the Petrosian match. He absolutely *will not come* to Reykjavik unless a letter of credit for the winner's share of the prize money is deposited in a New York bank. This letter must instruct the bank to pay Bobby the full sum, or a sum equal to the loser's share, upon certification *by me* that Bobby is either the winner or the loser of the match."

"By *you!*" Thorarinsson burst out laughing. "Who does he think we are—confidence men? This match is backed by the government of Iceland!"

"My client intends no disrespect, sir," Davis answered. "But the condition stands."

Thorarinsson's eyes half closed. Was Davis looking for a wedge to crack open the question of the gate? Or was he saying, "Let's get together and set up a minor victory to save Bobby's face."

"The prizes are ours to give, not yours or Mr. Fischer's. Under the conditions you suggest, you could force the bank to pay Mr. Fischer even if he had not played the match!"

Davis shrugged. "If you don't trust me, let's agree on a third party."

"Why should we let this money leave Iceland, where we know the law can protect it?"

Thorarinsson was nibbling and Davis knew it. "How about the Reykjavik branch of an American bank?"

"Doesn't exist."

"So put the money in a Reykjavik bank and give the U.S. chargé d'affaires power to release it. How about that?"

Thorarinsson was relieved. All Davis wanted was a convincing way to guarantee Bobby that the money would be paid. "I understand your problem, Mr. Davis," he said gravely. "I will speak with my government."

Davis leaned forward. "I hope you *do* understand my problem, gentlemen. Because it is your problem too. Mr. Fischer is demanding, perhaps unreasonable. This is unfortunate but we can't unbunch those coals now. We *can* reassure him that the prize money cannot possibly be withheld. If we do not do this, I can guarantee that Mr. Fischer will not play."

Thorarinsson smiled wistfully. "And if he is satisfied on this point, can you guarantee that he *will* play?"

Davis met his eye. "No. But I am here because I think there is a chance."

Thorarinsson nodded. "I will call you in the late afternoon."

"Not too late," said Davis, "please."

Tony Saidy came down to breakfast Saturday morning feeling worse than he had felt the morning before. All night he had squirmed and stared, waiting for the light inside his head to switch off. His mind kept making lists, rephrasing arguments, building little piles of things that could go wrong. Hunched over breakfast, Tony wondered if he could hold out.

First things first. Fred Saidy was going to the hospital today if they had to sprinkle Seconal on his cornflakes. So after breakfast, with the help of an excellent medical education, Tony threw a scare into the man who had paid for it. Then Tony got down to Bobby business.

He called Edmondson and they talked for almost an hour. Edmondson set everything in a practical perspective and came up with some wise suggestions. A little after 10:30, Tony started his countdown for the Second Reykjavik Expedition.

"Hello, Hans? It's on for tonight. The 9:30 plane . . . Can you and Tedd be here at, say, 7:00? And no limousine. Bobby says the press will be looking for it . . . Fine. Just so it looks like a private car . . . You mean skip the terminal? Drive straight onto the field? Perfect . . . Fresh fruit, milk, steak . . . For me? Just a good stiff drink."

By Saturday afternoon, rumors were flying around Reykjavik like baseballs at pepper practice.

Bobby was already in Iceland, hiding in the admiral's quarters at Keflavik airbase.

Bobby had flown back to California.

Bobby had gone insane at Kennedy Airport and was now in a private sanitarium on Long Island.

Bobby had agreed to play the match because the Ford Foundation had added $50,000 to the purse.

Bobby would arrive in Iceland on Sunday morning in a jet provided by Time-Life.

Bobby was already on his way to Iceland in Air Force One, accompanied by Vice-president Agnew.

Some reporters called Bobby the biggest sports scandal since the White Sox threw the World Series. Some agreed with Arthur Koestler, who was covering the match for the London *Sunday Times*. "I find it inexpressibly sad," he said, "that genius should be paired with such squalidity."

The Saidy phone rang steadily after Edmondson hung up. Some of the calls were from friends of Bobby's who wanted to help; some were from chess-club busybodies who had guessed where Bobby was and were hoping for juicy stories. About 11 A.M. Bob Hallowell phoned from a yacht basin near the tip of Long Island. Tony begged him to throw the weekend overboard and come help rescue Bobby. But Hallowell had had enough. Soon after that, a reporter called. Tony told him Bobby wasn't there, but he felt the walls closing in.

About 2 P.M., Tony went upstairs to his father. "This is the last time I'm going to ask. Either you tell me to call an ambulance right now, or I'm finished. I'm not going to waste any more time on you. What's it going to be?" Fred took a deep breath and then nodded unhappily.

Before the ambulance came, Tony had a few embarrassed words with his mother. Would she mind not coming home after leaving his father at the hospital? "Just for a couple of hours. The simpler the situation, the easier it will be to get Bobby off." Mrs. Saidy said she'd go visit her sister-in-law.

By 3:30 the ambulance had come and gone. It was high time to wake Bobby, and Tony knew it. In the next four and a half hours he would have to bathe, dress, eat breakfast, pack, take last-minute calls from Reykjavik—and make up his mind to go or not to go. Even so, Tony decided not to call him right away. If Bobby was slept out he would be more likely to wake up in a good mood.

Plenty of time, Tony thought, and ran up to do his packing.

About 5:30, Indridason and Hope arrived at the Saidy house in a Loftleidir station wagon with the company logotype carefully taped over. Peter answered the bell and made sure they weren't reporters before he let them in.

Tony look wrung out. Lombardy prowled restlessly, chewing on a cigar. Bobby, it seemed, was still asleep. The plan was to wake him in a few minutes. The bags were packed, Tony said, and they should be ready to leave by 8:00. In the meantime, would Hope and Indridason mind waiting in the car? Seeing them might put a flea in Bobby's ear, and he might knock himself out trying to swat it.

"I thought he was definitely going," Hope said. "We're not here to play games." He reparked the car where Bobby could not see them but they could see the front door, and then waited for Peter to stick his head out the front door "and wink."

An hour passed. No wink. "It was one of those sticky nights," Indridason remembers. "When we closed the windows, the heat killed us. When we opened them, the mosquitoes killed us." A little before 7:00, they rang the front bell again.

"Bobby's up," Peter told them in a low voice. "I don't know yet if he's going."

Hope called Loftleidir to hold the plane and the seats reserved for the Fischer party.

Back in the car, Hope and Indridason waited some more. Another car drove slowly past the Saidy house and parked just around the corner. A little later, Peter ran to the car and talked for several minutes with whoever was in it. Hope went to the kitchen door. No progress, so he let the first plane go.

Indridason meanwhile took a walk past the parked car. Two middle-aged women were sitting inside. One put her head out the window. "Isn't this terrible?" Mrs. Saidy asked. "Put out of my own house!"

Hope confirmed an indefinite delay of the flight for mechanical reasons. Mrs. Saidy said she would wait in the house of a relative, and drove off. Alternately stifling and swatting, Hope and Indridason waited.

The home of the Icelandic National Theater is an elongated cube, plated with red-black lava. A U-shaped lobby surrounds the auditorium, which seats about five hundred people. It was the same theater where Boris Spassky, several nights earlier, had sat in admiration of Margot Fonteyn.

Tonight the occasion was starchily official. For the last half hour men in tuxedos of the Eisenhower era and ladies in klunky Danish *couture* had been ducking out of Volvos and Moskvas and Mercedes.

They looked like rich farmers who had come to town for a do but weren't sure how to do it.

The president of Iceland arrived with his wife and several dignitaries. Fred Cramer came bouncing in. Jack Collins appeared in a shiny new wheelchair and Ethel steered him to a seat near the door. Theodore Tremblay turned up looking braced to grin and bear it. Viktor Bubnov, the K.G.B. man, strutted in with his chin covering the crowd like a pistol. About six feet behind him trudged his wife, who looked like a bodyguard in drag. Then a man with the build of a heavyweight wrestler came shouldering out of a black Zil, followed by a short thickset smiling man, the Soviet ambassador.

Benson was peering into the hall from a side door. "Have a look," he whispered.

Every seat in the hall was filled—except one in the front row. The president of Iceland, plus dozens of high officials and important businessmen, had shown up for the opening of a match that most of them now believed would not take place.

"It's the Emperor's New Clothes, isn't it?" Benson murmured.

Thorarinsson stepped to the rostrum. "Ladies and gentlemen," he announced, "in the name of the Icelandic Chess Federation, I welcome you to the match for the World's Championship of Chess . . . The match has now begun!"

About 7 P.M. the phone rang at Paul Marshall's house.

"Uh—Paul?"

"Yeah, who's this?" Marshall knew damn well who it was, but he needed time to get over his surprise.

"It's Bobby."

"Hi, Bobby. How've you been?" He let his voice be friendly but kept it noncommittal. He knew Edmondson and Lombardy were trying to get him reinvolved, but he had not expected this.

"Pretty good," Bobby answered. "Say, I was wondering, what's happening on that TV deal?"

Marshall smiled inside. Bobby wanted him back, but his pride wouldn't let him come right out and ask.

"I don't know," he said. "I assume Andy's taking care of it."

"Nyuuhhnn."

They talked awhile. Bobby expressed the sort of confusion that usually tempted people to take a problem off his hands, but Marshall held back. If Bobby was fussing over the TV deal, it meant he was going to play. When he hung up, Marshall was certain that Bobby was on his way to Reykjavik.

After the opening ceremony and a sip of champagne at the reception, Spassky went straight to his hotel suite. Geller, Nei and Krogius went with him, and for about an hour they sat around drinking Danish beer supplied by the Russian embassy.

For Spassky's sake they tried not to show it, but they felt let down, even a little silly, like knights who had taken a long journey to battle a dragon that looked them over and decided they really weren't worth fighting. They made nervous jokes ("Maybe we could sell some of our research to Petrosian?") and Spassky smiled.

"So it seems that all our work may come to nothing," he said, "but what can we do? It is Bobby's move. If he comes, we play. If he does not come, we do not play. I cannot force him to come. A man who is willing to commit suicide has the initiative."

Somebody said it was insulting to treat the champion in this way.

"I do not think that Robert James intends to be insulting," Spassky answered. "I do not think he knows what he is doing."

"He *knows*," Geller said.

"He simply doesn't want to play," Krogius put in.

"He *is* playing," Geller insisted, "and I do not think we should play Bobby's game."

After the others left, Spassky stared into the white night. Tomorrow, if Bobby did not come, Reykjavik would explode. Meetings, speeches, arguments, press conferences, flashbulbs, phone calls from Moscow. In all the confusion he would not be able to think. He must think now, calculate the variations, decide what he would do. At 1 A.M. he was still awake, playing Bobby's game.

At 10:50 Saturday night, Reykjavik time, Davis stared at his jangling phone.

"Lock the door as you leave," he told me. "For this one I don't want to be interrupted."

As the door closed, I heard him saying, "Tony? What's the story . . ."

I paced the corridor, hearing Davis's muffled rasp. It was torture not to hear the words. At 11:40, Davis had been talking for forty minutes.

Just after 8 P.M., New York time, Hope and Indridason rang the bell at the Saidy house again. "Bobby's talking with his lawyer in Reykjavik," Peter told them.

Hope called the airport and delayed the plane. Lombardy was downstairs, and they asked him if he thought Bobby would make the plane.

"I'll give you seven to one he goes," Lombardy replied. Indridason and Hope sat down to wait.

A little before 12:30 A.M., Reykjavik time, I passed Davis's door. After a full minute without hearing a sound, I knocked.

"Come in!" Davis shouted.

He was still on the phone but he waved me forward. "Well, that's how he *is!*" he said into the receiver. "Look, just take off your roller skates and get a good night's sleep. You can't do anything until tomorrow night anyway."

Bobby wasn't coming!

"No, *you* call Edmondson. The service here is lousy. And don't forget to send the medical cable."

The instant he hung up, Davis put through a call to Marshall. "Hello, Paul? It's Andy ... The word is, *he blew it* ... I did all I could. It's all yours, boy."

But what could Marshall do? Bobby had already missed his last chance to play the match.

"Saidy's expecting your call ... Bobby *what!* Called you already? Oh ..."

That hurt.

"Well, then, you're off and running ... All the luck, you'll need it ... I'll stay here and fight for the postponement ..."

Postponement! But could they get it?

"Chances? Practically zero, I figure. They all hate him too much now ... but we gotta try."

Davis set the receiver in its cradle and turned slowly. "How do you like them apples?" he asked quietly.

Hope and Indridason were in the living room talking with Peter Saidy. Bobby came downstairs in shirtsleeves, carrying a large glass of fresh-squeezed orange juice. He sat on the couch and leafed through a magazine. After a while he asked, "What are these guys doing here?"

Peter said, "Well, they came to take you to the airport. They're wondering if anything was decided."

"Yeah," Bobby said. "I'm not going." The others sat staring at him.

"There was no expression on his face," Hope said later. "To look at him, you'd never guess he had just destroyed his career."

"I'd better release the plane," Hope said. He went to the kitchen and called. When he got back, Bobby was still reading the magazine.

After a while Bobby said, "There's no more planes, right?"

"That's right," Hope said.

"Well," Bobby said, "I guess that's it, right?"

Hope and Indridason left.

Mrs. Saidy walked in. She had just got the message by phone. "I was devastated," she remembers. "When I thought of how we'd put ourselves out and then he's not going! I got so mad I could hardly speak to him."

Tony and Lombardy came downstairs, still stunned. Bobby was hot to play chess, so they ran through half a dozen blitz games. In one game Bobby spotted Lombardy one rook and put up a hell of a fight before he lost. Lombardy is a brilliant blitz player, but that night he couldn't keep his mind on the board. As soon as he decently could, he went home. Dying on the inside, Tony loyally played on until his big brown eyes looked like raisins with eyebrows.

6

Stop the World!
Bobby Might Get On

The lobby of the Loftleidir Hotel sounded like a giant television set with nothing on the channel but roar. At least three hundred over-excited chess officials, newsmen and rubberneckers were jammed into an area the size of a tennis court. "Fischer . . . Fischer . . . Fischer . . ." The word rushed through the room like a wind.

"The sonofabitch really did it . . . I mean, it's all over, right? . . . Cramer's talking about a medical postponement. Says Bobby has a bad cold. Ha! . . . You can't *get* a line to the States. Believe me, I've been trying for two hours . . . No, I talked to the stewardess on the Thursday-night plane. She said he refused to come because he didn't get a police escort . . . I'll bet you anything he'll show up for the drawing of the colors. This has got to be a publicity stunt . . . All I know is, one of the passengers said there was this U.S. Air Force jet, and a big car drove out on the runway and somebody got off the plane wearing civilian clothes . . ."

Chester Fox stood in a circle of reporters. "Mr. Fox," a British reporter was asking him, "are you concerned about the outcome of your investment?" Fox answered deadpan. "I haven't noticed if I'm concerned. I been trying too hard not to shit my pants."

Davis and Dr. Euwe, the president of F.I.D.E., walked into the lobby, looking grave. "Dr. Euwe," the question came from Harold Schonberg of the *Times*, "what is the situation now?"

"Yes, gentlemen, well—uh," Euwe said, "as you see, Mr. Fischer is not here. We are told that a telegram of explanation will come. But—uh—so far it has not—"

A reporter cut him off. "We all know Bobby *never* cops a medical plea. Who's kidding who?"

"Well—uh—Mr. Davis informs me that such a telegram has been sent and—"

"Mr. Davis," Schonberg began, "can you—"

Davis closed his face. "Sorry. Confidential."

"Well, I can tell you a telegram is *definitely* on the way." Cramer's bullfrog bass boomed from the general direction of Euwe's left elbow. "It was sent last night by Mr. Fischer's doctor and if the Icelandic communications system were worth a hoot in hell it would have *arrived* here last night or early this morning."

Davis glanced at a clock: 11:24. In six minutes Euwe, Schmid, Cramer, the Russians and the Icelanders would assemble. Under the rules, illness was the only valid excuse for a player who failed to show up for a game, and illness had to be certified by the match doctor, an Icelandic M.D. named Ulsar Thordarsson. Since Bobby was 2600 miles away, Thordarsson clearly could not examine him, but perhaps under the circumstances Euwe and the others would accept telegraphic certification from Dr. Saidy. The whole case for postponement, as Davis saw it, rested on that one perhaps.

At 11:26 chief arbiter Lothar Schmid walked into the lobby. Schmid was a cultured European with a civilized balance of interests. Born to millions, he lived graciously in Bamberg, West Germany, with an attractive wife, three children, the largest private chess library in the world, and a collection of chess sets, stamps and autographs that occupied 120 square meters. He was sleek all over, with soft brown eyes and beautifully styled tastefully graying hair, and he dressed in suave brown combinations that stressed the general impression of pussycat.

But when anything reminded Schmid of his official status as chief arbiter, the charming smile popped off his face. The expression behind the smile was rigid and humorless. When Schmid had inspected the playing hall, for instance, he'd sat on six or seven hundred chairs and wiggled back and forth in each to see if it made any noise. After more than an hour he had hauled his aching pelvis to Thorarinsson and announced with grave concern, "Chair number 222 squeaks."

Now Schmid's face was drawn with strain. All morning he had felt palpitations and a frightening tightness in his chest. Minutes later he told Gunnar Arnlaugsson, the assistant arbiter, that he was seriously thinking of resigning and going home. "Dreadful!" he muttered now. "Bobby should not have done this. Do you think his mind has given way?"

"He needs more time," I suggested.

"Time! But there *is* no more time! We cannot ignore the rules!"

Schmid, it seemed, would oppose postponement.

At 11:28 Thorarinsson crossed the parking lot and entered the other end of the lobby.

"Suppose the telegram doesn't get here," I asked him. "Are you going to fight for a postponement anyway?"

"It is no longer up to me," he said. "It is up to *them.*"

At that moment the Russians walked in. They paused just inside the entrance nearest us, five men standing close together as if to establish their separateness, their unity. Spassky was a step in front of the others, and stood looking at the scene before him with head held high and green eyes serene. He looked like a prince arriving at a follower's castle and waiting for the lord to greet him.

Thorarinsson went to meet the champion. The crowd fell back and made an aisle. Not even the brassiest reporters tried to question Spassky as he advanced to the conference room. Geller, Krogius, Nei, they recognized. The new man was an interpreter named Chamanin, one of many quasi-identical Russian bureaucrats of the island whose faces appeared to have been restored to almost human form after a fatal accident. Euwe, Cramer, Schmid and the assistant arbiter, Arnlaugsson, followed them. The door closed.

Davis looked like a man watching cannibals pot-roast his favorite child. Months of struggle, three days of pure hell—and now everything sent down the chute by some illiterate at Western Union who had probably sent Tony's wire to Ireland instead of Iceland. Davis blew out his breath and checked the time: 11:46 A.M. Four hours earlier in New York. "I'll be in my room," he said briskly.

As he hurried off, a reporter looked after him. "That's Davis," he told another reporter. "Now what kind of an asshole would be Fischer's lawyer?"

Max Euwe was a grandfather's clock of a man, tall and portly with a head so small it made him seem even taller. With his mild eyes, gentle smile, and wisp-strewn pate, he had something of the dear old party about him. He often tried to seem brusque and forceful, but in chess circles he was known as a stubborn Dutchman who just couldn't say no. All through the hassles with Bobby he had vacillated alarmingly, passing in a single conversation from dictatorial ultimatum to grandfatherly indulgence.

Euwe was stronger than he seemed. Any man who could win the world championship of chess—and Euwe won it in 1935 from Alexander Alekhine, before Bobby Fischer the most aggressive master in the history of the game—had plenty of force. But Euwe's force was like the power of water. He was easy to push around, yet in time the people who pushed him realized they were getting tired and he was still in the same place.

Euwe took charge of the meeting. "Gentlemen, a serious crisis has arisen. Great efforts and large sums of money have been invested in this match, which has aroused world interest in chess as never before. The prestige of two great nations is involved. We must be very careful in our decisions. They will affect the image of chess in the public mind and the future of F.I.D.E. for many years."

Then he came to specifics. Fischer was said to be ill, but a telegram from his physician had not yet arrived. Cramer broke in to assure the group it was coming. "I respectfully urge this meeting not to make any decision until it does."

Euwe said the situation would not be simple even if the telegram did arrive. "The rules state that medical certificates must be signed by an official doctor. Since the official doctor is here and Mr. Fischer is there—"

Cramer hastened to suggest that the rules had failed to envision the present situation. "Dr. Saidy is a properly licensed physician. Under the circumstances, I believe this meeting should accept his diagnosis."

Schmid brought up another point. "In Point Six of the match regulations it is stated that 'such certification should be given to the chief arbiter not later than noon of the day of the game.' It is now lacking only five minutes till 12:00."

Euwe raised a more fundamental problem. "Has the match started yet?" At the opening ceremony Thorarinsson had said, "The match has now begun." Euwe had other ideas. "Some think the match will only begin with the choosing of colors or the starting of the clock," he said. If that proved true, then Bobby's lateness would have to be referred to the president of F.I.D.E., who had a wide range of possible decisions.

Just then a substitute for the match doctor arrived. Fighting for time, Cramer started arguing whether or not the substitute was properly accredited. Euwe cut him off and put the question to Spassky —had the match begun or not? Spassky let Geller explain the Russian view: the match had been opened by the opening ceremonies.

Cramer interpreted that as a vote against Bobby. If the meeting ruled that the match had begun, the regulations would practically compel a forfeit of the first game. But Cramer had expected the Russians to cast the *only* vote against Bobby. He got a shock when he heard Schmid saying, "What is the purpose of an opening ceremony if not to open the match?"

Cramer spiked Schmid's answer. "An opening ceremony is just a social occasion, window dressing! In my opinion a match begins when the players choose colors. This match has not begun!"

Then came the crusher. "According to the Amsterdam agreement," Thorarinsson announced, "the match *must begin* no later than July 1st. July 1st was yesterday. Therefore in my opinion the match opened with the opening ceremony."

Thorarinsson stood to lose more than anyone else if the match were wrecked, yet he was saying the one thing that would hurt the match most! Feeling painfully alone, Cramer grabbed the first thought that came to mind, and took off on a filibuster.

"Gentlemen! Excuse me, but I have noticed that the rather large Russian delegation has been augmented by an interpreter, Mr. Chamanin. I wonder if his presence here is really necessary—and really fair. As we all know, Mr. Spassky speaks excellent English. On the other hand, if Mr. Spassky prefers to have an interpreter, I suggest that the American delegation should also have an interpreter to translate into English the comments Mr. Spassky and his friends have been making to each other from time to time in Russian. But perhaps, to be completely fair to both sides, the meeting should be conducted in a language *equally unfamiliar to everyone present!* Spanish, for instance!"

Color rose in the faces of the Russian delegation. Krogius spoke rapidly in Russian.

"Who are you exactly, Mr. Cramer?" Chamanin translated. "Who do you represent here?"

Taken aback, Cramer said that he was "Mr. Fischer's representative in all matters that have to do with the match."

"Can you show us your credentials?"

Cramer had nothing in writing to show that he was in fact Bobby's representative, but he tried to pass the question off lightly. "As is well known, the only pieces of paper Mr. Fischer signs are checks made out to him. Har, har."

"Since you have no document signed by Mr. Fischer, there is no reason why this meeting should accept you as Mr. Fischer's representative. The members of the Russian delegation do not know why you are in this room and why they should be forced to listen to what you say."

Euwe moved in smoothly to change the subject. "I see difficulties for the point of view that the match is already open. One cannot open a world championship chess match with a few speeches and a violin. I believe that the match will begin when the player who has chosen white makes the first move in the first game."

Euwe then presented the alternatives—none of them pleasant.

"First, if we shall decide that the match has begun, Bobby will forfeit the first game—and almost certainly choose to forfeit the match. Mr. Spassky will retain a championship that will have lost most of its meaning.

"Second, if we shall decide that the match has *not* begun, the match will probably have to be canceled." Spassky would have wasted eight months of preparation and the Icelandic Chess Federation would have spent a small fortune for nothing. "In both cases, a very strong and angry reaction will arise in the United States. There is great danger that F.I.D.E. will be destroyed by this quarrel."

Euwe then stuck his neck a long way out. "I have been thinking of another approach. *Suppose we postponed the first game of the match for two days!* This would give Mr. Fischer an opportunity to settle his problems and to appear in time to play the first game on Tuesday. At the same time, Mr. Fischer would be given a final ultimatum—if he does not appear in Reykjavik at noon on Tuesday, July 3rd, he will forfeit all his rights as the challenger."

For a long moment nobody spoke or even breathed. Euwe turned to Thorarinsson, who replied in impressive, slightly histrionic tones. "Gentlemen, if it is possible to have a two-day postponement of the match, the Icelandic Chess Federation will be very happy to agree."

All four Russians began speaking urgently in their own language. Spassky turned to Euwe.

"Dr. Euwe, my colleagues and I must discuss before we make a decision. Perhaps—" He glanced at his wristwatch. Euwe suggested a lunch break until two o'clock. As Spassky left, his face gave no clue to his intentions.

"Saidy didn't send the telegram!"

Davis did not elaborate on whether Saidy had asked Bobby's permission and Bobby had refused, or whether Saidy had been sure that Bobby would refuse and for that reason had not asked him. Davis by now had been bombed out so often he didn't seem to mind it any more. But Cramer was distressed that, without intending to, he had misrepresented the status of the telegram.

"That leaves us at the mercy of the Russians," he said bitterly, "and I can tell you that's no place to be. I'll bet you Geller's back there at the hotel right now, talking to Moscow. They know Bobby can beat Spassky and now they'll *never* let him get to the table."

Davis nodded. "So don't tell anybody the telegram isn't coming," he said. "Might be just the excuse the Russians are looking for."

The match was still alive, if only until after lunch, and for that reprieve Schmid and Cramer gave the credit to Euwe. They were amazed that the dear old monument had run the meeting so effectively. They might have been less surprised if they had known what Spassky and Thorarinsson knew.

At 8:00 that morning the wily Icelander had persuaded the champion to meet him secretly at the Esja Hotel. He told the champion that if the match fizzled, I.C.F. would be out about $140,000—at least $50,000 for preparation, more than $78,000 for Spassky's prize money. The Icelandic government, which would have to make up I.C.F.'s losses, might be seriously hurt, and he tactfully reminded Spassky that the government was a left-wing coalition friendly to Moscow. As matters stood, he said, the world would blame Bobby for destroying the match—why should Spassky go out of his way to share that blame?

Spassky knew that his bosses would want him to bust the match and he was tempted by the chance to win without fighting. On the other side was his ambition. Chess experts were calling Bobby the greatest player in the history of the game; if Spassky could beat him, what would they call Spassky? And then there were the financial considerations. "I think," he said with a sigh, "we must try one more chance for the match."

Thorarinsson showed Spassky how to achieve postponement while seeming to oppose it: let Euwe take the lead—and the responsibility. This was the scenario, and so far it had played with surprising smoothness. But what if Spassky had caught a call from Moscow during lunch?

Cramer was axed just before the 2:00 meeting began. Euwe took him aside and said as gently as he could, "It is better you do not come to the meeting now. We will call you later."

No explanation—none required. Obvious that the Russians had called Euwe during the break and told him Cramer had to go. The tactic was crude but legal and Euwe could not object.

Cramer took his dismissal hard. "If you insist," he answered. "But you realize that if you kick me out and then cancel the match, it will look as if Bobby was railroaded. And that will *really* split F.I.D.E."

Schmid opened the afternoon meeting with an eloquent plea for a two-day delay. Then Euwe turned to the Russians. "Gentlemen, have you reached a decision?"

Geller did a diatribe on the subject of Bobby Fischer. Then he denounced F.I.D.E.'s president for condoning Bobby's outrageous demands. As the speech wore on, Bobby's name was heard less and Euwe's more. The Russians were clearly taking up the case of Bobby Fischer as a cudgel and swinging it at Euwe's head.

Euwe's face went tight. He assumed that Geller was acting on orders from Moscow; in fact, he was acting on orders from Spassky, who felt that Euwe favored Bobby and had decided to punish the old man. At last Geller came to the point.

"The Soviet delegation does not support, neither does it oppose, to the proposal for a two-day postponement of the match or to any other proposal that has been made. The Soviet delegation has the opinion that the decision should be made by the president of F.I.D.E. *The president of F.I.D.E. is responsible.*"

It was clear that the Russians wanted the match—they just didn't want to admit it. They wanted Euwe to save their bacon by breaking F.I.D.E. regulations, and then they wanted to hang the old man for breaking the regulations! The dishonesty of the maneuver infuriated Euwe.

"*I* am responsible, you say? Very well!" He leaped to his feet. "I will say the match is off and Spassky is the winner, is that what you want?"

It was the last thing the Russians wanted. Spassky turned pale. Schmid grabbed Euwe's arm to restrain him.

"Dr. Euwe! Please! We cannot make the decision in this way. It is too important. Let us do it calmly."

Euwe cooled off but the Russians had been put on notice. Nei, speaking German, expressed the Russian position more tactfully. Euwe steamed up again. Thorarinsson said firmly, "I think we can all agree on a delay."

Euwe offered his hand to Spassky. "I will make the decision with the help of F.I.D.E. colleagues here in Reykjavik," he said.

All through both meetings, Spassky had maintained his serene and sober mask. But as he said goodbye to Euwe, his eyes were anxious. What if the Moscow bureaucracy discovered his role in the postponement?

Sunday afternoon unrolled like a rug.

The F.I.D.E. officers met at 4:30 in Euwe's hotel room and the postponement was approved. Euwe scheduled the drawing-of-colors ceremony for Tuesday, July 3, at 11:45 A.M. The first game of the match would begin at 5 P.M. the same day.

A reporter summed up the events of the day: "They all hated Bobby. He put himself in the hot seat and every man in the room would have gladly pulled the switch. But nobody could afford to let the sonofabitch burn. So what did they do? They stopped the world. Now if we all fall down on our knees Bobby might be willing to get on."

It was about 2 P.M. in New York when Davis told Tony about the postponement. "Great!" he said weakly. Bobby was still asleep, and that was about the only thing Tony had to be thankful for. "By Sunday," Tony's mother said later, "we were all hysterical. Every time we picked up a newspaper we were reminded that we were harboring a National Disgrace. It was crazy, infuriating, frustrating, awful. It was funny too, but it was hard to see it then. Having *that nut* in the house and then two phones ringing morning, noon and night! Some reporters had found out where he was and they were calling too. On Sunday a couple of them even came to the door. Tony was exhausted. Everything was up to him, and no matter what he tried, it didn't work."

When Bobby got up, still looking pale and dragged out, Tony told him the news from Reykjavik. "Yeah?" was all Bobby said. He was much more interested in breakfast.

Mrs. Saidy served him, but she wasn't her usual cheery self. Tony was either off making phone calls or lying down resting. As the afternoon wore on, Bobby became more and more tense. Pretty soon he was heard to mutter that he was "getting bad vibes around here." Whenever the phone rang, he would jump. "Was that a reporter?"

The answer was always no. When the call had come from Edmondson, Tony had to make up another name.

About 5 P.M., Bobby asked for a sandwich. When it arrived he lifted the top and checked the contents. He hadn't done that since Friday.

Partly to get him out of the house, Peter Saidy asked a friend to take Bobby bowling. After a couple of hours at the alleys, the friend decided that a little encouragement might not be amiss.

"You know, Bobby," he said, "I think you can beat that guy Spassky."

Bobby whirled at him. "I don't need *you* to tell me that!"

When they got back to the Saidy house, Bobby was still in a surly mood. Tony decided it was better not to talk about the match until Bobby was more relaxed. "I'll tackle him," he thought, "in the morning."

That evening an arresting figure presented himself at the Saidy's front door. He was short, dark, muscular and roughly dressed. He sported a bushy black mustache and talked like a prizefighter in a 1936 movie, dis and dat and duh.

"Evenin'. I'm Jackie Beers. Friend uh Bobby's."

He disappeared upstairs. Tony explained that Jackie was a sort of hanger-on of Bobby's. They had met as young chess players. Bobby had realized his promise, Jackie had not. Jackie worshiped Bobby. Bobby was patronizing, sometimes insulting to Jackie. A man who knows them both said that some years ago he heard Bobby tell Jackie off. "We all got genes, Jackie, but the difference between you and me is, I got good genes and you got bad genes. That's why I'm a great chess player and you're a piece of shit."

Jackie was aggressive. He had been barred from a couple of chess clubs for fighting on the premises. But he absorbed Bobby's contempt without complaint; he seemed to believe that Bobby could do no wrong. In return for this uncritical devotion, Bobby displayed a surly devotion of his own. No matter how late Jackie called to ask if he could come over, Bobby would invariably say, "We-ell, all right. But you can't stay long. I gotta rest up."

In fact, they stayed up till all hours watching television and playing chess and talking cars and girls. Bobby thought of Jackie as Sinatra thinks of his gang—somebody to have around, to dump on, to make him feel good by reminding him how much better off he is. In fact, Jackie was much more than a hanger-on. He was Bobby's friend.

Soon the Saidys heard laughing and talking up in Bobby's room. Had Bobby shifted his reliance from Tony to Jackie, from a man who said "yes, but" to a man who simply said "yes"? If so, prospects for the match were even darker.

Freysteinn Thorbergsson is a short square man in his early forties with red hair and a red face. His eyes burn with a ghostly intensity; they are the eyes of a visionary. But his strong little hands suggest a man of action.

In the autumn of 1971, Thorbergsson was gripped by a vision: the Fischer-Spassky match must be played in Iceland. In his usual dynamic way he helped Thorarinsson promote the match. But Thorarinsson was a visionary too, and during one of the crises their visions collided. Thorbergsson denounced Thorarinsson and late in April visited Bobby at Grossinger's to assure him that many Icelanders sympathized with his side of the argument.

When Bobby failed to show up for the drawing, Thorbergsson's predictions of disaster were vindicated, but the match he had fought for seemed destroyed. Then came the miracle of postponement. Thorbergsson resolved to take the next plane to New York and urge Bobby to play.

He told an Icelandic reporter what he was up to, and then rushed off to the airport. No suitcase. Not even a toothbrush. With a DC-8 for his Rocinante and a burning ideal for his armor, Thorbergsson flew off in the quixotic hope that where all others had failed he might succeed.

At midnight, Thorarinsson lay in bed reviewing the day. Time had been won, but it would take more than time to bring Bobby to Iceland. The moment had come, Thorarinsson decided, to break out his secret weapon. "In the morning," he told himself. "I will pay a visit to the prime minister."

In the morning Thorarinsson would talk to the prime minister. Thorbergsson would arrive in Douglaston. Tony would talk to Bobby —or would he? In the morning Bobby would be asleep, and he would stay asleep at least until early afternoon. Once again the people around Bobby were sitting on a time bomb. As on Thursday and Saturday, they would have no more than seven hours to get Bobby aboard a plane for Iceland.

Bobby's sneering indifference to the postponement took the starch out of the Saidys. "Tony was wiped out," Peter said later. "Physically and mentally he was on the brink." New people were needed in Douglaston; Lombardy had seen that clearly on Saturday night. But who? Lombardy decided there was only one man with the power to blast Bobby out of his Douglaston bunker—Paul Marshall.

Pretty sure now that if Bobby went to Reykjavik he would not take a second with him, Lombardy decided to accept an offer from Tele-PrompTer to analyze the match for cable TV. On Sunday he and Marshall met with TelePrompTer. The deal signed, Marshall invited Lombardy home for supper. Over drinks, Lombardy made his pitch.

Marshall shrugged. "I climbed out of that snakepit once. Why climb back in?"

"Because you want to!"

Lombardy was right. Marshall was bored with safe successes. Being Bobby's lawyer gave him the adrenalin jolts his temperament required.

"I'm out of my gourd," he said, "but let's try it."

Lombardy telephoned Douglaston at about 10:00 Sunday night. Bobby refused to take the call. "I'm watching 'Cade's County.' "

An hour later, Bobby still wasn't interested in discussing his plans. Marshall and Lombardy decided to drive out to Douglaston.

They arrived at the Saidys' just after midnight. The house was dark. They rang. Nobody came. They rang some more. Finally Bobby stopped raiding the refrigerator and came to the door. After shaking hands without energy, Bobby turned on the TV set and flopped on a couch. "Go ahead," he said. "I'm listening."

"I think you should go to Reykjavik and play the match," Marshall began.

"Yeah?" Bobby was watching television.

"Yeah. You got anything better to do?" Teasing him.

The sound track was just loud enough to be distracting.

"Well, what? You're not scared, are you?" Challenging him.

Bobby gave a derisive grunt.

"Well, that's what people *think.*" If anyone else had said it, Bobby would have told him off. "What's the matter—you don't like your deal?" Marshall was suddenly matter-of-fact, practical. That was his style with Bobby. Keep changing the pace, confuse him with footwork.

Bobby said he wasn't going until his terms were met.

Lombardy said the terms for the match were unimportant. "The money involved is peanuts, anyway. Once you're champion you'll make millions." Bigger things than money were involved and Lombardy called Bobby's attention to them again.

Bobby muttered something about "principles."

Lombardy decided to cut through the crap. "Bobby," he said in the calm, steady tone of a coach reassuring a star athlete, "you are one hundred per cent sure to win this match. There is no way that Spassky can beat you."

"Come *on!*" Bobby jeered. "Everybody knows *that!*"

"Everybody knows *what?*" Marshall was staring at him. "Twenty-five grandmasters know you can beat Spassky, and not even all of *them* are sure. The public doesn't know. All those people out there that you want to interest in chess—all they know is that Spassky showed up and you didn't. And that looks like he's got guts and you're yellow."

Bobby stared at the TV screen, bitter and silent. Marshall hadn't quite believed that Bobby was scared of Spassky. Now he realized he had been wrong. In a fatherly tone, he began talking about matters that lay at a safe distance from the problem of fear. "Let's talk about deals."

Bobby looked at Lombardy and mumbled about "private matters." Lombardy discovered something to do in the kitchen. Marshall went into his act.

He began with a machine-gun series of questions about the deals, trying to twist Bobby's head away from the movie. Like a trial lawyer making theater for a jury, he paced back and forth, waved his arms, struck an attitude twenty feet away, came crowding in to mug. And all the while he was spewing out an inspired tirade on the subject of Bobby Fischer and the glorious career that was opening before him.

In twenty minutes Marshall had slaughtered the late movie. In forty he had Bobby asking interested questions about possibilities that could only arise if he went to Reykjavik and won. Riding his momentum, Marshall veered back to the current crisis. He went over Bobby's deal, lingering longest on the television arrangements and the almost endless opportunities for exploiting the footage produced. As to getting the prize money in advance, Marshall said there were several standard ways to guarantee a payment. "The main idea," Marshall recalls, "was that he should concentrate on chess and trust me with the arrangements."

"Yeah, but what about the gate?" Bobby said. "I want that 30 per cent. I want the players to get that, not the organizers. It's their right!"

Marshall took the plunge. "It is *not* their right!"

"Wha-a-at?" Bobby gasped.

"It is *not* their right to drive the organizers into debt," Marshall insisted. The organizers had some rights too. "And the Icelanders," Marshall said, "are probably going to lose money even as it is."

Bobby said that was fine with him; the more money they lost, the better. "I'm gonna teach those Icelandic creeps a lesson!"

Marshall told him that was unenlightened capitalism. If he wanted chess to be a major sport, he had to accept the fact that people were going to make money out of it.

Bobby flared up. "I don't want *anybody* to make money out of *me!*"

"All right. But then you're not going to make money either."

They had a battle over that and Bobby wound up with the sulks again. Marshall took a deep breath and started on another tack. Lombardy came back in and the two of them kept after him. At 4 A.M., when they all said good night, Bobby was smiling and seemed glad they had talked. But he was still a long way from saying he would play the match.

On the way home, Marshall and Lombardy ricocheted between elation and depression. Given time, they were sure they could bundle Bobby off to Reykjavik—but time was the one thing they had not been given. Somehow they had to smoke him out.

Gray with fatigue, Marshall had one of those ideas that can wow a man at 4 A.M. "Let's get a private jet and fly him up!"

Back home, Marshall called some top executives of major corporations. They all said they would check their company jets and call back.

Marshall then asked his wife to call AP, UPI, the *Daily News* and *The New York Times* and tell them where Bobby was hiding.

At about 6 A.M., Lombardy dossed down in a guest room and the Marshalls fell into bed. Betty set the alarm for 11 A.M.

At 7:10 A.M. the phone on the bed table shrilled. Betty groaned and snatched it up.

"It's for you, Paul," she said. "Overseas."

Marshall lifted a numb hand to take the receiver.

7

"Chicken, Come On Out!"

At 10 A.M. Monday, July 3, Thorarinsson explained the situation to Prime Minister Olavur Johanneson.

"What can I do?" the prime minister asked.

"Can you get the White House to give Fischer a good hard push?"

Johanneson agreed to try. Some hours later, he told Tremblay that the Icelandic people and the Icelandic government would be affronted if Mr. Fischer did not play the match. His absence would be adverse to the U.S. position in Iceland. The prime minister said he hoped this would immediately be made known to the American government at the appropriate level.

At 9 A.M. Washington time, Tremblay briefed his superiors in the U.S. State Department.

"Marshall speaking."

"Is this Mr. Paul Marshall, Mr. Robert Fischer's solicitor?" The voice was faraway and British.

"That's right." Marshall looked terrible and felt worse. He had been asleep little more than an hour.

"Mr. Marshall, this is Robert Toner. I'm a producer for the BBC. An offer has just been made here by Mr. James Slater. If Mr. Fischer will go to Reykjavik and play Mr. Spassky, Mr. Slater has offered to add £50,000 to the prize fund."

"*What!*" Marshall sat bolt upright, startling his wife.

"To double the prize fund. That is, if Mr. Fischer will play."

Marshall blinked and checked the room. It was there. "Is this some sort of practical joke?" His face darkened. "Because if it *is—*"

"No, no, Mr. Marshall! I am here with Mr. Leonard Barden, the chess correspondent of the *Evening Standard.* Mr. Slater called Mr. Barden this morning, and authorized him to— Just a moment, here is Mr. Barden himself."

Barden said Slater had called him about an hour before, and asked about the chances of bringing Bobby to the table. Barden had told him Bobby was "sticking out for the gate money" and that the chances looked pretty bad unless some extraordinary gesture were made.

Like a shot Slater had said, "I'll double the prize money." Bobby could choose how the extra prize money would be paid: winner take all, or split the same way F.I.D.E. had—five-eighths to the winner, three-eighths to the loser.

Marshall was still suspicious. "Who is this James Slater?"

"James Slater of Slater-Walker, the—"

Marshall gulped. *The* James Slater of British Leyland, the great conglomerator of British industry.

"Got you," Marshall broke in, "but—please excuse me for being blunt, Mr. Barden. What's Mr. Slater's angle? Why has he suddenly turned into a little chess sugar daddy?"

Barden was shocked. Hearing the Maecenas of British chess called a sugar daddy was like hearing the sun called a light fixture.

"It's a tremendous sporting gesture," Marshall said when Barden had filled him in, "and it may very well save the match. But before I pass the offer on to Bobby I want to hear it from Mr. Slater's lips."

Ten minutes later, he did. Slater had one stipulation: he wanted the offer presented as a challenge. Marshall suggested the wording, "Chicken, come on out!"

Slater agreed and hung up. Marshall fell back on his pillow and laughed madly at the ceiling.

Forty minutes later Marshall called Bobby. In the meantime he had showered, shaved, dressed, had breakfast, and run a careful reconnaissance of the conversation he was about to have. This one had to be perfect.

"Paul?" Bobby asked blearily. "What's up?"

Marshall told him.

"Yeah?" Bobby was bowled over too. "That's *greeaaat!*"

Marshall told him the terms. Bobby said instantly, "I'll split it the same way as the regular prize."

Marshall was astonished. He had been sure that Bobby would bet the whole wad he would win. The money in any case was only somewhat impressive to Bobby. After his first surprise he had second thoughts. "Who is this guy Slater?"

Marshall explained, adding, "Slater says he doesn't think he'll ever have to pay up. He says he's doing this to prove that Bobby Fischer is chicken."

Bobby gave a slightly forced guffaw. Finally, torn between suspicion and elation, he said, "Sounds pretty good. I'll—uh—think about it."

"Call you back," Marshall said.

Bobby went back to bed after Marshall had hung up, but he didn't go back to sleep. It was as if a bomb had gone off inside his head.

Downstairs, meanwhile, the Saidys found themselves under siege. The news had broken in London at about the same time Marshall was calling Bobby; and half an hour later the bulletin hit every newsroom in New York City. About 9:30 the two Saidy phones had started ringing. By 10:00 the first reporter was at the door; by 10:30 a dozen reporters, photographers and TV cameramen were prowling the grounds. In the late morning, at a moment when Bobby happened to be downstairs, a photographer climbed up the ivy on the side of the house and aimed a telescopic lens through a window.

"Scram!" Peter yelled.

Bobby scampered into the next room, laughing. His mood had improved.

The phone rang for the thirtieth time. It was Thorbergsson.

Tony was appalled. The man had come all the way from Iceland and was now only two blocks from the house, at the Douglaston railroad station. But asking Bobby to see a visitor now was like asking a man in brain surgery if he felt like company.

Tony asked.

"Naa," Bobby said irritably, "I can't see *him.*"

Mrs. Saidy was furious. "Bobby," she burst out, "you can't let a man come all the way from Iceland and then not see him. That's not right!"

"I didn't ask him to come," Bobby replied.

Tony told Thorbergsson to call again in an hour or two. Eight hours later, Thorbergsson was still hanging around the railroad station. Toward the end of his vigil he was discovered by an NBC television reporter, Pat Collins, and had the doubtful consolation of telling his story to the American public on the *NBC Evening News.*

Not long after Marshall's call, Bobby had a rash of second thoughts.

"This Slater business doesn't change anything," he said. "I still haven't got my demands. How do I know the Icelanders are going to pay their share? And suppose I get up there—*how do I know I'm going to get out?*" When he said this, Mrs. Saidy reported, he rolled his eyes and looked "extremely strange."

"No! No!" he insisted when somebody pooh-poohed his fears. "Those Icelanders could keep me there indefinitely." He rolled his eyes some more. "*You never know!*"

For seven harrowing interminable days Tony had served with saintly patience, lighting little candles of hope. One by one, Bobby had blown them out and cursed the darkness. Then Slater, incredibly, had ignited a beacon fire so big that Tony at last could see the way clear to Iceland. Now Bobby was standing there pissing on the flames.

"My God, Bobby!" Tony exploded. "You had the best deal in the history of chess. Now it's been doubled. What more do you want!"

Bobby's mouth closed like a zipper. A minute later he went to his room. Tony slumped. Had he lashed out too hard? Seeing Tony's expression, Mrs. Saidy laid down the law. "I don't care if he goes to Iceland or not. But I know one thing, Anthony. *You're not going with him!*"

By 1 P.M. Reykjavik was a hive of speculation. A few minutes after Barden had hung up, Euwe had told Thorarinsson, Cramer, and a few others about Slater's offer. Cramer rushed through the lobby of the Loftleidir Hotel telling one reporter after another. Nobody believed him, but in ten minutes the calls were stacked ten deep on every line out of Iceland. At 2 P.M., Euwe appeared. A hundred reporters rushed him.

"Does this mean that Bobby's coming?"

"If you find out," said Euwe, "please let me know."

Sometime before noon, New York time, Marshall called Bobby to hear his decision.

"I don't know," Bobby said in a sullen voice. "I mean, there's nothing wrong with the offer, but it lets the Icelanders off the hook. And that's not right, you know? If I go, they get the benefit and they did nothing to deserve it. They're just using me to make money and I won't let them *do* that!"

After ten minutes of this, Marshall had had enough. "All right, Bobby," he said. "This is it. In five minutes, if you haven't said 'Yes, I'll go,' I'm going to hang up and that's that. I won't answer the phone again. This is a holiday and there's lots of very agreeable things I could be doing. I'm going out and I won't leave a number. So there it is. Five minutes. Make up your mind."

For two minutes, three minutes more, they argued. Then Marshall said, "Okay, time's up. Make up your mind or I hang up. Ya gonna go?"

"All right! All right!" Bobby burst out almost angrily. *"I'll go!"*

"Okay," Marshall said calmly. "You want to talk to Bill?"

"Y-yeeaahh . . . But I want that return ticket *in my hands* before I get on the plane, unnastan'?"

Lombardy came to the phone.

"Are you coming?" Bobby asked.

"You haven't asked me. Besides, I've contracted to do the match on TV."

"Somebody else can do that," Bobby answered airily. "See you later."

Marshall grinned. "Bill, you just had the shortest career in the history of television."

Henry Kissinger called Bobby about half an hour after Marshall hung up. The call had been suggested by James Slater and arranged by David Frost, Slater's partner in a company called Equity Associates. The operator told Tony "a White House aide" was calling, and Tony ran upstairs to tell Bobby.

"*What* aide?" Bobby wasn't going to pick up the phone for any old White House aide. Tony checked and said the call was from Kissinger. Bobby went to the phone.

Kissinger as usual was adroit. "This is one of the two worst chess players in the world speaking to the best," he began, and went on to say he understood that Bobby was having some difficulties with the arrangements for the match. He said the match was very important to the international prestige of the United States. He had not discussed the matter with the president, but he was sure the president would join him in urging Bobby to overcome his difficulties and play the match for the sake of his country "In short," Kissinger later recalled, "I told him to get his butt over to Iceland."

Bobby listened quietly to all this, obviously impressed. Then he respectfully thanked "Mr. Kissinger" for calling and said he would "certainly think very carefully" about what Kissinger had said. Kissinger heartily wished him good luck and hung up.

A little after 3:30, Marshall and Lombardy arrived at the Saidy house in a Loftleidir station wagon. By now there were maybe twenty press and television people and eighty or a hundred people from the area standing in the street or on the neighbors' lawns. Two cops were directing traffic.

Tony said Bobby was still upstairs. Marshall called the president of TelePrompTer.

Marshall: "But Bobby won't go without Lombardy!"

TelePrompTer: "I'm warning you, I'll sue!"

Marshall: "You'll sue! For what? For not narrating a match that won't take place if he narrates it?"

In the end, TelePrompTer agreed to release Lombardy and accept grandmaster Arthvr Bisguier instead.

The phone rang again. It was Hans Indridason, saying that he and Tedd Hope were now parked at the Douglaston railroad station—what should they do?

"Wait there. We'll call you."

"Here we go again," Indridason thought. It began to rain—hard.

An hour later, Indridason made another call. "Come on over," Marshall said. Hope parked the wagon in the Saidy driveway and found Bobby's bags stacked just inside the back door. In the living room everybody looked excited but scared too, like kids watching a balloon get big and wondering when it would pop. Marshall said the chances looked good—"But don't bet your ass on it unless you've got a spare." Hope gave Marshall four round-trip tickets to Reykjavik—one for Bobby, one for Lombardy, one each for Marshall and his wife. Mrs. Saidy talked in a worried murmur about Tony, who lay on a couch in the living room like a man breathing his last.

At 5 P.M. Peter went up to Bobby with some orange juice. Ten minutes later Bobby came down. Still in shirtsleeves, he was surly and haggard. When he saw Hope and Indridason he went straight to the back door to make sure his bags were there.

"Don't you dare move my bags! Not under any circumstances, unnastan'?"

Tony was awake now. But Bobby did not speak to him. Nobody said much, for fear of jiggling the nitroglycerin in Bobby's head. In a little while Bobby went back upstairs. Everybody breathed again.

Warned that "Bobby never likes wives around," Marshall changed plans. "I'd better not take Betty," he told Indridason and Hope. "Would you call the airport and send her back home?" Then he went up to see Bobby.

Ten minutes later, Marshall was down again, beaming. "Call the airport again!" he told Hope. "Bobby said Betty could go."

About 6 P.M., Bobby came downstairs unbidden. Dressed as if for the trip, he looked hyper but resolute.

"I wanna see the press! I wanna make a statement!"

Hope and Indridason couldn't believe their ears. All week long, at Bobby's insistence, they had been cooking up elaborate schemes to bypass the press. Now, for no known reason, Bobby was going out of his way to meet the beast he had been baiting.

Marshall asked smoothly where he wanted to hold the conference—perhaps in the living room?

"Naa! Naa!" Bobby said. Being in a constricted space with that mob was more than he could face. He would stand in the front door and let the press fire questions from the lawn.

As the door opened, reporters crowded around. Bobby appeared —and was doused by the blowing downpour. His new red slacks were getting spattered. He turned and rushed back inside.

"That's no good!" he said. "We gotta do it some other way! I'll see *one* reporter, in here—that's all!" But no one reporter could satisfy all the media. Marshall suggested a series of smaller press conferences and Bobby reluctantly agreed.

When the ABC-TV team came in, Bobby had a moment of panic. "Who's that woman?" he gasped, peering at a middle-aged female who had appeared in the living room. She was only a few feet away and her face was toward him but he did not recognize—Mrs. Saidy!

When the first session began, Indridason and Hope came in from the kitchen.

"What are *those guys* doing in here?" Bobby demanded. "I want them out of the room or this press conference stops right here!"

"Those guys" stormed out the back door, heading for their car.

"Fuck him!" Hope said.

"That's *it!*" Indridason agreed. "After five days of chasing his ass all over creation we don't have to take that!"

Lombardy rushed after them. "Please don't take it personally. It's just the way he is. Consider the source and let it roll off."

Hope asked why the whole world had to adjust to Bobby instead of the other way around, but they let themselves be persuaded.

Bobby was jittery when the questions started coming but his answers were direct and forceful.

Asked if he was going to play, Bobby answered, "I'm going to play and I'm going to win."

Asked if his battle with the Icelanders had been a battle over money, Bobby answered, "Not only money. There were other problems."

Asked if his public behavior had really been an attempt to psych his opponent, Bobby answered, "I don't believe in psychology. I believe in good moves."

Asked if he was playing the match for himself as a chess player or as a representative of his country, Bobby answered, "First as an American, second as a chess player."

After three sessions Bobby said, "Okay, that's it."

Just then the boys from Metromedia got back from a coffee break and discovered they had missed the main event.

"Too bad," Bobby said, stone-faced. "That's it."

Bobby's friends crowded around and congratulated him. As he began to smile and strut, Marshall began to feel really sure he was going. 7:10. The plane left at 9:00 on Monday night instead of 9:30. Why not strike while the iron was hot? If they got ready now, they could start for the airport by 7:30.

Just then Hope reported that the flight would be delayed one hour. Bobby sagged and went upstairs.

"Damn!" Marshall thought. "Just when we had him moving!"

In Reykjavik the death watch began again. At about 9 P.M. Davis called Cramer to his room.

"If Bobby comes," Davis said, "there's going to be one hell of a mess at the airport. Five thousand reporters and photographers, and if Bobby sees one of them he may never get off the plane. Somehow we've got to avoid all that. Any ideas?"

Cramer described a plan to have the Loftleidir plane stopped on the runway, maybe a mile from the terminal. "Take Bobby off. Put him in a private plane. Fly him to Reykjavik airport. Put him in a private car. Drive him to his house—or to his hotel suite. By the time the press realizes what has happened, Bobby'll be sound asleep."

The police and the airline had agreed to cooperate. So had immigration and customs. The U.S. embassy had offered two cars and a two-engine Cessna had been reserved. "All we need now," Cramer said, "is a driver for the car at Keflavik airport, a driver for the car at Reykjavik airport, and a man to take the baggage through customs. That's three."

Davis asked if the three members of the *Life* team in Reykjavik would help out. In addition to Benson and me, *Life* had hired the best guide in Iceland, Kristjan Arngrimsson.

I.C.F. suggested one change in the plan. Stop the plane on the runway, yes, but transfer Bobby to a car instead of a plane. "We want to give him an official escort." The plane was canceled. Reykjavik was ready.

In the Saidy living room, the clock was edging toward 9:00. No sign of Bobby. Every five minutes for about twenty minutes now, somebody had told him it was time to go, but he was still up there "getting ready," he said. Drinks were set down. People kept looking at their watches.

Suddenly Bobby was there, colorful and natty. He was wearing his red slacks, a pastel shirt open at the neck and his dark-brown Argentine leather jacket. In his hand were some chess magazines and a little red book of Spassky's games.

"All set?" he asked. Pale, faintly blue, he looked like a small boy on a high diving board wondering why oh why he had said he would take the leap.

"All set," Marshall said. Moving quickly through the rain, Marshall and Tony Saidy loaded the bags in the rear of the Loftleidir station wagon. "Bobby watched like a hawk," Indridason remembers, "to make sure Tedd and I didn't touch a thing, especially not the sacred Sony."

It was time to go. Marshall turned to Bobby. Bobby drew back. The press gathered around the station wagon.

"No more pictures!" Bobby announced. The press was told. Marshall turned to Bobby again. He was still hanging back.

"How about covering the car windows?" he asked anxiously. "Like with masking tape."

The matter was gravely discussed. In the first place, the Saidys didn't have enough tape to do the job. In the second place, there wasn't time to tape the car windows. In the third place, they weren't going anywhere near the press or the crowds this time.

Giving in suddenly, Bobby hurried out to the station wagon and jumped in the back seat. A few cameras clicked. Marshall and Beers eased in on either side of Bobby. Hope took the wheel. Indridason and Lombardy sat beside him. The car began to move.

"Wait! Wait!" Bobby called out in alarm. "My seat belt isn't fastened!"

There was a two-minute pause while Marshall and Beers rummaged for the ends of the seat belt, found them and locked them together.

The car eased out the driveway. Tony followed a few steps, walking very slowly, like a man coming out of a cellar after a hurricane.

It took Tony a week to get himself together. Mrs. Saidy was too busy to collapse—she spent the next nine weeks commuting to the hospital. Peter printed a large sign and that night when the Saidys sat down to dinner they found it on the dining-room table. The sign read:

FUCK CHESS

It was about twelve miles from the Saidy house in Douglaston to Kennedy Airport. Traffic wasn't bad but there was another irritation. When Hope turned out of the Saidy driveway, a green Ford moved in behind him, and it stayed on his tail.

Bobby made a couple of remarks about the press, but the Ford kept its distance and he soon began to think of other things.

"Are you with the airlines?" he asked Indridason as though they had just met for the first time.

A bit startled, Indridason described his job and Hope's.

Bobby was impressed. "Yeah? You guys look young."

Indridason said they were both twenty-nine.

"That's young to have responsible jobs. Do you get to fly much?"

Talk about the green Ford, which was still following them, led to more talk about newsmen. Bobby said he preferred television to the daily paper as a news medium. "You really get to see the people in the news. I like that."

"You won't see any TV in Iceland," Hope told him. "They've only got one station and it's shut down for the month of July."

"No kidding!"

Teasing Indridason, Hope said Iceland wasn't all bad. "They've got a tree up there, you know. It's the national tree of Iceland."

Bobby belly-laughed. All wondered how long his mood would last.

At the outskirts of Kennedy Airport, Hope swung into a parking lot. The Ford followed. The Fischer party moved from the Loftleidir wagon to a Mercury wagon, Hope's personal car. "Nobody'll spot us in this." Hope then drove the Mercury back onto the parkway. The Ford followed. Bobby was outraged. Hope reassured him. "We'll lose him at the entrance. He can't go on the field without Port Authority plates."

The prospect of seeing the gates slam in the face of his pursuer appealed to Bobby. He guffawed and said he really liked chases. "Like the chase in *Bullitt.* That was great." Bobby said he liked Steve McQueen. "There's no expression on his face, you know? But you can tell what he's thinking." The Ford closed in a little. In the mood of a movie chase, Marshall turned in his seat, pointed his finger through the back window, and said, "Bang! Bang!"

"Don't do that!" Bobby said. "He might report it."

At the gate to the field, Hope spoke to the guard, then pulled onto the field. Bobby turned to watch the gates slam in the reporter's face. The Ford stopped at the gate. The guard leaned down to speak with the driver—and then the Ford came barreling after them!

"Hey!" Bobby hollered. "What's goin' on here!"

Hope made directly for the nearest exit and left the field. The Ford followed. Hope turned around and approached the gate again. This time he told the guard what had happened at the other gate and warned him strenuously that the green Ford was not to be allowed on the field. As Hope started up again, everybody in the Mercury wagon turned to watch.

The Ford pulled to a stop. The guard put his head down close to the driver's window and began to speak. The Ford took off. The guard reeled back. The green Ford was on the field again!

Now Bobby was really appalled. "What kind of security is that! No wonder you get hijackers!"

"I'm going straight to the plane," Hope said grimly. "There are guards there."

Hope drove close to the plane and parked. The green Ford parked a little way off. Indridason went aboard to make sure that the crew was ready. Hope instructed the Fleet Service crew to load the baggage for the Fischer party. By the time it was aboard, the reporter was waiting near the foot of the passenger stairway.

Marshall eased out of the car and struck up a conversation. The reporter agreed not to bother Bobby—"I just want to make sure he really does take the plane."

When Indridason came back, Bobby got out and followed him toward the stairway. Lombardy and Marshall moved in behind. It was happening. Bobby was boarding the plane. He was going to Iceland! He—

He stopped short, staring at a red-haired man standing at the top of the stairway. Thorbergsson was smiling cordially, pleadingly. He could understand that his friend had been too busy to see him earlier. But surely, after coming all this way, he could at least be the first to welcome Bobby to Icelandic territory?

Bobby reddened. Pointing up the stairs, he shouted, "Remove that man!"

Thorbergsson's smile crumpled. Indridason hustled him politely into the plane and a stewardess escorted him to his seat.

Indridason gave the all-clear. Bobby went up the stairs, followed by Lombardy and Marshall.

The plane was a stretch DC-8, a 249-seat jet, the largest plane Loftleidir flies. Bobby insisted on sitting in the last row. As Lombardy explained to Indridason, "He wants to see what's happening in front of him!" As Indridason later put it, "He wanted to be damn sure nothing was happening behind his back!"

In the last row, Bobby demanded the window seat. Indridason explained tactfully that this particular window seat had certain disadvantages. In fact, it was the worst seat on the plane. The seat back could not be fully lowered, and the ceiling was so low that the occupant could not tilt his head to the right.

Bobby didn't care. That was the seat he wanted.

Lombardy gave Indridason a 240-pound nudge. "Hurry up," he muttered. "Let me sit next to him. With me there he won't be able to get away."

Bobby sat down. Lombardy squeezed into the next seat. Marshall took the aisle seat.

Bobby carefully fastened his seat belt and lifted his head. Diagonally across the aisle, two rows ahead, he saw a familiar face smiling tentatively in his direction. Thorbergsson.

Bobby's eyes hardened. "I want that man removed!" he announced loudly.

Thorbergsson's mouth made little goldfish motions of astonishment. Indridason hustled him politely to a seat farther forward.

A shapely Icelandic blonde took his place.

"There," Indridason asked with a wink. "That better?"

"All right," Bobby said.

"And this," Indridason said, "is Ingibjorg, your personal stewardess. She will take extremely good care of you." He stood aside to reveal an attractive young woman in an airline uniform.

"Loftleidir wishes to welcome you aboard," she said sweetly, and handed Bobby a huge bon voyage basket of fruit.

Bobby's eyes went wide. "Thanks! Thanks!" He examined the fruit carefully. "Very good!"

Indridason wished him a good trip and a great victory. Bobby nodded absently. He couldn't take his eyes off the fruit.

As the DC-8 trundled heavily toward the runway, Hope and Indridason stood on the concrete ramp, watching it go.

"We can't be this lucky," Indridason said. "Any minute now, the right outboard motor is going to fall off."

It didn't.

8

Hello, Bobby— Bye-bye, Boris

The island Bobby was bound for is one of the grimmer points on the planet. Iceland is a gale-swept cinder the size of Kentucky that juts into the North Atlantic at the edge of the Arctic Circle. Volcanoes constructed it, and the world's most intense volcanic activity still terrorizes its inhabitants. Vast ice sheets cover many of the craters, and when they erupt the land is wrecked by floods that spew out more water every minute than the Amazon carries to the sea at the height of the rainy season. Three-fourths of the island is covered by a desert so ghastly that U.S. astronauts trained there for their moon walks.

Without the Gulf Stream, nothing could live in Iceland; with it, a gray-green coastal ledge sustains a population of about 200,000. Their winters are long black nights ripped by blizzard winds that come howling off Greenland's mountains. Their summers are long gray days that pass in intermittent drizzle.

People have been living in Iceland since the eighth century. Irish monks came first, then some Viking refugees. In 930 the local chieftains established the Althing, the world's oldest parliament. Bloody brutes, the early Icelanders terrorized the coasts of Europe with their looting, raping, slave-raiding. But they were also magnificent seamen—an Icelander, Leifr Eiriksson, discovered North America—and the greatest poets of the Middle Ages. The Icelandic sagas are fascinating epics composed in verse forms unequaled for intricacy and sophistication.

All this culture flowered in the shadow of death. Iceland was regularly struck by natural disasters that slaughtered the livestock, destroyed the forests, covered most of the country with an armor of

115

lava and killed off so many people that in 1900 Iceland's population was the same as it had been in 900. Only the toughest, the meanest, the stubbornest, the smartest survived—the modern Icelander is an evolutionary triumph. In a land where a fly can hardly make it, the Icelander has built up a prosperous modern nation. Since 1944, when Iceland broke free from Denmark, the population has increased by 40 per cent and the gross national product has more than quadrupled. Reykjavik, the political and commercial capital, has hoicked itself up from a fishing village to a modern city of 80,000. Private enterprises flourish: the fishing industry, which brings in four-fifths of the national income, is owned by hundreds of small-business men. At the same time, a welfare state has been set up and it works. There is no plutocracy, no poverty. Medical care and education are excellent and cost nothing.

Success has at least partly tamed these Vikings. In this century only nine murders have been committed in Iceland, and in the whole country at any given time there are usually fewer than fifteen people in jail. The berserk feelings seem to be sublimated into commercial competition, bourgeois emulation and the national passion for obeying the rules—Iceland is a paradise for bureaucrats.

A few direct expressions of aggression are still in evidence. The per capita consumption of hard liquor is shocking even by Scandinavian standards. On Saturday night two-thirds of Reykjavik is drunk, and by 2 A.M. so many people are staggering about or sleeping it off in the street that they constitute a major hazard to driving. Sex is the other national pastime, and the women are if anything more aggressive than the men. On Friday, Saturday and Sunday nights thousands of Icelandic girls cruise the bars and hotels. With a couple of drinks under the belt they walk up to complete strangers, look them straight in the eye and say, "What are you doing later?"

"On a small island," a cultivated Icelander told me, "people have to have plenty of alcohol and sex. We also travel a lot. The average Icelander spends several months every year abroad." But they seldom stay abroad. Wherever they go, the silence of their eerie and primordial fells calls out and brings them home again. Their patriotism carries a primeval charge that makes it dangerous to challenge —and Bobby had challenged it.

At 7 A.M. Tuesday, July 4, Davis, Cramer and Benson ducked into my vermilion Volkswagen and we rolled off to Keflavik under cement-gray skies. We had sat till after 5 A.M. reviewing the horrors of the week and marveling again at how many people and events had come together at just the right time to save Bobby from himself.

Davis didn't get to sleep till 6:00. A few minutes after we left him, he had telephoned Theodore Tremblay, the U.S. chargé d'affaires, and routed him out of a deep sleep to hear the news. Kissinger, Davis announced, had called Bobby, who was now on his way to Iceland— "no thanks to you." Davis then suggested that Tremblay appear at the airport to welcome the distinguished visitor "if it isn't too much of a strain on your limited resources." He also threatened to let Washington know Tremblay had been dragging his feet.

Davis had a practical reason for chewing out the U.S. chargé. In Tremblay's opinion, as Davis read it, Bobby was a bad boy who might harm the U.S. image. The U.S. embassy therefore intended to stand well back from Bobby while he was in Iceland. But if word got out that Bobby could not count on official support from his own country, all sorts of people might be encouraged to push him around. Davis's diatribe was intended to let Tremblay and his State Department superiors know that if they didn't do right by Bobby they would face some unattractive consequences.

The clouds seemed lower and woollier at Keflavik, and there was a cold scrape in the air. Talking, laughing, sucking up coffee, close to two hundred press and TV people were standing in the main waiting room of the terminal. Now and then a reporter would duck his head to peer out a window, hoping to be the first to see the plane.

A shout went up—there it was! a faraway silverfish crawling up the southwestern sky. Benson and I ran for the Volkswagen and took off across the airfield.

"We've got to get this!" Benson said. "The only pictures of Bobby landing in Iceland!"

As the Volkswagen idled toward the plane, we kept an eye out for the police convoy. Any minute now, according to plan, it should go roaring across the field. We wanted the convoy to reach the plane first. Just as the door of the plane opened and Bobby started down the ramp, Benson could go to work with a telephoto lens and we could scoot away before anybody objected.

The plane rolled to a stop. We checked the field—still no convoy. The plane turned and taxied toward the terminal. The plan had been changed!

"They've foocked us!" Benson yelled in a broad Scots accent. "Shake a leg or we'll miss the party!"

The plane was almost as close to the terminal now as we were. We hit seventy going back, reaching the terminal seconds before the plane parked. The ramp rolled up to its side. Two hundred reporters and photographers surged out. The crowd was so thick the convoy halted about thirty feet from the ramp.

Cramer was standing beside the first car, looking nervously toward the plane. "It's that sonofabitch Sigurdur Magnusson, the Loftleidir press agent," he said. "He told the police they couldn't meet the plane on the runway. The hell they couldn't! He just wants pictures of that Loftleidir plane all over the front pages!"

The police made no effort to control the press. The only way from the plane to the convoy was through the very center of that swarm of staring eyes and clicking cameras!

Benson winked. "Tough bastards, these Icelanders. Bobby made 'em sweat. Now they're gettin' a bit of their own back."

Two men ran up the ramp. One of them opened the door of the plane. The other, an Icelandic grandmaster named Fridrik Olafsson who also happened to be a big gun in the Ministry of Justice, disappeared inside.

Two minutes passed. There was a small commotion inside the plane. A pretty blond woman stepped out, looked confused, stepped aside. Then all at once Bobby was there.

After a day of foreshortened frenzy, the trip had gone so well it made Marshall and Lombardy nervous. Once the plane was in the air, Bobby stopped worrying about spies and settled almost comfortably into his corner. "But his eyes," Marshall said, "looked strange."

Betty Marshall, who had been seated toward the front of the plane, walked back once to say hello. A Broadway and television actress, Betty is tall, blond and dramatically attractive. The sight of her made Bobby uneasy, so she didn't come again. In about two hours, excellent steaks and a good red wine were served to the Fischer party. Bobby slept a little but most of the time he was awake, working at his chess wallet, talking with Lombardy and Marshall. "He seemed to be reasonably aware of what was happening," Marshall said some months later, "but I'll tell you a funny thing. After the match was over we talked about the trip up, and you know, nothing I said could convince him that I had been with him on that plane!"

As Bobby hit the top of the ramp he froze for an instant, eyes wide and unfocused.

"It's Bobby!" I thought. "He's really here!" Then came an uncomfortable second thought: "That's not Bobby—it's somebody else!" The body was Bobby's and so were the movements, but the red slacks and brown leather jacket were unexpectedly mod, and the face was a gray smear that might have been almost anybody's. I had seen him in panic and exhaustion before, in Buenos Aires, but I had never seen him this far gone.

For an instant Bobby paused and then, ducking his head, ran the gauntlet. He took the steps at such a gallop the photographers saw him getting away before they could take their pictures. "Aaaaaaa!" they yelled and came crowding toward him. Hunching his shoulders, Bobby plunged on.

As he hit the bottom of the steps, a wall of dignitaries appeared at his right. He rushed past them without noticing. The last man in the line was Thorarinsson.

"Bobby!" he said quickly, leaning close to Bobby's ear and extending his hand. "Welcome to Iceland!" Startled, Bobby slowed and, reaching back, shook hands. "Yeh," he said. Then he rushed on to the first Mercedes, scattering photographers like chickens, and jumped in. Olafsson followed. The largest policeman in Iceland closed the door and stood in front of it like a seven-foot wall.

Just then Lombardy came puffing up and told the officer that as Bobby's second he had to get in too. The policeman, who spoke no English, paid no attention to that 240-pound midget. The caravan began to move. Smiling and smarting, Lombardy joined the Marshalls in the second car.

Benson and I beat the convoy to the gate and stayed ahead all the way to Reykjavik—in a Beetle, that took some doing. Top lights flashing, the police cars set the needle at 150 km (about 90 mph) and kept it there.

Bobby normally hollers when the needle hits 55 mph, but Cramer said afterward that he didn't notice the speed. He seemed to enjoy the flashing lights and the idea of having a police escort—"like a president," as Cramer put it.

Cramer briefed him about the time and place of the drawing (12 noon) and of the game itself (5 P.M.), then gave him some pocket money—I.C.F. had agreed to pay the players $70 a week for incidentals. Bobby pocketed the cash without looking at it. When Cramer suggested he sleep at the house instead of at the hotel, Bobby blankly accepted direction. Cramer felt a surge of confidence. Bobby was going to be easier to handle than he had expected.

At the house, a large, rectangular, two-story building made of concrete and painted a rich orange-gold, Bobby reasserted his grip. From the moment he entered there was only one thing on his mind: get the others out so he could get to sleep. But both Cramer and Lombardy had assumed they would be living there with Bobby. "After all," Cramer had said, "it would be ridiculously inconvenient if I had to jump in the car and drive four miles from the hotel every time he wanted anything."

So Lombardy and Cramer went nosing all through the house, checking out the rooms and the furnishings. "It's brand-new," Cramer explained. "Never been lived in. It's the first prize in the next national lottery. Cost about $60,000." There was a good-sized living room with a Danish modern sofa and a hi-fi, a big kitchen with all the latest Danish gadgets, two tile baths and four bedrooms. Plenty of room, Lombardy and Cramer were thinking, but they were much too polite to say what they were thinking.

Bobby meanwhile tried the lock on his bedroom door, checked the catch on his bedroom window, made sure that not even a crack of light showed around the window shades. Then he took a quick snoop through the refrigerator, which was jam-packed with cold cuts and apple juice. Finally, he yawned.

"Well, so long," he said absently. "I gotta get some sleep."

Crestfallen, Lombardy recovered quickly and reminded Bobby that the drawing was at noon. They would have to wake him in two hours.

"Naa, I don't want to go to the drawing. You do it. I gotta sleep."

Lombardy turned to Cramer. "Is the second allowed to draw?"

Cramer wasn't certain, but it wasn't the moment to cross Bobby, so he said he was pretty sure anybody could draw if he had a letter of authorization from the player.

"So write a letter," Bobby said.

Cramer tore a couple of sheets of ruled paper out of a notebook he was carrying and hastily wrote out two authorizations, one for Lombardy and one for himself. Still touchy because Cramer had taken his place next to Bobby on the ride from the airport, Lombardy felt Cramer was trying to grab more authority than he was due. Bobby didn't want to sign either note, but when Cramer assured him the notes would carry no weight if they weren't signed, he scribbled his signature on the bottom of Lombardy's note. Lombardy pocketed it with some satisfaction.

After they left, Cramer began to make bossy noises about the note.

"That's my job," Lombardy lashed back, "and I'll thank you to let me do it my own way!"

"I was just trying to be helpful, Bill."

"I don't need any help."

Ten minutes later Bobby called. "Hey, Fred, where's my other bag?"

"It's probably outside in the police car," Cramer told him.

In a T-shirt and slacks, Bobby went paddling out to the police truck that was guarding his house. While reporters gawked and cameras clicked, a policeman who spoke English radioed headquarters and put a tracer on the suitcase.

Then the house was silent. When a neighbor two doors away began to drive some nails, the policeman strolled over and asked him to do it later. The reporters left. Bobby had marked out his turf.

"You Americans think the only problem is to get Bobby here," Thorarinsson said. "You don't understand it is just as important—and maybe more difficult—to keep the Russians here."

On Monday, at another private meeting in the Esja, Spassky had hinted to Thorarinsson that his superiors were infuriated by the postponement and might call off the match. Excited by Slater's offer, Spassky came up with a plan to outmaneuver Moscow.

Spassky said he would resist pressure from Soviet officials. Thorarinsson said he would ask Prime Minister Johanneson to lean on the Soviet government. But Bobby held the key to success, Spassky said. "If Bobby does not come to the drawing, I am sure it will not be possible to save the match."

Late that night, a telegram sent by the Soviet Chess Federation to Lothar Schmid, care of I.C.F., arrived at Thorarinsson's house. It savagely scolded Euwe and Bobby and concluded that if any more rules were broken, "USSR CHESS FEDERATION WOULD CONSIDER MATCH WRECKED."

Thorarinsson kept the telegram secret—if it were published, Moscow might maintain its position to save face—and gave it to Schmid the next morning. Agreeing that "Bobby must make the drawing himself," Schmid summoned Lombardy and Cramer.

"Out of the question," Cramer protested. "He was up all night on the plane." Nothing Schmid or Thorarinsson said could change the Americans' minds. They simply failed to read the danger signals.

The drawing of colors was to take place in a conference room at the Esja—the best setting available on short notice. The room, pleasantly paneled in dark wood, was about twenty feet wide and thirty feet long and could be tripled in width by the removal of partitions. Even so, it offered too modest a setting for the occasion. "Rather like launching a battleship in a bathtub, isn't it?" a British reporter remarked.

The drawing was scheduled for noon. By 11:45 Euwe, Schmid, Lombardy and Thorarinsson were in the conference room. A little before noon seven Russians moved in single file through the crowd of reporters in the lobby. Spassky led the way, wearing a tweed jacket and a dark tie and looking calm. Geller, Krogius and Nei wore their usual masks. Chamanin, the interpreter, was in the party, and so were two officials from the Soviet Chess Federation. After a lot of handshaking, the doors were closed.

Spassky said he had noticed that Mr. Fischer was not present. Was he perhaps on his way? Schmid explained that Bobby had arrived exhausted and was trying to get some rest before the game. Grandmaster Lombardy had a letter authorizing him to act on Mr. Fischer's behalf at the drawing.

In that case, Spassky said, he would like to read a statement. Rising, he took a document from his coat pocket and read about ten sentences in Russian. Chamanin made a rapid translation that left everyone still confused but now alarmed. Words like "violated" and "insult" and "indignation" and "punishment" came through. As Chamanin returned the letter to Schmid, Geller rose and handed an envelope to Euwe. Then the whole Soviet delegation rose and bowed stiffly. With faces as blank as bowling balls the seven Russians crossed the room in single file and went out the same door they had come in.

A reporter caught Spassky at the head of the stairs.

Reporter: "Are you walking out on the match?"

Spassky, grimly: "I do not know."

Geller's letter to Euwe, typewritten in English, was a milder version of the Moscow telegram. Spassky's letter, translated at top speed by a Reykjavik University professor, said Bobby had "insulted me personally and the country which I represent." Spassky said further that Bobby had "put his moral rights to play the match under the question" and must be "justly punished." The letter concluded, "Only after this I might discuss the possibility of holding the match."

Euwe glowed. "Well! It is not *so* bad. They have walked out but they have not closed the door."

"They have closed the door *tight*," Lombardy said. "If anybody tries to punish Mr. Fischer, he will simply go home. Everybody knows that. So in refusing to play the match unless Mr. Fischer is punished, Mr. Spassky is simply refusing to play the match!"

Schmid hedged. "Perhaps the Russians are just trying to save face. After all, Mr. Spassky is the champion. His dignity must be preserved."

Marshall cut him short. "Where in the rules does it say that the players have to attend the opening ceremony? Nowhere. The Russians are wrong."

"We must not offend the Russians, Mr. Marshall!" Schmid answered nervously.

Having no knowledge of the Moscow telegram, Marshall and Cramer were shocked by Schmid's appeasing attitude.

When Euwe called a press conference, almost two hundred newsmen rushed in.

"As you can see," Euwe said when the letters had been read, "the situation is very confusing. Before we can respond to these letters, we must find out what the Russians really want."

A reporter asked, "How bad do you think the situation is?"
Euwe replied, "I do not know if the match will be played."

The Americans huddled right after the Russians walked out. After the horrors of Kennedy and Douglaston, this new crisis was hard to take seriously. Surely the team that had brought Bobby Fischer to Reykjavik would have no difficulty with such a minor matter as an enraged Soviet Union.

"I guess we've got to see the Russians right away," Marshall said. Arrangements were made, and at 2 P.M. nine men met in the Saga's cocktail bar.

The meeting went well. Geller laid down a hard line at first, but when Marshall began to compliment ("I can assure you Mr. Fischer has the highest respect for Mr. Spassky and for the great Soviet people"), Geller began to grin. Finally Marshall offered a quick solution. "What if Bobby wrote a presonal letter of apology to Boris?" Geller and Nei looked immensely relieved, and the meeting broke up in smiles.

Ten minutes later Lombardy told the press that the Russians were demanding a written apology from Bobby.

"Is that all?"

"Whaddya mean, is that all? When was the last time you heard Bobby Fischer apologize? To anybody. For anything."

While Marshall and Lombardy were meeting with the Russians, Davis was packing.

I was shocked. "You're not leaving!"

"Sure am." His tone was light, but his eyes had the shades pulled down.

"But Bobby's still in serious trouble. The match—"

"Paul can take care of it."

Was there a touch of bitterness in that?

Before he left, Davis wrote Cramer a note.

Dear Fred,

Good luck on a tough mission. Remember that Bobby may well be very sick and must be provided for in all events.

Best regard,
Andy

Then he carried his bag to the taxi. Only the room clerk knew he had left.

At about 11 P.M., two Icelandic policemen were sitting in a Land Rover outside Bobby's house. The last reporters had straggled away about half an hour before and the two cops were resigned to a long dull night.

All at once the front door opened and Bobby lurched out. He was wearing the same outfit he had worn that afternoon on the trip north—red slacks and brown leather jacket—and as he hit the night air he turned his collar up. Seeing the police in the Land Rover, he hurried over. The policeman at the wheel, who spoke excellent English, said good evening and asked if there was anything he could do.

"Yeah." Bobby looked both ways along the street, his eyes wide. "Any reporters hangin' around?"

The policeman said they had just left.

"Hnnn. Which way is it to town?"

The policeman pointed the way.

"Thanks." Bobby charged off.

The young officer watched anxiously. Sure enough, Bobby took the wrong turn at the corner. In five minutes he would be wandering along a main north-south highway at an hour when every third driver in Iceland was drunk. The policeman flipped on his two-way radio.

"Hello! Officer Saemundur Palsson here. Bobby Fischer has left the house. On foot. He says he's going to walk downtown but he's heading toward Copavogur. What shall I do?"

"Follow him. Get him in the truck. For God's sake, don't let him out of your sight."

Bobby by now was in fact out of sight. For thirty desperate seconds, Palsson thought he had disappeared. But there he was, an incredible distance down a dirt track that was taking him back toward the airport.

"Good evening, Mr. Fischer," Palsson said as he drew abreast. "I was wondering if I could take you where you want to go."

"Naa. I need the exercise," Bobby answered, and went barreling on. He was being followed and didn't like it.

Palsson kept right up with him. "In that case, would it be all right if I wrote out your address on a piece of paper? You might get lost but if you had your address you could tell a taxi driver where to go."

"Yeah, good idea," Bobby said brusquely—anything to get rid of the guy—and kept on going.

Palsson stopped the truck and wrote out the address. Just as he finished, Bobby seemed to change his mind and came charging back. Palsson handed him the note.

"Would you like me to take you on a little tour in the country?" Palsson asked pleasantly. "It's beautiful at this time of year. Very relaxing."

Bobby hesitated. "Nnyaaa," he said. "Maybe take me back to the house. I left my sweater inside."

Bobby climbed hesitantly into the front seat, but before they reached the house he gave a quick little sigh and said, "Yeah, okay. Let's take a tour."

And that's how Bobby Fischer, cast up like Robinson Crusoe on a desert island, found his man Friday—the smiling, cunning, tireless Nordic aborigine, loyal as a tapeworm, who from that moment enveloped him in a private atmosphere as a baby is wrapped in a bunting. Bobby has an affinity for men like "Saemi" (pronounced Symie) Palsson, for soft, agreeable, motherly men who allow him to feel all-powerful. Beers and Saidy are variations of the type, and even a man as complex as Edmondson, recognizing Bobby's need, had sung him a constant lullaby of reassurance.

At thirty-two, Palsson looked like a Norse sun god in a children's picture book. He stood just under six feet in height and he was gold all over. His hair was a thick mass of tumbling gold, his body lithe and rippling with muscles. His face was not quite handsome—he had a lantern jaw and a horsey smile—but his eyes were huge and soft and looked at the world through long dreamy lashes.

Most of time Palsson's eyes look sleepy, and it was widely assumed in Iceland, where intelligence is generally equated with intellect, that he was not very bright. His parents were uncultured—his father, who at fifty-one had a fifty-eight-inch chest and a thirty-eight-inch waist, was once the heavyweight champion of Iceland—and Palsson himself never graduated from high school. In fact, Palsson was gifted rather than intellectual. He could take up almost anything and do it well.

In his middle twenties, Palsson was a well-known pop singer and Iceland's leading rock dancer. At twenty-seven, he won his diploma as a master builder, a title that certifies proficiency as a carpenter, mason, roofer, electrician and plumber. When he joined the police force he took judo training and in less than a year, though he rates only an orange belt, defeated several black-belt players and placed second in the Icelandic championships. But Palsson's strongest talent was political. He had an almost eerie sensitivity to situations and personalities, and he functioned at all times like a chameleon, changing to conform with the pressures he felt.

Palsson presented himself as a simple, friendly cop with a pretty wife and four very pleasant children. But most Icelanders knew about Palsson's lifelong hunger for fame. "Turn on a spotlight anywhere in Reykjavik," said a man who had known him for years, "and in five minutes Saemi will be standing in it." Palsson was also a born manipulator, but there was nothing mean in the man. He did not deserve the nickname he was given by the press, Slimy Saemi. On the other hand, he was far from the Simple Saemi he tried to appear. He knew instinctively that Bobby was the chance of his lifetime, and he moved in suavely to make the most of that chance.

That first night, Palsson sensed that Bobby was like a motorcyclist in a centrifuge who had risen to the rim. If he couldn't slow down he was going to flip out.

"I talked to him very quietly," Palsson said later, "like to a frightened child." As they started out on the tour, Bobby wanted to know where Palsson had learned to speak such good American. Palsson explained that about two years ago he had spent six months in California.

"No kidding! I just came from there!"

They talked about California for a few minutes and then about Palsson for almost half an hour. Bobby was fascinated to hear about his rock career. "I used to really keep up with all the groups," he said, "but lately I lost track."

Palsson explained how he had come to be a master builder and Bobby was really impressed. "You mean you can build a whole house all by yourself?"

"Oh, yes," Palsson said casually, and passed on to his judo record.

Bobby's eyes widened. "Second best in Iceland! With somebody like you around I'd be safe from those aggressive photographers, huh?"

"Well, yes," Palsson murmured with a little Clark Kent smile, "I think I could make it a little difficult for them."

By now the truck had traveled through eight or ten kilometers of insane geology. Torrents of black lava squirmed over the landscape like crocodiles. Here and there a sheep flickered against the low white sun.

"Let's go that way," Bobby said, pointing toward some black mountains. He was still jerky in his movements and sometimes fleered his eyes at nothing in particular, as if he were seeing something scary in his mind.

A herd of Icelandic ponies, pale gold and orange-brown in the midnight sun, turned and fled.

"Really beautiful out here, y'know?" Bobby said. "Clean air, beautiful animals. Really different from New York. It's terrible in New York, y'know? The concrete jungle."

They talked about cities then. They had both been in Vancouver and in Paris. Bobby said he liked Vancouver and hated Paris and somehow it turned out that Palsson felt the same way.

Near a town called Hveragerdi they saw some sheep. Bobby wanted to pet one, so Palsson stopped the car and they ran all over a rocky meadow trying to catch a lamb, but the animals were too quick. Bobby and Palsson stumbled back to the Land Rover laughing and out of breath. Palsson told Bobby about a delicious Icelandic dish called *hryggur* (back of lamb) and said his wife made the best *hryggur* he had ever tasted. "I would be very honored," he said, "if you would come to my house for dinner sometime."

"Yeah, yeah." Bobby was in high spirits now. When they started off again he wanted the truck to go faster, but Palsson had a good thing going and didn't want to spoil it. "With that valuable cargo," he explained later, "I wanted full control of the machine. So I told him a Land Rover couldn't go any faster than seventy or eighty kilometers an hour."

On the way back, Bobby asked about tailors—who were the best ones and how much would it cost him to have a suit made up? "I want something mod. Not too mod but a little, y'know?"

Palsson promised to check out a British tailor who had set up shop in Reykjavik.

"But I don't want him using my name in ads or anything, unnastan'?"

Palsson understood.

By the time the Land Rover stopped in front of Bobby's house it was almost 6 A.M. With somebody to boss around, Bobby had already begun to act more confident. He felt he had put down a root in Iceland; maybe the place wasn't as bad as he had thought.

"You be here tonight?" Bobby asked as he started toward the house. His tone was airy, as if to indicate that the question was of no importance.

"Oh, yes, I'll be here," Palsson replied, jumping out to shake hands respectfully.

For five and a half hours, Bobby had not said a word about the match. Had he been thinking about Spassky's demand for an apology? Had he decided to refuse the demand and bust the match—or had he decided for the first time in his public life to say he was sorry? When Bobby went to bed that morning, nobody knew.

9

In the Clutch of the Bear

In the last week, wondering had replaced fishing as Iceland's principal industry. Which way would Bobby jump? Did Spassky really want an apology or had Moscow forced him to ask for it? Would the Russians also demand the forfeit of a game?

Marshall and Lombardy had no answers as they rolled toward Bobby's house at 10:00 Wednesday morning, July 5. They knew only that if they couldn't persuade Bobby to apologize, the Russians could walk off with the title without moving a pawn.

Revived by a five-hour sleep that brought his total to eight hours in the last fifty-two, Marshall roughed out a note intended to smooth Spassky's feathers and at the same time save Bobby's face. But there was a risk involved. Banging on Bobby's door in the middle of the night, or what Bobby considered the middle of the night, was going to shock him into rattled acquiescence—or into a tantrum.

When Marshall knocked on the front door, it swung open! The house was silent. He tapped at Bobby's bedroom door—no answer—then pushed it in. The room was pitch-black.

"Bobby?" he called.

There was a long moan.

"It's Paul, Bobby," Marshall continued. "We've got to talk about this thing with Spassky. Do we talk here or in the other room?"

The body thrashed.

"Okay, we talk here. Now you understand the situation. Spassky refused to draw because you weren't there. He said you had insulted him and the Russian people and demanded some form of *indemnity*. Bill and I . . ."

This time the whine was irritated. "C'mon, Pau'! I'n'wan' talk now! Wan' sleeee . . ."

"You gotta talk, Bobby. The Russians are looking for an easy way out and we gotta stop 'em. They said Spassky wanted an *apology* from *you* for being late for the match."

"Apology!" The covers jerked down and a pale face appeared.

"Yeah, we're lucky. They could have asked for the forfeit of a game and maybe they will, but if we give 'em something fast they might forget about the forfeit."

"Wha—?"

"Right. Because when we refuse the forfeit they'll back out of the match, claiming you've lost your right to play."

Bobby's eyes were big staring circles. But was he really awake? Marshall decided to batter him with complications and then tempt him to yield the apology by promising to take the problem off his hands.

"The Russians would have a pretty strong case," Marshall went on rapidly. "That's why we should throw them a bone now. They want an apology. We give 'em an *explanation* instead. They can call it what they want. Costs us nothing, makes us good guys. Makes them bad guys if they don't accept it. So all we need from you now is an okay to issue a statement of explanation. Unsigned. Then you can sleep. When you wake up, you can look it over and we can talk about signing it."

"I don't know," Bobby said in a voice still thick with sleep. "I don't like this thing about an apology."

"No apology!" Marshall said. "Just an explanation of the situation, made by Bill Lombardy for the American side. Your name will not be involved. Later you can look it over and sign it if you want to. But we've got to make a statement. If we don't—"

"All right, all right!" Bobby burst out. "Do what ya gotta do to get the match started. I gotta sleep!"

"Okay, Bobby. See you later." Marshall and Lombardy rushed away before Bobby could change his mind.

"An' lock the front door!" Bobby called after them. "Don' wan' any reporters gettin' in here . . ."

Bobby tried to get back to sleep but couldn't. He kept hearing words in his head. Forfeit. Indemnity. Apology. For ten minutes he tossed and turned. Then he swung out of bed, picked up the phone, and dialed the only number he knew in Reykjavik.

"I want to speak to Fred Cramer."

"Mr. Cramer is in a meeting," the hotel operator answered. "May I take a message?"

"No! Get him out of the meeting. *This is Bobby Fischer!*"

On Wednesday Cramer woke up feeling shaky. In three days he had lost so much face that "now," as one reporter remarked, "he's beginning to lose neck." The Russians had attacked him, Bobby had ignored him, Marshall and Lombardy had pushed him to the sidelines. Depressed and angry, Cramer was determined to win back somehow the position he felt was rightfully his.

Cramer showed up at noon in the Loftleidir auditorium for a press conference held by Euwe and, as a F.I.D.E. vice president, took a seat on the stage. Euwe had called the meeting, he announced, to report a new and careful translation of the Spassky note.

Marshall and Lombardy arrived from Bobby's bedside and were invited to the stage. At almost the same moment, Cramer was called to take his phone call from Bobby. By a painful coincidence he was forced to walk off the stage just as his rivals walked on.

After a quick exchange in low voices, Euwe announced that Grandmaster Lombardy had a message from Mr. Fischer. Lombardy took the microphone and read the statement Marshall had written in the car.

We are sorry that the world championship was delayed. The problems causing the delays were not with World Champion Spassky, whom I respect and admire as a man and as a player. If Grandmaster Spassky or the Soviet people were inconvenienced or discomfited I am indeed unhappy for I had not the slightest intention of this occurring.

Lombardy added that Bobby "wrote this statement himself about fifteen or twenty minutes ago," that he was "really unhappy" that Spassky felt he had been insulted, that he was "anxious to get the match going."

At that point, Cramer hurried onstage and there was quick exchange in low voices. Cramer moved toward the microphone but Lombardy got there first.

"While Mr. Marshall and I were en route here," he resumed, "Mr. Fischer called Mr. Cramer. Mr. Fischer now says that he would also like to make his explanation to Mr. Spassky in person when the drawing takes place."

As Lombardy transmitted it, Bobby's message sounded like a reaffirmation of his apology. In fact, it was a frantic attempt to cancel the apology.

"Fred!" Bobby had shouted to Cramer. "I want you to stop those guys from releasing that statement. If I make a statement, I want to make it myself. I'll talk to Spassky myself, maybe at the drawing. I don't know."

Cramer had hurried back to the auditorium to forestall Lombardy's moment of glory, but Lombardy stole Bobby's words out of his mouth and left him standing to one side like a messenger boy.

A little after 1 P.M., Benson and I showed up at Bobby's house to take pictures for *Life*. I had called Bobby ten minutes earlier and explained that if we could shoot him in the next half hour, the pictures could be rushed to the 3:15 plane to reach New York in time for the upcoming issue.

Bobby answered the door in his Jockey shorts. He was trying to look surly, but he couldn't hold back a smile when he saw Benson's Nikons. Let the world believe that Bobby hated photographers. We knew better. He loved to have his picture taken by Benson because he knew it would appear in *Life*—and because Benson let him think he was running the show.

Bobby closed the front door behind us. "Hey, what's goin' on here? This door doesn't lock!" He stared at us. "You mean I been lyin' here asleep and this door's been open? Oh, *no!* What's the matter with these Icelanders! They tryin' to get me killed in my sleep?"

"I'll tell Thorarinsson," I said.

"Wow!" He stumbled back to the bedroom and fell facedown on the bed. "You guys got here too fast. I gotta look my best, y'know? Don't want to have my picture in *Life* lookin' tired."

Suddenly he rolled over. "You hear that?" We heard nothing. "Hear that truck?" Faintly in the distance a motor moaned. "All last night I kept wakin' up. Look!" He pulled aside the black window shade I.C.F. had installed to guarantee him photon-free sleep. About forty feet away we saw the back of a house and about a hundred feet farther a residential street.

"A *main artery* goin' right past my bedroom window! And look!" He thumped out into the hallway and pointed at some small windows set so close to the ceiling that someone standing on the roof of the house next door could have seen no more than the head of someone standing inside Bobby's house. "The house is surrounded by reporters—but no curtains! And look out here!"

He stomped into the kitchen and pointed at another row of small windows set high in the wall. "No curtains here too. It's like a zoo! What do they think I am, some animal for people to watch while it eats?"

He went to a corner of the window and peeked out. "Photographers!" he gasped, pulling his head back.

We looked. One man in civilian clothes was standing beside the police car. If he had a camera we could not see it.

"Come on!" Bobby said. "We gotta cover these windows now!" He hurried back to his bedroom and tugged a pile of sheets and towels out of the bureau drawer. Keeping his head out of sight, he held the sheets at arm's length and tried to cover the windows. Benson and I helped him.

"Looks terrible," he grumbled, "like some cheap place." Then his eyes lit up. "All right! Now we gotta do these pictures!"

"I've got a suggestion," Benson said quickly. "The public knows that as soon as you arrived in Iceland you came to the house and went to bed. If you don't mind, I'd like to get a picture of you sleeping."

"You mean the way I am *now?*" Bobby was horrified.

"Under the covers, of course. Just your head showing."

"Oh, I don't know about *that,*" he said. "I gotta preserve my dignity, y'know? Whatever I do affects chess."

He hurried into the bathroom and closed the door. "Gotta get fixed up," he hollered. "Don't wanna look sloppy in *Life* magazine." Then he gave a big chesty laugh. "How many readers they got now?"

"They claim thirty million people read every issue."

"Yeah? That's good!" We could hear him spluttering at the sink. "What about the cover?"

"Not this time. We figure they'll put you on the cover when you're the new champ."

"Yeah? Well, how many pages am I gonna get?"

"We're asking them for eight but we can't guarantee it."

"Eight, huh?" He appeared in the bathroom door, rubbing his face with a white towel and blinking solemnly.

It took him at least fifteen minutes to dress. He picked his trousers without hesitation but changed his shirt and tie twice before he was satisfied. Then he opened a huge suitcase and burrowed through dirty shirts, torn underwear, crumpled letters, rolled-up toothpaste tubes, all woven together by twenty or thirty ties. Finally he came up with a fairly clean handkerchief, stuck it in the pocket of the brown leather jacket, put the jacket on and straightened his tie. On second thought, he took the tie off. Then he gave his hair a final comb-through, sat on the bed, and lay back.

"Okay," he said. "You want some pictures of me in bed?"

Benson blinked. But he's a pro. He aimed the bed lamp to catch Bobby's face and the chessboard beside the bed, leaving the over-dressed body in semidarkness. It was a good newsy shot—Bobby Fischer flaked out in Iceland after a week that shook the world—and *Life* spread it across two pages in the next issue.

As Benson clicked away, Bobby began to make improvements. He stretched his arms out wide and let them fall. He moved the fatal digital clock farther into the picture. Catching sight of a book that lay on the dark side of the bed, he shifted it to the night table so *Life*'s readers could read the title. THE BIBLE.

We left a little after 2 P.M. Bobby had cooperated happily for maybe half an hour, suggesting pictures, refusing pictures, thinking every minute of his image and all those people who would see him in *Life*. Suddenly he went ashen and collapsed in an easy chair. "Gah 'nough?" he mumbled. "Gah res' up now."

We were used to Bobby's abrupt collapses, but this one was unusu-ally severe. As we left, Benson shook his head. "My money's on Spassky. This boy'll never stand up to a twenty-four-game match."

After Euwe's press conference, Cramer offered to type Bobby's explanation and Xerox some copies for the press. Lombardy said he'd do it himself. All Cramer got to do was unlock Bobby's suite so that Marshall could leave a copy there.

What Cramer needed was a massive shot of the morale vita-min—reassurance that he was a member of the team, if possible acknowledgment that he was the captain. Unfortunately, there was no team. Cramer, Lombardy and Marshall all acted like chiefs; there weren't any Indians.

After Marshall left, Cramer called his wife in Milwaukee. Then he started a diary. After a while he took down a bottle and had a couple of nips.

At 6 P.M. the Russians gave a press conference at the Saga. More than two hundred people were jammed in an ugly little cocktail lounge designed to hold forty. All the Russians were there except Spassky—they sat in a row like finalists in a self-effacement contest. TV cameras were set up, ready to whirr, but as Geller rose the room was as still as a funeral parlor. In a few minutes we would know if there was still a chance that Bobby and Boris would somehow, someday, sit down and play chess.

The first paragraphs of Geller's statement were an angry indictment of Fischer and Euwe and a list of the F.I.D.E. and match regulations they were accused of breaking. The match would not continue, Geller said, unless three conditions were met:

"First, Robert Fischer must apologize to the world champion.

"Second, the president of F.I.D.E. has to condemn the behavior of the challenger.

"Third, the president of F.I.D.E. has to admit that his two-day postponement violated F.I.D.E. rules."

A reporter questioned Geller on the first point—hadn't Bobby made an apology that morning?

"We have seen the document described as Mr. Fischer's apology," Geller answered. "It was a duplicated copy, it was not signed and it was delivered to us by a messenger."

A deliberate slap in the face!

Euwe cleared his throat. "Well! Since I seem to be the subject of two of the conditions which Mr. Geller has ordained, perhaps I should respond." Edging through the audience, he sat down next to Geller. "As to the first condition, that I should condemn Mr. Fischer's behavior—there is no difficulty there. *Everybody* condemns Mr. Fischer's behavior!

"Now the second demand, that I should admit that the postponement of the match was a violation of F.I.D.E. rules. All right, I apologize! But if I had not violated the rules there would be no match!"

A reporter asked Geller if the Russians were satisfied with Euwe's answers. After a muttered conference, Geller replied, "We would like the statement to be made in writing, and we would like him to state that the rules will not be violated again."

Euwe shrugged. "I can write it *now*," he said, and drafted a letter on hotel stationery.

While he was writing, a reporter asked Geller, "Is it true that the Soviet Chess Federation has demanded that Mr. Fischer forfeit the first game to Mr. Spassky as a penalty for his late arrival?"

"*Da,*" said Geller.

This was news to everybody.

"I believe," Euwe said quickly, "that there has not been an *official* request."

Geller smiled mysteriously. "I don't think Mr. Spassky would accept the forfeit," he said, "even if Dr. Euwe offered it."

What the hell did *that* mean?

"Let me be sure I understand that, Mr. Geller," the same reporter went on. "You're saying that you don't think Mr. Spassky would *accept* a forfeit, but you're also saying that the Soviet Chess Federation is nevertheless *demanding* a forfeit—is that right?"

"*Da,*" said Geller.

So Moscow was asking for a point and it didn't really matter whether or not Spassky would give the point back, because Bobby would never accept a forfeit and Moscow knew it. In demanding the point, Spassky's bosses were trying to win the match without playing it.

Euwe cleared his throat again, and read his apology, which Geller nervously accepted.

"Assuming that you receive Mr. Fischer's signed apology by tomorrow morning," a reporter asked, "is there any reason why the drawing should not take place tomorrow at noon and the first game begin at five o'clock?"

Geller had been trapped.

Quick like a politician, Euwe turned the moment to his advantage. "No, no!" he broke in. "That would be unfair to Mr. Spassky. He has been very much upset by all this, and I would not like to make him play tomorrow. If I allowed a postponement for Mr. Fischer, I can certainly do no less for the world champion. I would like to give him a week to settle his nerves."

Appalled by Euwe's capitulation to the Russians, Cramer asked in a whisper if he might make a few remarks for the American side.

Euwe was shocked. This was a Russian press conference. Couldn't Cramer see that it would be grossly provocative if Cramer used it as a forum for pro-Fischer remarks?

Cramer's impulse solidified into an angry resolve: he would hold a press conference of his own within the next half hour!

Cramer announced his conference by buttonholing reporters in the lobby of the Saga. "Fellows!" he declared, bouncing from foot to foot as he spoke, "There's more than one side to these questions, as you'll find out!" Then he nipped back to his room at the Loftleidir and wet his whistle.

When he arrived in the auditorium, Cramer was by no means ossified, as many reporters claimed, but his anger had changed to a flush of indignation, and the point of his press conference had blurred in his mind.

He started by stating that he wanted to set the record straight. Then he admitted lamely that most of his objections had already been made by the reporters. But that was all right, he said, because "the seats are somewhat more comfortable at our press conference than at theirs."

Nobody laughed.

"The Russians aren't the only ones who feel that a lot of F.I.D.E. rules have been broken. No, sir! We want an apology from Euwe too! Bobby is getting his suit pressed for the drawing right now! We're ready for a—"

"What do you mean by 'we'?" a reporter asked.

"You guess!" Cramer shot back.

"I wish you would treat these matters more seriously," a well-known master rose to say.

"Throw that guy out!" Cramer muttered at the microphone.

"I beg your pardon, Mr. Cramer," a British reporter asked, "but would you please explain your credentials here?"

"Ha ha." Cramer had heard that question before. "I'm here as an assistant to grandmaster Fischer. At this minute his suit is being pressed—"

The British journalist cut him off. "You have this unbelievable hangup about Mr. Fischer's sartorial equipment. This is simply the most irresponsible press conference I have ever attended."

"Gentlemen," a chess master concluded, "we must not listen to this man."

Laughing, shaking their heads, the reporters filed out, leaving Cramer on the stage alone.

Salt was promptly rubbed in Cramer's wounds. At about 7:45, Bobby called.

"Where ya been? Didn' ya get my message? . . . Yeah, well, I want you to *be* there when I need ya, unnastan'?" He said he wanted some hot food sent over from the hotel. As an afterthought, he asked casually, "So what's new?"

Cramer was in no shape to give an objective account. His reflex was to defend what he had done, and in telling Bobby about the afternoon meeting he portrayed himself as the good Cordelia and Marshall/Lombardy as the other two.

"Yeeaah?" Bobby was alarmed. "Wha'd they say?"

As Cramer described it, the apology was not one that *he* would have made. It was too humble for one thing, and it was made in Bobby's name.

Bobby was even more appalled when Cramer told him the Russians had rejected the apology because it wasn't signed. He wanted to know more—Cramer had at last found the credulous audience he had hoped to assemble at his press conference. Sensation piled on sensation. As the conversation ended, Cramer felt reasserted but Bobby was in a frenzy. Two minutes later he was on the phone to Marshall.

"What's this I hear about you and Lombardy making an abject apology to Spassky *in my name?* I never told you to apologize! What's goin' on? You can't put words in my mouth!"

"You heard wrong," Marshall told him. "In the first place there was *no* apology. There was an *explanation.*"

"I never told you you could say *anything!*"

"Oh yes you did. Bill and I came to your house at 11:45 this morning."

"Oh. Yeah."

"In the second place," Marshall went on, "the explanation we made was *not* abject. It was dignified and straightforward. In the third place, it was *not* made in your name. That's why the Russians objected! They want you to sign the statement and I strongly advise you to do so. It's a minimum statement. It gives them nothing."

"Naa! Naa!" Bobby said.

Marshall's heart sank.

"I wanna write it in my own words," Bobby went on.

Marshall was staggered. Had he actually heard Bobby agree to apologize?

"Great," he managed to say. "Better."

Five minutes later, the phone rang in Cramer's room. "You come over here around ten o'clock," Bobby told him. "I wanna work on that letter to Spassky."

It had been a heavy day for Spassky. In the late morning, some seven hours before the Soviet press conference, the chairman of the Soviet Sport Committee had called from Moscow. A man of immense power answerable only to the Politburo, Sergei Pavlov had clashed with Spassky more than once, and the word was out in Soviet chess circles that Pavlov was looking for a chance to nail Spassky's hide to his door.

Pavlov said he had decided it might be better if the Russian team came home immediately. Grammatically, he was making a suggestion; actually, he was giving an order.

Any reasonable Russian would have swallowed his pride like a very small fishbone and taken the next plane home. But as usual in a crisis the reasonable man in Spassky gave way to the stubborn, crafty muzhik. He decided to interpret Pavlov's order as a suggestion.

The prematch position, Spassky said, had clarified "with advantage to our side." He argued forcefully that the match should be allowed to proceed. Iceland needed it, Russia's honor required it, Spassky himself wanted it. "I cannot leave," he is reported to have said. "The world will forget Bobby's foolish behavior and remember only that he came and I ran away. If he refuses the punishment and goes home, that will be his tragedy. Better his tragedy than mine."

Pavlov agreed to wait and see how Bobby and Euwe reacted to the Soviet demands, but he ordered Spassky to insist on the forfeit of the first game. Spassky could give the point back, but the Soviet Union could not be pushed around.

At least for the time being, Spassky had fought Moscow off. Bobby remained a problem. Damn Bobby! Spassky's sense of form had been violated, his creative rhythm broken. Exhausted now by Pavlov's call, the champion felt an urge to get even with his opponent. "Bobby must pay a penalty," he told Geller. "I want the point. And then," he added with a cold smile, "I want to give it back."

About 10:00 Wednesday night, Geller summoned Euwe, Schmid and Thorarinsson to a midnight meeting at the Saga.

"Midnight!" Euwe muttered as he hung up the phone. "I confessed, I apologized, I condemned. Now they want me to die."

Cramer's car crunched to a stop in front of Bobby's house at 10 P.M. Bobby was dressed and had company.

Saemundur Palsson, out of uniform, had arrived about an hour earlier with his seven-year-old son, Asgeir. Palsson noticed that Bobby was keyed up and restless. "D'ja call the tailor?" he wanted to know right away. Palsson said the tailor had agreed to open his shop any night that suited Bobby. "Not bad," Bobby answered.

Squeezing close to his father, Asgeir sat staring at Bobby with big scared eyes. Whenever Bobby looked back, he stuffed his head in his father's armpit.

"Asgeir!" Palsson protested in Icelandic. "Why are you so shy? Mr. Fischer won't hurt you. He's a *very* nice man."

Asgeir said something to his father's armpit.

"Aw!" said Palsson, and explained to Bobby, "He is shy because you are so famous."

Flattered, Bobby noticed the child. "Hey, Oscar," he said, "ya want some apple juice?"

Palsson translated. Asgeir blushed and nodded.

Bobby got the juice and Asgeir sat drinking shyly. He had a broad rosy face and enormous brown eyes set far apart, like a lamb's. Bobby decided he liked him and Palsson insisted that Asgeir liked Bobby too.

"Yeah," Bobby said, "I get along good with kids."

Palsson noticed that Bobby seemed to be in some sort of shock. His eyes were unfocused and once or twice he jumped at a slight sound that Palsson had scarcely heard. "What's that?" he asked anxiously. Occasionally he was captured by his Sony shortwave radio, and for four or five minutes sat slack-lipped, twisting the knobs. Then he resumed the conversation as if there had been no interruption.

When Cramer arrived, Bobby switched Palsson off. "I got some work to do," he said.

Thanking Bobby profusely, Palsson took his son and left.

"Okay," Bobby said, whirling to Cramer, "we gotta write this letter to Spassky, right? You got somethin' to write on?" He rushed back and forth, speaking in an urgent, almost hysterical voice. "Okay! They don't think I'll apologize and they *know* I'll never take the forfeit! But I'm gonna surprise 'em, see? *I'm gonna apologize!* Start writin'.

" 'Dear Boris, please accept my sincere—my sincer*est* apology for my insulting behavior—for my *crude and insulting* behavior in not attending the opening ceremony.' " In Bobby's voice there was a sound of confessional exaltation.

"Read it back."

Cramer read it back, being careful not to look up—he was appalled at what Bobby was dictating.

"Now write this. 'I did *not* intend to insult you but simply became *carried away* by my *petty dispute* over money' . . . got that?"

"Ye-es."

"Write faster, Fred!"

"All set."

". . . 'my petty dispute over money with the Icelandic chess organizers.' Make that 'petty *and* undignified.' Okay? Read it back."

Cramer read it back.

"Good. Now comes the surprise! 'For many months, this dispute has distracted public attention from the true purpose of the match, which is . . . which is a contest between two great chess players for the world championship.' Got that? 'Therefore, I now propose to you that *we both will give up all prize money and play the match for the sake of chess alone!'* "

Cramer jerked with amazement. Bobby's face was shimmering with excitement. Cramer gave a little shudder.

"How about that!" Bobby demanded triumphantly, coming to a stop in front of Cramer. *"That'll* prove I'm not greedy like they been sayin', right?"

"Right!" Cramer answered with a big false grin. It was one thing to charm the media with tales about what a nut Bobby Fischer was. Quite another to be shut up in a room with him when he was freaking out.

After half an hour of dictation, Cramer tried to escape. "There's a typewriter back at the hotel. I'll—"

"Not yet! I gotta write about the forfeit! They *know* I'm not gonna accept that!"

Bobby was talking numbers now—the number of games he needed to win, the difference a forfeited game would make. In some frantic but logical way he demonstrated that the forfeit would actually put him three games behind and that Spassky would be a bad sport if he insisted on it.

A little before 10:45, ears ringing from forty minutes of unpunctuated Fischer, Cramer stumbled into the bright silence of an Icelandic summer's night.

"What in hell," he thought, "am I going to do now?" This was suicide and it had to be stopped, but Cramer knew he didn't carry the clout to change Bobby's mind. Marshall might, but Cramer was so threatened by Marshall's power that he couldn't bear to bring him back into the picture. Somehow he had to ride out the storm alone and then steer Bobby back to more reasonable shores. He typed the letter rapidly, smoothing and shaping but not changing the writer's voice, and was back at Bobby's house by 11:30.

Bobby fell upon the letter with ferocious joy and began to read aloud like a priest declaiming a sacred text. When he came to the end he looked disappointed that there wasn't more.

"Pretty good!" he said.

He read the letter again, this time silently. Suddenly he gave a start.

"Hey! I didn't say that! You changed what I said!"

Cramer explained why. Bobby didn't like the idea that His Letter had been tampered with.

Soon he found other changes. Then he made a change himself. It gave him a new feeling of power. He began to make changes all over the place. Soon the smooth letter became patchy. Bobby sensed the roughness and blamed Cramer.

"I need a professional writer," he said. "Get Brad."

Euwe and Schmid arrived at the Saga in a sour mood. Four days in the pressure cooker had sweated the last strength out of Euwe. Schmid's heart had been acting up, and now he was developing a toothache. Thorarinsson was grim. All he could do was delay and pray that Moscow would call off the dogs.

Geller, Krogius, Nei and Chamanin were there for the Russians. They all seemed embarrassed, but Geller did his duty. "The USSR Chess Federation therefore demands that Mr. Fischer shall forfeit a point for the first game."

Euwe threw up his hands. "How can a game be forfeited if the clock has not yet begun? If even the match has not begun?"

Cramer said, "The Soviet Chess Federation believes the match was opened by the opening ceremony. The forfeit will be legal."

Euwe protested; Geller persisted. "If F.I.D.E. will not give this forfeit, the world champion will not play the match."

Two hours later, Euwe gave up. "Very well, I will give you the forfeit."

The Russians sat with lowered eyes. They had not dared oppose Moscow, but they felt a mistake was being made.

Accurately estimating their mood, Thorarinsson brought his right fist down on the table like a bludgeon. "No! I will not permit this forfeit. It will not happen in Iceland!"

It was as if his fist had hit every man in the room.

"Dr. Euwe," Thorarinsson went on, "must draft a telegram to the Soviet Chess Federation—tonight."

Since Schmid and Euwe were exhausted, Thorarinsson wrote the telegram himself. Cunningly, he let the Russians believe they had won, but suavely put Moscow on notice that the forfeit would be illegal and could cost them the title at the next F.I.D.E. Congress. "WOULD APPRECIATE UTMOST EFFORT ON YOUR PART IN SMOOTHING THE WAY FOR THE START OF THE MATCH."

Geller beamed. Euwe signed the message.

Five minutes later, Schmid told Jim Ward of UPI that the drawing would be held at 8 P.M. that day, Thursday, July 6. Euwe added that the match would begin "on Sunday or, at the latest, Tuesday."

When Thorarinsson slipped into bed he was still chuckling. He might not win but he had put up a hell of a fight.

It was 1 A.M. when I arrived at Bobby's house. Cramer opened the door. "Jesus," he said, "am I glad to see you! I just finished my eighth version." Then he leaned in close. *"Watch out! He's crazy!"*

Bobby was sitting in an alcove off the living room. As he looked up from the handwritten sheets, I saw his eyes. They looked as if he had been caught in a terrific flash of light and his pupils had locked shut.

"Okay, Fred," Bobby said. "I don't need you any more."

Cramer left instantly.

"I'm writin' this letter to Spassky, see?" Bobby went on. "I'm gonna read it and you polish it up, right?"

He began to read in an excited voice, in love with his own prose.

When he came to the part about giving up the prize money and playing for the love of chess, his voice skidded up the scale and hit a note of earnest lunacy. I got a fearful glimpse of what Davis and the others must have gone through earlier. But there was a difference. In New York, Bobby had converted fear into anger, telling himself that he was standing up for principles and fighting evil men. But in coming to Reykjavik without winning the conditions he had said were essential, he had lost the feeling that he was in the right, and without it he was like Samson shorn. At the first test of his will he had collapsed.

Take the money, he was saying. Take the stardom. Take the contracts I can't understand and the sharpies who want to exploit me. Forget that I wanted to be rich and powerful and famous. Just let me be Bobby Fischer, the kid who loves chess and plays it so well he doesn't have to do anything else in his whole life, ever.

Suddenly it was clear what had to be done. Bobby could no more grapple with Spassky without aggressive qualities than a tiger could fight without claws and teeth. His ferocity had to be reactivated, his self-righteousness dug out, his anger unclogged, the bubble of his vulgar ambitions reblown. In one night the intricate chess machine called Bobby Fischer had to be rebuilt and there was only one man who could even begin to do the job. How could I persuade Bobby to see him?

"Whaddya think? Whaddya think?" Bobby asked urgently.

"I think it's a very strong letter."

"Yeah? Yeah?" A little smile kept climbing onto his mouth and getting pushed off.

"It's very clear, very forceful. The apologies are direct and generous."

"Yeah?" The smile was holding on. "What about the forfeit?"

"Sharp. If the Russians insist on a forfeit after that, they'll look bad."

His face became careful. "And—uh—what about where I give up the prize money?"

"It really shook me. The public thinks you're greedy. With one blow you kill that idea. You raise the whole match to a higher level. But . . ."

"Yeeaahh?"

"But it worries me. It involves the whole question of money and chess, the rights of the players. For twenty years you've been fighting for these things. An action like this can have another twenty years of consequences. Why not put Marshall's head to work on this too, just as a precaution?"

Bobby looked put out. "Marshall? What does *he* know about this?"

"He knows about consequences. That's what lawyers know about. You've got a top lawyer, David Frost's lawyer, and he's right here. *Make him work.* Hear what he has to say. Then *you* decide."

It was "make him work" that did it.

"Yeah . . . we-ell . . ."

On the way to the Loftleidir, Bobby sat with one arm over the back of the jump seat and one elbow out the window. Every few seconds he glanced at the letter in his right hand. His smile was a little sappy. It was pep-talk time and Marshall had better come up with a good one.

Marshall come to the door in his pajamas. It was 1:45 but his eyes were clear and unsurprised. "Sssh! Betty's asleep. What's up?"

I explained in whispers.

Three minutes later Marshall knocked at the door of Bobby's suite. I said I'd be in my room, and left. Thank God he was Marshall's problem now.

"So what can I do for you?" Marshall asked in a matter-of-fact tone.

Bobby read him the letter. Watching his eyes, Marshall got goose flesh too. "I felt like a cop talking a jump case off a ledge," he told me later.

When Bobby asked him how he liked the letter, Marshall said yes and no. "The offer to play for nothing is a serious mistake."

Bobby looked as if he had been struck. "A mistake?"

Marshall asked what he hoped to accomplish by giving up the money.

"Well, this'll really give 'em a jolt! They're all sayin' I'm greedy and materialistic. This'll kill that idea and raise the match to a higher level. The chess'll be important, not the money."

"The jolt'll last about ten seconds," Marshall said. "Is that worth a hundred and fifty thousand dollars? No way will it kill the idea that you're greedy. They'll just think you're greedy *and* crazy."

Marshall hoped the shock wouldn't blow Bobby's circuits.

"People have made up their minds about you, and only one thing's gonna change their minds. Win and they'll say you were right to demand the money. Lose and nothing you do is right."

Bobby resisted. "But I want the *chess* to be important, not the money."

"The minute you start to play, they'll forget *everything* except the chess—"

"Nnnnyuuhhhh." A little light was filtering through.

"—and so will *you*. You know what the Russians would do if you offered to give up the money? They'd accept! And they'd laugh at you because you had 'em in a trap and you let 'em out."

Marshall reminded Bobby that the Russians had fought for years to keep chess prizes so small that Western players could not hope to make a living from chess alone. In this way the Russians prevented the rise of Western chess professionals who could challenge the state-supported chess bums of the Soviet Union. The Russians, Marshall explained, feared Bobby as much for the huge prizes he could command as for his feats at the board.

In Bobby's eyes a glint of meanness appeared. The anaconda was stirring; Marshall threw it another rat.

"And how about the organizers—why let *them* have all that money?"

"That's right!" Bobby said in a sharp voice. "I forgot about them."

At 2:45, Bobby and Marshall knocked at my door. Bobby fell into a chair and sat blinking like a man coming out of a cave.

"Can you help us with this thing?" Marshall asked.

I set up my portable. As we began to go over the letter, Bobby took charge. He knew exactly what he wanted to say and he wanted every word to be his. By 3:45 A.M., he had constructed a jalopy of a letter that bumped and sputtered but moved right along to where it had to go.

"Much better!" he said. His eyes were almost normal now and there was color in his cheeks. He sat down and wrote the letter out in big childish print.

Dear Boris

Please accept my sincerest apology for my disrespectful behavior in not attending the opening ceremony. I simply became carried away by my petty dispute over money with the Icelandic chess organizers. I have offended you and your country, the Soviet Union, where chess has a prestigious position. Also, I would like to apologize to Dr. Max Euve President of F.I.D.E. to the Match organizers in Iceland, to the thousands of chess fans here, to the millions of chess fans around the world and especially to the millions of fans and the many friends I have in the United States.

After I did not show up for the first game, Dr. Euwe announced that the first game would be postponed without prejudice to me. At that time you made no protest. Now I am informed that the Russian Chess Federation is demanding that the first game be forfeited to you. The timing of this demand seems to place in doubt the motives for your Federation's not insisting at the first for a forfeit of the first game.

If this forfeit demand were respected, it would place me at a tremendous handicap. Even without this handicap, you will have an advantage to begin with of needing twelve points out of twenty-four, to retain your title whereas I will need twelve and a half to win the world title. If this demand were granted, you would need only eleven points out of twenty three but I would still need twelve and a half out of only twenty three. In other words I must win *three!* games without losses, just to obtain the position you would have at the beginning of the match. I don't believe that the world's champion desires such an advantage in order to play me.

I know you to be a sportsman and a gentlman, and I am looking foward to some exciting chess games with you.

Sincerely

Reykjavik, July 6 1972   Bobby Fischer

"C'mon!" Bobby burst out, striding to the door. "We gotta take this to Spassky!"

At 4:40 A.M., the Volkswagen rolled up to the Saga.

"Wanna come in?" Marshall asked Bobby.

"Naaa."

Marshall took the letter and hurried into the hotel. Bobby sat fidgeting, then burst out of the car and rushed into the lobby. Marshall was already on the way up to Spassky's room. Bobby paced the lobby muttering, "C'mon! Hurry up!"

Spassky's room was at the end of a dim corridor about 150 feet long. Marshall and the bellboy escorting him tiptoed the last twenty steps to Spassky's door. Raising a finger to his lips, Marshall knelt. His knees cracked like party pull-outs. Marshall winced, but no sound came from inside. Then he leaned forward and, sliding the letter gently across the carpet, tried to push it under the door. No go. Dropping his head to the floor, Marshall closed his left eye and tried to peer under the door with his right eye.

The door opened.

Cheek on the rug, Marshall rolled his eyes upward, expecting to see Spassky.

The bellboy tapped him on the shoulder. He had just opened the door with a master key.

Heart thumping, Marshall eased to his feet. In front of him, across a shallow foyer, sat a small table. He took one step into the suite. Another. Hearing a noise in the room to his right, Marshall stopped short. Run away? Go ahead? Tiptoeing swiftly to the table, he dropped the letter on it, then spun and tiptoed out. The bellboy turned the key and side by side they went scooting for the elevator.

Ten minutes later, Bobby was settled for the night in his Loftleidir suite. He looked tired but satisfied. As we were leaving, he switched off his shortwave radio and asked, "So when's the first game?"

10

An Evening in
Thor's Jockstrap

The playing hall was possibly the ugliest public building north of the Weehawken Ferry Terminal. Somebody described it as "Thor's Jockstrap," and it was known to the press as "the playing hell." It was a big bare steel and concrete shell that looked like an airplane hangar, and every noise bounced off its surfaces like a nail clattering around in a tin can. The only effective way to heat and light the place was to burn it down, but it was the best auditorium Reykjavik could offer and I.C.F. was trying to make the best of it.

A new stage had been built and a balcony to house the electronic equipment, a huge screen had been mounted above the stage to show the moves as they occurred, and closed-circuit television had been installed all through the building. Fifteen thousand square feet of red carpet had been laid and one thousand green chairs set up. Six thousand square feet of light-resistant curtains had been draped over the baleful skylights. The most striking object in the hall was the lighting unit, a rectangular box almost twenty feet long, ten feet wide and four feet deep that floated over the stage like a truck body inexplicably levitating.

Gathered in the hall for the drawing of the colors, chess experts were impressed. Harry Golombek, A British international grandmaster who had seen five championship matches, said I.C.F. had provided "the best playing conditions in the history of chess."

When the Russians arrived, three hundred journalists, chess buffs, autograph freaks and sleeve-feelers were clumped around the stage door. Spassky stepped out of his white Jeepster. A cheer went up. In gray slacks and a tan pullover, he sent out vibrations of tennis star. He rippled affably through the crowd into a foyer and then through a

149

brown curtain that shut off the backstage area. Spassky's three assistants followed him.

The Russians were a few minutes early for the ceremony, scheduled for 8 P.M. Schmid and Thorarinsson met them and all five stood laughing and talking in the corridor that ran past the dressing rooms. Spassky was splurging charm and seemed relaxed. His friends knew better.

Spassky had found Bobby's letter about two hours after it was dropped on his hall table and he had read it, he said later, with "strong feelings." He felt relief and then a burst of affection for the straight-line little-boy mind that had written the letter. As he studied the challenge in the last paragraphs he began again to imagine Bobby as a Galahad of chess and the match as a chivalric spectacle.

Eager now to play the match, he was glad to hear of the Thorarinsson/Euwe telegram. But it made problems. He owed Pavlov a difficult explanation and the Soviet Chess Federation some advance notice of the drawing. Cunningly, he decided to telegraph a report on the midnight meeting to the Soviet Chess Federation—but to make sure it did not go off too early. With any luck, the drawing would be over and the match under way before his bosses could order him home.

By lunchtime all this anxious jiggering, coming on top of four days of the same, had scooped the marrow out of Spassky's headbone. Waiting backstage, he told Thorarinsson and Schmid that he could not play before Tuesday. But he was eager for the drawing. All day long, at intervals, Spassky had been thinking of the moment when he and Bobby would meet—eye to eye, hand grasping hand, men of honor on the eve of battle. He discussed the scenario with his companions and then came up with an impish notion.

"I'll squeeze his biceps," Spassky said, "and ask him what sort of condition he's in. Then I'll tell him to squeeze mine." Geller and the others laughed. Bobby's arms are almost girlishly soft; Spassky's had been stripped to pure sinew by several months of determined tennis.

But now it was 8:10 and the historic encounter had not come off. What had happened—why was Bobby late? Spassky flushed. After what had happened at the last drawing, it should have been clear even to Bobby that the slightest lateness could be read as an intentional insult.

Spassky told himself the delay was routine. But what if—an unthinkable thought. Turning pale, Spassky broke away from Schmid and the others and paced the corridor, eyes flashing.

What if Bobby did not come?

Watched anxiously by everyone in the corridor, Spassky made seven or eight tigerish transits. It was 8:22. How much longer could a world champion wait without loss of dignity? Schmid caught up with him, spoke reassuringly and hurried to a phone. Spassky strode on.

Suddenly the crowd outside the stage door roared. Spassky stopped just inside the curtain, listening.

About fifty feet from the stage door Bobby's cab ran into a wall of flesh. The two policemen on duty made no move to clear a path.

Bobby burst out of the cab wearing a glitter-green slubbed-silk suit with wide pointy shoulders, the sort of outfit Irish gangsters used to favor in Pat O'Brien movies. Lombardy and Marshall scrambled after him—too late. Bobby was twenty feet away, alone in the crowd, streaking toward the stage door through a barrage of cheers and catcalls.

As he darted inside, his head came up—no trace of the panicky child we had seen the night before. His cheeks were rosy, his eyes bright as he whooshed past the cops and burst through the curtain, almost running into Spassky.

Smiling broadly, Spassky extended his hand. But Bobby's eyes were dazzled by the evening sun, and his head was full of the roar of the crowd. He rushed past without noticing the champion.

Spassky stood staring at the broad green back, his smile crumpled, his tan two shades lighter. Big and vital and overdressed, Bobby looked every inch the arrogant superstar. In a sweater that had lost its casual flair, Spassky looked like a guy who had asked for an autograph and been told to buzz off.

Charging down the corridor, Bobby ran head on into Schmid, Krogius and Geller and handed them a big hello. Krogius tactfully indicated Spassky, who now realized that Bobby simply had not seen him. Bobby stared blankly at Spassky for about two seconds before recognition came. Then his face split in an all-American smile and he hit Spassky with a handshake that came in like a peg from right field.

"Hi, Boris!" he called out in a Brooklyn street voice. "How ya been?"

It was hardly the courtly encounter Spassky had imagined. The champion shrank back. He was startled, he admitted later, by Bobby's energy and size.

"Say," Bobby said, "you look"—he was about to say "great" but, pulling back a little, he looked Spassky over with sudden concern —"you look *thiiin!*" The word carried intimations of Buchenwald or maybe terminal cancer—also a trace of relief that Spassky wasn't as big as he had remembered, sort of puny actually, maybe not so dangerous after all. The father image that had always put Bobby in awe had magically vanished with Spassky's blubber. Ironically, the training intended to make the champion more dangerous at the table had made him less formidable in Bobby's eyes.

Spassky produced a wilted smile. Shifting smoothly to the attack, he explained that he was down to his best fighting weight. Then he reached out and squeezed Bobby's left bicep. "How about you?" he asked.

Bobby gave a puzzled glance at the arm Spassky was squeezing. Apparently his mind had wandered during Spassky's explanation about his physical condition, and now he couldn't understand why the champion was feeling his arm.

"Uh? Oh, yeah," he answered. "It's one of those new synthetic fabrics."

Spassky blinked. "Fabrics? Excuse, my English—"

Just then Schmid and Marshall whisked Bobby away. In his dressing room, with the door closed, Schmid produced a stack of documents. "These are the match rules," he told Bobby. "According to the regulations, both players will approve them by signing a copy. It is necessary that you do this now, before the drawing will take place."

As he spoke, Schmid uncapped his fountain pen and offered it to Bobby along with the papers. Bobby jumped as if he had been asked to autograph a tarantula.

"Whaddya mean, sign?" he exploded. "I never heard that rule! I don't hafta sign anything!"

Schmid set his face. "Please, Bobby," he said with determination. "Read it only. Then we will discuss."

"Wait a minute, Lothar," Marshall cut in. "Bobby can't just sign a thing like this on the spur of the moment. What are there—eight pages? He's got to read this carefully."

"Please." Schmid felt he had to establish his authority now. Moscow had stated unequivocally that the next breach of the rules would cause Spassky to be called home, and as chief arbiter it was Schmid who would be blamed. He set his lips in a tight official smile. "Perhaps then Mr. Marshall can read the rules and—"

The papers had lodged somehow in Marshall's hands. "Certainly, Lothar," he said, "I'll be happy to read the rules—tomorrow morning.

It's not the sort of thing I can do fast. I mean, I wouldn't want my client to wake up and find out he'd bought a parking lot in Greenland. So, why don't you keep these until after the—"

But Schmid would not take the papers back. "Please, Mr. Marshall," he said, "as chief arbiter I must insist that you—"

Holding the papers at waist level, Marshall simply dropped them. They landed on the floor with a cold smack. "See you later, Lothar," he said pleasantly, and followed Bobby out.

For a full minute Schmid stood still, fighting off shock and indignation. Later he told a friend, "What animals Fischer and his people are!" There would come a time, he told himself. He would not indefinitely let himself be made a fool of.

At 8:45 the ceremony began. When Spassky strolled onstage, he got a big hand. Bobby was given a much fainter ovation. Spassky drifted to the chess table and inspected it calmly; he had seen it once before. Bobby, who had never seen the physical arrangements for the match, glanced quickly about the stage. Bland green carpeting underfoot, écru drapes on the walls. Spotting the handsome new chess table at stage center, he cut across to it like a kid making tracks for the ice cream store.

The table was an angular, modern piece of heavy mahogany, rubbed to a red-gold glow. Cream-colored leather cushions had been let into the edges for the players to lean on, and in the center, in a square mahogany socket, sat a jewel of a chessboard made of black gabbro and white marble squares.

Bobby stared down at it for at least a minute without moving. The hall fell silent. Everyone sensed that something uncanny was going on, a mysterious union and communion. Then Bobby's hand moved slowly toward the chessboard until at last, lovingly, he touched the White King.

When Geller had announced that the champion's conditions had been met and he would play, Schmid invited Spassky to choose one of the two envelopes he was holding. Spassky picked the envelope containing Bobby's name. This choice gave Bobby "the right to choose colors from Pawns held in the hands of the other player." Spassky picked up a Black Pawn and a White Pawn, turned his back and then turned to face Bobby with his fists closed.

Bobby confidently reached out and tapped Spassky's right hand —Edmondson had told him that about eight times out of ten a player will hold the White Pawn in his right hand.

Spassky opened his right hand and displayed—a Black Pawn. Bobby gave a little start, then looked away.

"Mr. Fischer has selected Black," Schmid announced. "Mr. Spassky therefore has White and will make the first move in the first game of the match, which will begin on Tuesday, July 11, at 5:00 in the afternoon."

Loud applause. The Russians on the stage clustered around Spassky, the Americans around Bobby. His green suit had lost its electric crackle, his face was the texture of a wet saltine. Something was wrong and everybody in the hall knew what it was. Losing anything to Spassky at this point was like losing his life. Marshall later guessed, "Bobby was thinking that Spassky had a jinx on him."

Dreamily, Bobby wandered back to the table, where he stood alone, fingering the chess pieces.

11

Iron Logic Meets Sculptured Frenzy

It was the day of the first game—Tuesday, July 11. Five days had gone by since the drawing. Was the match really going to happen?

At 4:54, a woman in the uniform of a chambermaid crossed the stage and dabbed the chessboard with a dust cloth. Then she hurried off. Chief arbiter Schmid went quickly to the table, made sure that every piece was exactly in the center of its correct square, then hurried back to his table at stage right.

At 4:56, the curtain at the back of the stage parted and Spassky appeared. Loud applause. Looking calm and confident, he bowed acknowledgment. Schmid showed him to the table, where Spassky laid out pencils and score sheets. In his white shirt, sincere tie, and dark-gray three-piece suit, Spassky was the picture of a young executive setting up for an important conference.

Spassky had used his long weekend well. On Friday morning at breakfast, seeing him worn and irritable, Nei had proposed a weekend vacation at Borgarfjordhur, a small town on a salmon river about fifty miles from Reykjavik.

"Do I have the permission of my commanding officers," Spassky had wondered with a straight face, "to catch myself a pretty little fish?"

"Fishing," he was informed, "is very tiring. You may catch a pretty little fish when you are two games ahead."

So Spassky took long walks in the country and slept till his eyes were fat. Saturday night he went to a dance at the local hotel and risked a couple of slow numbers with a pretty farm girl.

Sunday night, he was back at the Saga, his priorities reasserted. To beat Bobby Fischer and retain the world championship was his third objective. His second was, as he put it, "to play myself into form." His main aim was "to have the connection with the things we are calling the ground, the most deep things in a man's life. Without this, an artist is nothing."

Grounded or not, as he sat down at the chess table he felt dizzy. At 4:57 he walked carefully back to his dressing room to steady his nerves.

Two minutes before game time, Schmid made a silent prayer: "Please, Bobby, no more trouble!"

On the playing table, in full view of the audience, sat a chess clock—a pair of timers, one for each player, geared together so that when one stopped the other started. Both were now motionless at twelve o'clock.

At 4:59.45, Schmid walked to the playing table. Stretching out his right hand, he held it above the plunger that would start Spassky's clock. The Match of the Century was about to begin ... but where was Bobby?

Physically, Bobby was in his hotel room. Metaphysically, his whereabouts were anybody's guess. In the press the delay had been called "manna from Moscow," and no doubt Bobby needed it far more desperately than Spassky. But could he take advantage of the delay?

At 11 P.M. on Thursday, about two hours after the drawing, Bobby had phoned me.

"This house is no good," he said. "I wanna move to the hotel. Can you get here fast?"

I was there in ten minutes. Bobby looked haggard and upset.

"Help me carry the stuff out," he said. We carried out his TV set, his radio and one of the supersuitcases. An Icelandic reporter was there with a photographer, who took pictures. Bobby ignored them and went back for the other suitcase; we carried it to the car. I started the motor.

"No, wait!" Bobby ran back into the house and reappeared with a tray of cold cuts. "Some freeloader might get 'em."

We drove off, followed by the reporter and photographer.

"Get rid of them!" Bobby said. "I don't want anybody taking pictures of my things."

I drove through a red light, an infraction Icelanders consider roughly as naughty as wiping dishes with the national flag. The two newsmen stared after us in astonishment, and next day there was a four-column story in *Visir* about how Bobby had run a red light.

Ten minutes after I left Bobby in his room he called again.

"I left a pair of shoes over there," he said in an anxious voice. "I wanna get 'em right away. Some souvenir hunter might break in."

When we found his shoes, he looked relieved and asked me to let him drive Cramer's Fiat, which I had borrowed.

"But it's a stick shift," I warned. He had informed Thorarinsson that he would never drive a car unless it had an automatic transmission.

"We-ell," Bobby said.

For the next half hour I sat clutching the dashboard and wondering if I was about to become the first reporter ever killed while covering a chess match. Bobby was erratic enough in a car with automatic transmission—in 1971, just after he got his license, he ran through a fence onto somebody's lawn, and even after a year of driving he whimpered when he had to make a left turn across oncoming traffic.

After four or five stalls, he got the Fiat moving with a series of eye-loosening jolts. When he tried to shift to second the gear box sounded like a power mower leveling a lawn of eightpenny nails. For the next five minutes we zipped along at about eighteen miles an hour. Bobby was pretty good at steering, but when he changed gears he looked down at the gearshift and forgot where he was going.

"Oop! Oop!" I kept saying as the car swerved.

"I got it! I got it!" he would answer. But the minute he looked down again we were off on the shoulder. I'm not sure he ever achieved high gear.

"Uh-oh," he said suddenly. A car was coming toward us on the other side of the road, not very fast. Bobby narrowed his eyes and edged his right wheels off the road. Just before the car reached us, the asphalt came to an end with a bounce that loosened the steering wheel in Bobby's hands. The Fiat swerved slightly toward the oncoming car but missed it by almost six feet.

Bobby went pale. "What's the matter with that guy! Wow! They got reckless drivers here!"

A little later he said he was tired and we changed seats. Back at the hotel, he fell into bed, completely played out.

The next day at about 5 P.M., Benson and I took Bobby to the country to shoot some photographs. All the way out he was surly and silent. About ten miles from Reykjavik we saw a field of sturdy little Icelandic horses that ran after the car, their blond manes streaming in the sun.

"Hey, they're pretty!" Bobby said. "Can you pet them? Will they bite?"

We pulled off the road and Bobby waded through deep grass to the fence. Fourteen horses trotted up boldly, bumping each other aside in their eagerness to sniff this interesting visitor. Bobby, delighted, broke into big smiles as the horses thrust their soft muzzles into his hands. Then he jumped back.

"Hey! They're drooling on my best coat!"

He took off his precious leather jacket from Argentina and gave it to me to hold. Benson asked him to go into the field and let the horses gather around him.

"Think it's safe?" he asked anxiously. "I got this far. I don't want to die before I get all that money."

We reassured him and separated the barbed wire. The horses veered away at first, but when Bobby sat on a tussock they came back and stood around him in a rough circle. The attention pleased Bobby, who seemed happier with these animals than we had ever seen him with people. He began to talk to them, and they listened.

One of the horses, bolder than the rest, leaned forward as if to kiss Bobby's cheek. Instead, very gently, the horse nipped his earlobe.

Bobby jerked back in terror. "He bit me! Did you see that? Wow! Lemme outa here!" He hurried back to the fence. The horses watched him with gentle eyes.

"This is dangerous, y'know?" he went on. "They got dirty teeth. I could get blood poisoning from a thing like that!"

It was only on Monday, the day before the match was scheduled to start, that the fraidy cat began to turn into a tiger.

About 10 P.M. Sunday night, Bobby went for a swim in the Loftleidir pool. He was appalled to find some hair and what looked like bits of skin floating on the water. In a fury he summoned Cramer and ordered him to inform the Loftleidir management that the public must be excluded from the pool for the duration of the match. "They promised me that this pool would be reserved for my exclusive use and I *demand* that they live up to that promise!"

Cramer was speechless. The hotel had promised Bobby merely that he could have the pool to himself after 10 P.M. Cramer presented the demand with so many apologies that the hotel manager understood he could easily refuse, but when he did, Bobby was outraged and said he was being cheated.

This outburst put him in a bold mood, and at 1:00 Monday morning, only forty hours before game time, Bobby at last showed up to make his official inspection of the playing hall. Four nights in a row, he had promised to check it out. Four nights in a row, six film technicians had waited at the playing hall from 9 P.M. to 3 A.M. Four nights in a row, Bobby had failed to show.

"Bobby had been putting off the inspection because he was scared of it," Cramer explained later. "It was his first real confrontation with the organizers since coming to Iceland. He wanted to give 'em hell, make 'em pay for everything they'd put him through, but he was scared they might be tougher than he was. So when he first got there he was very timid."

The openers were pleasant. The first thing Bobby saw onstage was a handsome black leather chair with a chrome frame and a swivel base, a $550 luxury item designed by Charles Eames for the lobby of the Time-Life Building. Just in from New York, a token of Edmondson's continuing solicitude, the chair was a duplicate of the one Bobby had used in Buenos Aires when he beat Petrosian.

"Oh, wow! My chair from B.A.!" Bobby sat down and swiveled happily.

Feeling expansive, Cramer suggested that the stage might look better if both players had the same kind of chair.

"What?" Bobby shot back. "Why do anything for *them?* They never did anything for *me!*"

Still glowering, he began to inspect the chess board. "These squares are too big," he said. "They make the chessmen look tiny."

Two elegant custom-made wooden boards were brought out. Bobby found one too shiny and said the light and dark squares of the other looked too much alike.

"I don't know what you're gonna do," he said, "but these boards you got are no good."

Bobby then turned his attention to the table the chess board was set in.

"It sure is a beaut," Cramer volunteered. Thorarinsson said it had cost about $1200 to build. Just that day a wealthy Icelander had offered to buy it for $10,000 at the end of the match.

"Yeah, well, it's too high," Bobby said. "You can't see the board right. Can't you cut the legs off or something?"

Thorarinsson assured him that something would be done.

Bobby got around to the lighting next. Leaning back, he peered up at the huge suspended box and then ducked his head protectively.

"It makes me nervous, that big thing up there," he said. "How do I know it's not gonna fall on me?"

Thorarinsson swallowed hard. He had just received a $5000 invoice for the fixture.

"See those bolts?" he answered. "There are four of them, and they are anchored in heavy metal beams that would easily support a large truck. There is no danger of anything falling."

Bobby grunted and went on. "The light isn't bright enough. Can't you make it brighter?"

Fox beamed. The more light he had on the stage, the easier it would be to shoot the film. Hurrying over to Agustsson, he whispered, "Start it with fifty footcandles. That way he'll keep asking for more, see? I need minimum a hundred and twenty or I can't shoot."

Cramer overheard. "Nonsense, Chester," he said. "I know Bobby. He likes lots of light. Start with a hundred and twenty. He'll *still* ask for more."

The light level was set at 120 footcandles.

"Naa, that's too bright," Bobby said. "Cut it down!"

Fox moaned. Agustsson cut the light to 100 footcandles.

"Still too bright." Bobby cut the power to 80 to 50 to 30 footcandles. Finally he had it down to 20.

"That's good," he said.

Fox could stand it no longer. "But Bobby," he said, "twenty footcandles—that's *moonlight!* We need—"

"That's your problem," Bobby said. "I like it."

Fox started to speak, stopped, walked away, and stood staring at the cameraman with his mouth open.

"All right, Bobby," Cramer carried on, "how about the color of the light?"

"Too blue," Bobby said. "I want more yella."

Soon everybody began to look Chinese. Finally Bobby said there was enough yellow but now the light wasn't bright enough.

Agustsson turned the power to 30, 40, 50, 80, 100. Fox was striding up and down in triumph. When Bobby stopped the dial at 180, Fox stood there with his chest out like Washington crossing the

Delaware. But pretty soon the level was down to 80 again. Fox glumly gnawed on his little finger.

"By George, Gudmundur!" Cramer exploded. "This is the finest lighting setup I've ever seen for a chess match. Bobby's put it through every trick in the book and there was nothing it couldn't do!"

Bobby glowered at Cramer. "I don't like that thing up there with all the little holes in it," he said.

He meant the diffuser panels. After a long discussion the technicians repaneled the whole underside of the light fixture with translucent plastic. Bobby liked it better. Agustsson took a chance and without telling Bobby turned the dial back to 100. Bobby never noticed the difference but Fox did. His confidence rose.

"And now, Bobby, if you're ready," Fox said with a big smile, "I'd like to show you the film setup. Three cameras will be covering the game at all times. One—"

"What's those things up there?" Bobby asked suspiciously, pointing to two tiny cameras fixed to the back of the big screen that hung over the front of the stage.

"Oh, they're just the closed-circuit TV monitors. They don't move or anything."

"Yeah? Well, I don't like them pointing at me," Bobby said, pulling his eyebrows down like shades.

"We will cover them with cloth," Thorarinsson offered smoothly. "Only the lens itself will show and it will not move."

"Right," Fox said. "Now the film cameras, as we promised, will be concealed at all times, one in that small opening in the rear wall of the stage, the other two—"

"Yeah, I noticed it up there. I don't like it. It's been pointing at me too. Put somethin' over it, I don't want to see it, unnastan'?"

"I understand, Bobby," Fox answered in a consoling voice. He had turned an odd shade of yellow, and not only because of the overhead light. "Only the lens will be visible."

"And no movement either."

Fox swallowed hard. "Right, Bobby." He signaled wildly to Thorarinsson with his eyebrows, but Thorarinsson had decided not to be a hero.

"Okay," Fox went on more hesitantly, "the other two cameras are completely out of sight—"

"Yeah, I noticed those things," Bobby broke in, swiveling toward the burlap-covered camera towers. They were sitting on the floor of the auditorium, one at the left, one at the right of the stage, both about thirty-five feet from the playing table. Fox had wanted to put them right up on the stage, about twenty feet from the players, but Thorarinsson had tactfully suggested that the towers were not in keeping with the rest of the stage decorations.

Bobby said what Thorarinsson meant. "They're ugly."

Dead silence. Even Fox knew that the towers looked like something built by an eight-year-old boy in his backyard. Thorarinsson kicked himself for not keeping a closer watch on Fox, but he just hadn't had the staff or the time.

"Yes, well, it is true, of course," Thorarinsson said, seeming to support Bobby's point, "that the cloth is not perhaps as attractive as we would like to have it. But the color was chosen to be inconspicuous, you see, to blend in. It is a very dull color."

"It's not just the color," Bobby said. "It's the whole thing. They look cheap. I can't play with those things there."

"But, Bobby!" Fox burst out desperately. "Where we gonna put the cameras? Where we gonna put the cameramen?"

Bobby looked horrified. "You mean there's gonna be *people* in there? Oh, no! Those things gotta go!"

Fox was speechless. Some other place might be found for the movie cameras, but without the towers there would be no place at all for the still photographers—and there were pots of money to be made from the sale of stills to newspapers and magazines.

Cramer rashly tried to mediate. "Let's go with them for the first game, but have something better for the second."

Bobby glared at him again.

Thorarinsson came up with another compromise. "Perhaps we could keep the towers but move them back a little farther."

"Yeah," Bobby said. "Move 'em back where I can't see 'em. Back to the wall."

The wall was 110 feet from the playing table. Fox spun toward Thorarinsson, who defended sturdily. "I did not mean all the way to the wall, Bobby. From that distance the film would simply be a blur. But certainly we could try it from—"

"No!" Bobby said in a hard flat voice. "You wanna use those things, you put 'em all the way back against the wall, unnastan'! I don't wanna look at 'em. I don't want *anything* up close to the players—and that reminds me!"

Bobby was in a paroxysm now.

"Those seats"—he stabbed his arm at the front rows of the audience "—are much too close to the stage!"

Thorarinsson rounded on him—this had to be stopped. "Those seats are forty feet from the playing table, the exact distance specified in the Amsterdam Agreement. If you like, I will measure it now." He did.

"Exactly forty feet."

"Yeah ... well ..." Bobby had lost momentum but he had to go on. "Anyway they're too close to the players, *much too close!*" He glared at Thorarinsson, who looked back calmly, as a grown-up might look at somebody else's child who was having a tantrum.

Bobby said the most outrageous thing he could think of. "I want the first ten rows removed!"

Thorarinsson blinked. There were only *twelve* rows of seats altogether! It was time to go home.

"I understand, Mr. Fischer," he said gravely. "We will do what we can."

Tight-faced, Bobby left. With a shrug, Thorarinsson ordered the front row of seats removed and two more rows added at the back of the hall. On the cameras he compromised, ordering them to be set up fifty feet from the players.

Driving back to the hotel with Cramer, Bobby wasn't sure he had really settled Thorarinsson's hash, but he was obviously pleased with his performance and disappointed with Cramer's. He told Cramer he wasn't being tough enough with the organizers. "I don't like their attitude," he said. "I want to see 'em jump through hoops."

Cramer had watched the scene onstage with rising outrage, all his sympathies following Fox and the Icelanders. Now he was in no mood to take a scolding from "a jerk kid" who, as he said later, "really needed a spanking." Bobby sensed his resentment.

At 3:30 A.M., brooding over the tic of independence his millionaire slave had developed, Bobby woke Lombardy and dragged him out to hike around the airport that adjoined the hotel. Lombardy agreed that Cramer was not the man Bobby needed and said bluntly that Edmondson was.

"No! I got rid of him." But Lombardy had a hunch that Bobby was secretly pleased by the suggestion.

Some time after 4 A.M., Bobby woke Cramer out of a deep sleep. "I'm not feelin' too good about the way you're doin' your job," he said. "Whaddya think about Edmondson? Think we should get him?"

If Cramer had simply said yes, Bobby might have told him to send for Edmondson, and the final insanity of the coming week would likely have been eluded. But Cramer did not say yes. God knows a part of him wanted someone, anyone, to take this impossible person off his hands. But another part still wanted the glory of being Bobby's assistant and was afraid of what people would say if he got yanked in the first inning.

"I've talked with Ed several times about that," he said. "He'll come only if you agree to play chess and let him take care of everything else."

Bobby stiffened. "Yeah, well, I'll think about it." He left without making a decision.

The conversation confirmed Cramer's impression that Bobby was unable to make a sane decision about the simplest things and had to be discreetly manipulated by wiser heads. The only way to deal with Bobby, Cramer decided, was to say yes to everything and then do what you thought was right.

But Cramer missed the main point of everything Bobby had done that night. In bullying everybody in sight he was working himself up to a pitch of frenzy that would overcome his dread of the match and hurl him like a wild beast at Spassky's throat.

By the time Bobby went to bed on Tuesday morning he was in a rage, as ready for the match as he was ever going to get.

At exactly 5 P.M., the chief arbiter's hand fell. The hands on Spassky's clock began to move. The match had begun. Without Bobby.

Spassky walked quickly to the table. Applause. He sat down, studied the board, then advanced the pawn in front of the White Queen two squares. The move was flashed on the screen above the stage and on the twenty-four closed-circuit television screens scattered through the building.

"Pawn to Queen Four!" Harold Schonberg of *The New York Times* sang out in the press room. There was a stampede to the Telex machines and the international telephone lines. A murmur of excitement rolled over the playing hall and in the analysis rooms a hubbub of discussion rose. Then silence.

At 5:01, Spassky strolled backstage. Schmid followed him, then reappeared. At 5:05, Spassky reappeared and gravely studied a position that as yet scarcely existed. Saemundur Palsson stood backstage in well-pressed plainclothes, looking smug. Half the force had wanted to bodyguard the players, but Palsson had got the job.

Cramer kept rushing to the stage door, where he paced and muttered and stood on tiptoe as if hoping to see Bobby over the heads of the crowd. Thorarinsson waited silently at the back of the hall. Inside the burlap tower that faced Bobby's chair, Benson sweated it out with two other photographers and a cameraman. The towers were about forty feet from the playing table, even closer than Thorarinsson had suggested.

I called the hotel. "Mr. Fischer's room does not answer," the operator said.

"Goddamnit!" Cramer exploded. "I woke him up at four but the dang fool went back to sleep. Then Bill tried to get him up. At 4:30 I had to come over here and check the cameras and the lighting. When I left he was starting to get up—I *think*."

"What do you think?" Schonberg asked grandmaster Evans, who knew Fischer as well as any man in Reykjavik.

Evans smiled. "I think he's scared of Spassky."

Bobby had good reason to be scared of Spassky. Of the five games they had previously played, Spassky had won three and drawn two. Many grandmasters thought he had the Indian sign on Bobby. All agreed that Spassky's talent was massive and mysterious. Tal could attack and Petrosian could defend and Geller was letter-perfect in the openings and Smyslov played the end game like a computer, but Spassky could do everything—follow any strategy, reproduce any style.

In chess temperament, Spassky was sometimes compared to Kutuzov, the Russian general who destroyed Napoleon. Slow, heavy, searingly cold, he played in a peculiarly Russian style of passionate lethargy. In the early stages of a game or a match he was inclined to hang back a little, trading space for time and time for position while he prepared his counterstroke. When it came, Spassky's assault was furious and usually irresistible.

"He has an incredible depth of imagination," said grandmaster Robert Byrne, "and an Asiatic patience that gives me the creeps. He can begin with nothing and develop a long-range sustained attack that slowly grows all over you like poison ivy. He doesn't insist on beating you in six moves. He is perfectly happy to do it in sixty-six."

Spassky's imagination was fantastic but disciplined; his frenzies were sculptured. On the whole his style was subtler than Bobby's. "At the climax of every game they have played," said grandmaster Lubomir Kavalek, "it became clear that Spassky had seen further than Bobby." Spassky's feeling for combinations, for setting up sudden spectacular slaughters, was wilder and luckier. Bobby sometimes got befuddled in a complex position that offered him no clear theme; chaos was Spassky's muse. "Bobby is like Bach," a man who has played them both explained. "Boris is more like Kandinsky."

Spassky was a fighter, too. He had often compared himself to a bear—slow to arouse but, once he got up on his hind legs, almost impossible to stop. Resistance only brought him on stronger and he was never so dangerous as when in a weak position or after a defeat. The stubbornness that infuriated everyone who had to deal with him was the root of his power as a chess player. And stubbornness was supported by cunning. Unlike Bobby, who played the position, Spassky played his opponent. "He's a brilliant psychologist of the game," said Byrne. "He doesn't just look for the best move. He looks for the move that will disturb the man he is playing. He has done this every time he has played Bobby, and every time he has thrown Bobby off his game."

Spassky's weaknesses? Technically, there was only one, his opening game, and eight months with Geller might well have whittled Bobby's advantage in that area. "Geller is the key to this match," said Byrne. "If Geller has cooked up half a dozen really wicked variations for Black, and found busts for Bobby's main lines in the Sicilian, Bobby is in big trouble."

Bobby knew it, and his preparations for the Spassky match were the most exhaustive in chess history. By April 1, he had replayed more than five hundred of Spassky's games. "And after that," said Edmondson, "he really began to work." Bobby worked harder than Spassky—he works harder than any grandmaster except Lajos Portisch of Hungary. "One reason I beat 'em is I know more," Bobby once told me. "I know as much chess as the top ten Russians put together."

Genius helped, too. Bobby's natural talent was one of the most formidable in chess history. He could envisage continuations and subcontinuations with a speed and accuracy nobody had ever equaled. He was never in time trouble. In the first half hour of a game he often gained twenty or twenty-five minutes on his opponent, and when the opponent's time ran out Bobby usually had sixty or even ninety minutes left.

Bobby's technical skills were immense. Byrne called him "the best Bishop player in history," and in the match with Taimanov he rewrote the textbook on the uses of the Knight. As for the Rooks, Kavalek said he used them like well-trained watchdogs—"they keep turning up where you don't want them to be."

All these skills were coordinated by supreme chess judgment. Since nobody had ever climbed so many of the logical trees that make up the forest of chess, nobody had ever so firmly imprinted the map of that forest in his mind. Chess was Bobby's habitat and his opponent was his prey. In the heat of the chase, he was objective and practical, never hesitating to face the truth of the situation and follow any line that would lead to capture. But even his most practical moves could meet the test of theory; he never stooped to conquer with bad chess. "An iron logic orders every move," said Kavalek. "He thinks in systems and combinations of systems. Bobby has the most powerful reasoning mind in the history of chess."

The force of Bobby's logic lent his play a clarity and a unity rarely seen in chess since Capablanca was in his prime, but Bobby's logic was passionate, and what drove his mind was a maniacal will to kill. "Bobby is the greatest fighting machine the game ever saw," said grandmaster Evans. "He plays to win—always. He will play a hundred extra moves to avoid a draw. Chess as he plays it is total war."

Spassky described to a friend the effect of Bobby's force. "It was the game at Siegen, you know, the last game we played. We were in the fifth hour. He was lost, ruined, not a chance! I knew it, he knew it. But he sat there—almost an hour!—calculating, calculating, calculating! Inside, he was screaming. He was pale, like a dead man, but this force was going through him like millions of volts. I could feel it smashing and smashing at me across the board. Well, it had an effect, I can tell you that. Five or ten minutes—all right. But an hour! In the end, *I* was the one screaming inside. When you play Bobby, it is not a question if you win or lose. It is a question if you survive."

Curiously, what made Bobby so menacing was also what made him vulnerable. His rage to win made him try to win impossible games, and when he rashly overextended he could sometimes be chopped off, as he was by Spassky at Mar del Plata, Los Angeles and Siegen. Adventures, he argued, kept him on his toes; quiet positions put him to sleep.

Bobby's other weakness was the narrowness of his opening repertoire. With White he almost always opened Pawn to King Four and when possible eased into a Ruy Lopez. With Black he usually defended Pawn to King Four with a Sicilian Game. Pawn to Queen Four he answered more often than not with a Grünfeld or a King's Indian Defense.

There again Bobby considered the weakness a strength. By playing only what he knew best—in fact, knew better than any player in history—he had achieved unprecedented control over a few vital approaches to victory. But now Bobby was facing Spassky and Geller, the Soviet grandmasters who had achieved the greatest success against him. And he was facing the financial and informational resources of the most formidable chess establishment on the planet. What Bobby could do in the Sicilian and the Ruy, the eight or ten grandmasters who had assisted Spassky in his training might be able to undo. Several American grandmasters had urged Bobby to broaden his opening game. "But when Bobby is convinced of a chess strategy," Byrne told me with a sigh, "it takes dynamite in large quantities to blast him loose."

Publicly, almost all the Soviet experts said Spassky would win. Publicly, most of the Western experts said Bobby would win. Privately, the top chess people were iffy, and the people around Bobby and Boris were iffiest of all. The big question was condition: after the hurly-burly of the last few weeks, which of the two players was in worse shape?

"We knew that Boris was not quite ready," Geller later told a friend in Russia, "but Boris is never quite ready. He is like an actor who looks very bad in rehearsal. It is the match that brings out his strength. We counted on that."

Cramer, on the other hand, was afraid that "now we've got Bobby here he's too crazy to play." Byrne smiled at the notion. "Every good chess player I know is a little bit weird, and their emotional problems always hurt their chess. Bobby is different. He's *real* weird, but the emotional problems magically drop off when the game begins. When he sits down to play, he's one of the sanest men I know. I won't worry until I see him make a crazy move at the chess board. Then I'll know we've finally lost him."

At 5:07 the curtain across the rear of the playing area whirled aside and Bobby strode onstage. A great "Ahhhhhh!" filled the hall, and then a barrage of applause even louder and longer than the ovation for Spassky. Maybe they hated Bobby, but they were sure glad to see him.

Knees flexed, shoulders forward, elbows flapping, Bobby charged the playing table. Cornering hard, he dropped halfway to his chair before he saw Spassky.

"Uh!" He straightened up to give Spassky's hand one quick shake. Then he dropped into his chair, hiked it closer, scribbled Spassky's move onto his score sheet and settled down, eyes flicking lightly over the board.

Twenty seconds passed. In the sudden silence the spectators heard an irregular clicking noise, quite loud, and under it a sound like growling. It was the clicking of the hand cameras in the tower and the whirring of the movie cameras, and it was irritating.

Bobby's head jerked up. For a long moment he stared at the tower facing him. Even in the yellowish light the sudden reddening of his face could be seen. Pushing back his chair, he jumped up and strode over to Schmid.

"There's noises comin' from that tower!" he said. "I want 'em stopped, unnastan'? I want 'em stopped right away!"

Offended by Bobby's aggressive manner, Schmid nodded stiffly. Bobby strode back to his seat and studied the board again. After waiting about ten seconds, apparently to restore his composure, Schmid moved to the corner of the stage and made hushing motions in the direction of the offending tower. The clicking died down but the growling went on.

Bobby leaned forward and made his first move. Knight to King's Bishop Three.

The clicking burst out as loud as before.

"Omigod!" Evans muttered. "Schmid better do something quick! Can't he see Bobby's looking for an issue?"

Bobby rushed across to Schmid. "That noise is still coming from that tower, Lothar. I'm telling ya again, I want it stopped. They're disturbing my concentration, unnastan'? If they can't stop that noise they can't have cameras in there. This is a chess match and the rules say the players must *not be disturbed!*"

Bobby lurched back to his chair, looking sour. Schmid made more hushing motions.

Spassky was focused totally on the board. Bobby's move had startled him. It looked like an offer to play the Nimzo-Indian Defense, not one of Bobby's favorites in the past. If Spassky accepted the offer on his next move, Bobby could carry the action immediately into a sharp line—just the sort of country where an ambush might lie in wait for White. Spassky was not interested in sharp lines. When Geller had suggested one for the opening game, Spassky had refused it. "Why should I show him anything good the first time? Robert James is in an emotional state. Perhaps I am playing for a draw—maybe he will be bored. Maybe he will try too hard to win. Yes, I will rather steal this game than win it. Then he will think I have some strange power over him."

Slyly, with Pawn to Queen's Bishop Four, Spassky invited Bobby to set up the same Grünfeld Defense that had lost for him at Siegen.

Bobby declined, but the move he made (Pawn to King Three) was cautious—it was almost as if Bobby were looking for a quiet game too. Finally Spassky accepted the Nimzo. The fight was on. Any minute now a real punch might be thrown.

Noticing a fresh burst of clicking, Bobby looked up and saw something sticking out of one of the holes in the burlap—a face! Bobby stomped over and this time really boiled the chief arbiter's ear. Schmid left the stage in a hurry and tiptoed to the noisier of the two towers. Leaning close, he heard a loud click.

"*Aha!*" he announced in a stage whisper, and poked his head through the curtain. "I've got you! Come out!"

In the tower were three people Schmid might have grabbed. With his usual luck in human relations he grabbed the wrong one. Harry Benson was the only photographer in the house who had taken the trouble to silence his camera. Remembering an old *paparazzo* trick, Benson had removed his jacket and stuffed his camera in his sleeve until the lens stuck out the other end. At a distance of three feet, his shutter was about as audible as a loud wristwatch.

Schmid nevertheless ordered Benson out of the hall and permitted the two other photographers, whose cameras were noisy, to keep on taking pictures.

From the first moment, Schmid was remiss in his handling of the camera problem. For the last four months he had assumed, along with most people, that Bobby's demands were just obnoxious nonsense, and now he assumed that this latest demand was more of the same. The noise of the cameras did not bother the chief arbiter; why should it bother Bobby? In fact, the clicking and whirring were an irritation to many people whose ears were less sensitive than Bobby's and whose need for concentration was far less acute. No doubt Bobby was looking for something to object to, and if it hadn't been the cameras it would have been something else. But Bobby's objection to the cameras was entirely reasonable, and his anger fully justified when the problem was not promptly dealt with.

In the melodrama now beginning to unfold, Schmid was not the only fall guy. Chester Fox had been a wreck ever since Bobby had forced his cameras to retreat. Monday afternoon, after a conference with Stein, he had defiantly ordered his crew to place the towers forty feet from the players—only five feet farther than they had been when Bobby protested. He also took a hard line when his head cameraman warned him that one of the cameras had a broken gear and would make "a devil of a clatter" if it were not replaced. "The hell with it," Fox answered. "Bobby don't cooperate with us, we don't cooperate with him."

Half an hour before the start of the game, Fox and his entire crew had arrived onstage to rearrange the potted plants and fiddle with the light level. Suddenly the head of I.C.F.'s technical staff arrived with a six-foot-six assistant and unceremoniously booted Fox and his people off the stage. Fox spent the afternoon looking for a nice little ego-building battle he could win.

The Schmid-Benson run-in was right up his alley. *Life* was paying Fox/Stein $1000 for a single picture of the first game, and if Benson didn't get his picture Fox wouldn't get his money. "You go right back in there and take your pictures, Harry!" Fox announced in a voice that could be heard from one end of the crowded lobby to the other. "And if Lothar Schmid bothers you, I'll settle his ass!"

Spassky meanwhile had settled into his famous playing posture. His huge head was lifted high above the board. Supporting his chin, the thumb and forefinger of his right hand pushed his mouth so far out of shape that Bobby couldn't possibly read its expression. Though it made Spassky look like a caricature of Rodin's *Thinker,* in the past this pose had awakened Bobby's father complex and stressed his feelings of inferiority. But now, with his elbows on the edge of the table and his face in his hands, Bobby looked as if he had forgotten Spassky was there. In comparison with Spassky's imposing crest, Bobby's head looked small and pointy. Where Spassky sat straight-backed and proud, Bobby hunched. Where Spassky's hands were calm and controlled, Bobby's wandered restlessly.

But when Bobby sat still he sat much more still than the Russian did. Spassky had an athlete's body; its stillness was movement carefully controlled. Bobby's body had the total stillness of a thing left for dead. All his energy, all his life was in his eyes, which skittered about the board like demented roaches.

The game developed with curious blandness on both sides and soon arrived at a "standard position" in the Nimzo. Spassky had often reached the position before, Bobby never. Why had Bobby urged the action into this form now? When was the zinger coming?

The zinger never came. Slyly repeating, move for move, a game that Spassky and Krogius had played in 1958, Bobby brought the position dead even.

Spassky sat staring at the board for twenty minutes. American grandmasters thought he was dismayed because Bobby had equalized. In fact, Spassky had wanted Bobby to equalize—and be tempted to scramble for a win. What bothered Spassky now was that for almost the first time in his career *Bobby had not tried to win!*

Why not? Had he dumped a lifelong principle? If so, what other principles might he also be ready to abandon? A flexible and therefore unpredictable Bobby would be a far more dangerous Bobby . . .

Spassky decided there was nothing to do but nudge the game gently toward one of those sleepy standoffs known as a grandmaster draw. After the twenty-eighth move, the position was so hopelessly drawn that five hundred ticket-holders went home. Another five hundred were jostling in the lobby, some picking up souvenirs, some buying commemorative stamps. In the mezzanine above at least three hundred customers were sitting at cafeteria tables watching the game on closed-circuit TV screens or standing in lines. One line led to a steaming vat of fat beige grublike objects, the Icelandic version of the hot dog. The other passed a glass case displaying single slices of white bread on which Taj Mahals of ham, egg and pickle had been constructed over a half-inch foundation of commercial mayonnaise.

"Too bad," Thorarinsson was saying to a Yugoslav reporter. "We had hoped for an exciting game to get the match going."

"I don't know what's got into him," Lombardy was mumbling to another grandmaster in the press room, where most of the Western experts were sitting. "Maybe he's just too worn out to play. Well, I better go backstage. Couple more moves, they'll call it a draw."

As Lombardy rose, Bobby made his twenty-ninth move.

Bishop takes Pawn!?

Spassky jolted like a man hit by a bullet and stared at the board.

Four seconds later, the move was flashed on the closed-circuit TV. Lombardy's jaw dropped.

"What!" Byrne yelled, and went pale. At the other end of the lobby, Geller gasped and grabbed Krogius' arm. "It's a mistake!" grandmaster Gligoric told grandmaster Olafsson. "They put the wrong move on the screen!"

But it wasn't a mistake. Geller, Nei and Krogius stared at the nearest TV screen, heads together, mumbling excitedly. Byrne and Lombardy began shuffling pieces in Byrne's chess wallet. A dozen reporters clustered around them. "Jesus!" Byrne gasped. "Maybe Bobby's got something!" Down in the analysis room, an Icelandic master was moaning, "I don't get it! What does he see that I don't see?"

A roar filled the lobby. People in the restaurant were yelling so loud the noise could be heard in the playing hall. In sixty seconds every entrance to the hall was choked with people charging back in. *"Bobby's attacking! Bobby took a poisoned pawn! Bobby busted the game wide open!"*

Thorarinsson stood in the center of the lobby, his grin spreading from wall to wall. "One move," he said blissfully, "and we hit every front page in the world!"

"Look! Look!" Byrne was yelling into his chess wallet. "He's pulled a sleeper! Spassky traps the Bishop, right?"

"Okay," Lombardy said fiercely, "and Bobby moves Pawn to Rook Four."

"Spassky, King to King Two!" Byrne rushed on.

"Bobby, Pawn to Rook Five!" Lombardy replied.

"Spassky, King to Bishop Three!"

"Bobby, Pawn to Rook Six!"

"Spassky, King to Knight Four!"

"Bobby, Bishop to Knight Eight!"

"Spassky, King takes Pawn!"

"Bobby, Bishop takes Pawn—and he's got a way out!" Byrne almost shrieked. "Bishop to King Eight and he's got a— *Oh my God!*" Byrne's voice sank to a horrified mutter. "No! Look!"

"Jesus!" the priest croaked. "Spassky can stop it! Bishop to Queen Two before Bobby can do Bishop to King One!"

The sleeper, the fiendishly cunning combination, turned out to be the most godawful goof of Bobby's chess career. Byrne and Lombardy stared at each other, their faces collapsing like jack-o'-lanterns a week after Halloween.

"He played too fast!" Lombardy said glumly.

Byrne took a deep breath and tried to be matter-of-fact. "Bobby's got to lose the Bishop," he said. "Two Pawns for a Bishop—not good. But let's see what else he gets . . ."

"He cleans out Spassky's Kingside Pawns," Lombardy went on.

"He gets his own King in the center. He gets Spassky's King boxed in on the King side, probably. But Spassky's Bishop is going to give him hell. No," he sighed, "it wasn't worth it. He had a book draw to start with. Now if he's got a draw he'll have to fight like a tiger for it."

Softly, as if to himself, Byrne asked the next question. "Then why did he *do* it?"

Their eyes met, then quickly dodged away. The move was not an ordinary miscalculation. There was something freakish about it, something almost—crazy.

On the stage, Bobby gave a little start, went white, then glared at the board with special intensity. The hall was cool, but in a moment drops of sweat showed on Bobby's forehead. As he wiped them away with his handkerchief, his hand was visibly shaking. With an effort, he tightened his face and, vibrating his left foot frantically, brought all his force to bear on the mess he had made. At that instant, seeing the abrupt change in Bobby's face and gestures, the photographers produced such a squawking of shutters that an American in the audience said the tower facing Bobby sounded like a henhouse with a weasel in it.

Bobby gave the tower one long look of pure hatred before he went back to the game. The photographers saw the look and clicked away even faster, trying to record it.

Meanwhile both players were rocketing through the consequences of Bobby's blunder. Bobby still had a draw in hand, but on the last move of the day, he made a fatal miscalculation: Pawn to Bishop Five.

"Ooops!" said Lombardy. "He's weakened his central Pawns! Now Spassky's King can spear them one at a time!"

Gloom flattened the grandmasters in the Western press room. Out in the lobby, Geller was strutting up and down on his little chimpy legs, grinning so broadly you could see all that brand-new Siberian gold in his mouth.

Spassky saw Bobby's error too, but decided to play safe. There were thirty-five minutes left on his clock. Rather than risk a miscalculation in what now looked like a winning position, he ran out the clock and then handed his final move of the day to chief arbiter Schmid in a sealed envelope. The win could be worked out by his seconds overnight.

Rising silently, Spassky left the hall. Lasered in on the board, Bobby apparently did not notice Spassky leave. When the crowd rose, a bellow of conversation filled the hall. Bobby gave a start and blinked.

He had obviously forgotten there was anyone else in the room—maybe even in the world. Then with a sigh he rose and tore himself away from the board.

Bobby burst out the stage door like a hornet looking for something to sting. Striding angrily through the crowd, he jumped in the Polish Fiat, Lombardy at his heels. Cramer was at the wheel.

"Get goin', Fred!" Bobby said. "I wanna get outa here!"

Cramer eased through the crowd onto the main exit road—where the car was blocked by another crowd of spectators.

Teeth clenched and eyes rolling, Bobby gripped the back of the front seat. "Run 'em down, Fred!" he yelled. "They don't belong here! Run 'em down!"

Cramer sat on the horn.

"I don't like the way you drive, Fred," Bobby said coldly when the car had cleared the crowd.

For the next sixty seconds he sat scowling out the window and jiggling his left leg. Suddenly he glared at Lombardy.

"Did you hear those cameras? All that clicking and that whirring noise? And they *promised* me I wouldn't hear a thing. Wow! An insult to the players! Nobody could concentrate with all that racket. I *told* Lothar to stop 'em—how many times did I tell him?—and he didn't do a thing, right? *Hnnnnnh!*"

Back at the hotel Bobby ordered Cramer to write Schmid a letter demanding that the cameras be removed from the playing hall until further notice. "I want those towers out too, unnastan'? Out!"

Horrified, Cramer hurried away. "Good God almighty!" he told me a few minutes later. "That'll *ruin* Fox and it'll put the Icelanders in a hole they'll never climb out of! And that's what he *wants* to happen! Damnation, it's not right!" When I left him ten minutes later, Cramer was still looking for a way to save Fox and the Icelanders from Bobby's vengeance.

Bobby and Lombardy meanwhile were tearing the game to pieces. Bobby brushed aside the alarming matter of that freakish twenty-ninth move. "I moved too fast," he said with a wave of his arm. "All that noise." Then Lombardy showed him the move he should have made just before the game ended. Bobby strode up and down clutching his head and crying out, "Oh! Oh! Why didn't *I* think of that! I'm a fish! I played like a fish!"

How come Bobby was so upset about his fortieth move, a crucial but subtle mistake he might have made on the best day he ever had, yet hardly interested in his twenty-ninth move, which was clearly the worst blunder of his career?

Whatever the reason, Bobby's mind for the first time in weeks was totally occupied by chess. From 10:30 that night until 6:00 the next morning, Bobby and Lombardy worked like maniacs to find a draw for Black. No luck. White won in every variation.

"Well," Bobby said at last with a shrug, "I gave him half a point." And went to bed.

The Russians had turned in two hours earlier with a win done up in ribbons.

Cramer slept the sleep of the just. On his dresser was a letter to Schmid that said what Bobby had told him to say. In the back of his mind was a sly little dodge he was sure would keep Fox in business and the organizers in the black. After all, you had to say yes to Bobby's face, and then do the necessary behind his back.

12

"You! You Lied to Me!"

Cramer's letter was what the press called a "bombshell." Bobby, it said, "asks that the burlap-covered scaffolding containing camera equipment be removed [and] will not enter the hall until the work has been completed."

Schmid was outraged. "But the contract gives to the organizers the right to film!" Fox turned green and spent fifteen minutes in the men's room. Thorarinsson was shaken. He had hoped Bobby would stop fighting I.C.F. when he began fighting Spassky, but it looked as if Bobby wanted war on two fronts.

"What if we refuse?" Thorarinsson asked. "Do you really think he will abandon the match because of a little inconvenience with these towers?"

"He has abandoned it before," Cramer answered, "and I've gotta believe he'd do it again. But look." Cramer leaned in close and set in motion the scheme he had cranked up the night before.

In giving Cramer his instructions, Bobby had said, "You tell 'em I don't even come over unless those towers are out of the hall!" Bobby had meant, "I want *all* cameras taken out and *all* filming to stop." But he had neglected to mention specifically the third camera that peered down at him through the rear wall of the stage.

Cramer now told Thorarinsson, "Bobby didn't say anything about the third camera. Why not use it for the rest of this game—and then talk things over when he isn't so riled up?"

Thorarinsson decided to play along. "The towers are bad—we must do better. Let us remove them for one day as a friendly gesture."

Fox and Stein sang a five-hour duet of agony but at 4:45 Cramer called Bobby and told him his demands had been met. "The towers are out of the hall and so are the cameras."

"D'ja check the whole hall? Way at the back?"

"Including the back."

Technically, Cramer was not lying. The third camera was literally "out of the hall," behind the rear wall of the stage. But in effect he was deceiving Bobby. The camera was in full view of the playing table and not more than twenty feet away.

At 5:06, Bobby clomped onstage to inspect the arrangements, but when the audience gave him a big hand he made a surprised little bow and sat down to play. After brief study, he replied to Spassky's move. Both men made two more moves. Then Bobby sat back and looked around. In front of him, no tower. In back of him, no tower. Leaning back in his chair, he glanced up at the hole in the rear wall of the stage—and jerked forward.

"Excuse me, Boris," he said grimly and leaped to his feet. Looming over the chief arbiter, he flung an arm at the camera and began flapping his lips angrily. Then he thrust through the curtain and disappeared backstage. Schmid trotted after him.

"You! You lied to me, Lothar!" Bobby yelled. "You *promised* to have all those cameras out of the hall!"

"Now Bobby," Schmid began soothingly. "There—"

"I don't wanna discuss anything with you! You find Fred Cramer, Lothar, and find him—"

"There is no need to get Cramer, Bobby. I—"

"—*fast* if you don't want this match to end right here! I want that camera out of this hall and I mean all the way out and I'm not going to believe they're out until Fred Cramer says they're out!"

Schmid tried to make a stand but Bobby's fury blew him down.

"Yesss, Bobby, yesss!" he was hissing as he rushed up the stairs that led to the corridor where the cameras had been set up.

Bobby chased Schmid to the bottom of the stairs. "I don't trust you any more!" he screeched.

Cramer hurried in from the auditorium, a man trying to whistle as he walked to his execution. "He's *shaming us* in the eyes of the world!" he whispered. "How can I face my friends back in Milwaukee after *this!*"

Bobby bore down on him. "I thought you said there were no cameras in the hall!"

"To my knowledge there—"

"Yeah, well, they snuck one in. Get up there and throw it out!"

Cramer scuttled upstairs. At the camera station he found Schmid tangled in another battle of wills. Gisli Gestsson, the tall, blond, blue-eyed Icelandic cameraman, had agreed to stop shooting at Schmid's request, but refused to move the cameras. "I am sorry, Mr. Schmid. Mr. Fox ordered me to place the camera here. *Only* Mr. Fox can order me to remove it."

Schmid sent for Fox. Five minutes passed on Bobby's clock. Fox could not be found. Groaning, Schmid sent for Thorarinsson.

Bobby meanwhile was swirling in wider and wilder circles of frenzy. Every twenty seconds he rushed to the foot of the stairs and shouted, "What's goin' on up there, Fred?"

"We're making progress, Bobby," Cramer kept telling him. "It takes a few minutes."

"Where's Sammy?" Bobby demanded angrily.

Palsson was in the room behind the upstairs corridor sawing an inch or two off the legs of an extra chess table I.C.F. had furnished, just in case the game had to be moved out of the playing hall. He was sent downstairs. Bobby sent him back up to find out what was really going on. Palsson told him that the cameraman was obstructing.

Bobby sprinted up the stairs three at a time. "What's goin' on here?" he demanded.

As Iceland's top cameraman, Gestsson felt he had no need to take anybody's dust, and as a human being he had decided long since that he was worth six of Bobby Fischer.

"Shut up!" he said. "Mind your own business. This camera is my responsibility. You just go down there and play chess."

Bobby gasped, stared, whirled at Schmid. "You hear that? Wow! Arrogant and rude!"

As Bobby stomped downstairs Thorarinsson arrived and told Gestsson quietly in Icelandic that the cameras must be removed. Shaking with anger, Gestsson ordered his assistants to take the camera into the ping-pong room just off the corridor.

Downstairs Bobby exploded again. "That's not enough! I want that camera out of the building and I want that crew out too!"

Gestsson refused to move his camera one inch farther. It took Thorarinsson several minutes to cool him off. Finally Schmid told Bobby that he could resume play because the camera was on its way out. Bobby answered stiffly, "I don't trust you, Lothar. I'm not goin' back in there till *Sammy Palsson* tells me that camera's out of the hall."

At 5:46 Bobby got the word from Palsson. Thirty-two minutes after he had broken off the game, he was back at the table.

Spassky had been considerably disturbed by the interruption, but he had kept cool, resting in his dressing room and sometimes strolling onstage to study the board—"It was quieter there," he said later, "than it was backstage."

The endgame was played calmly and faultlessly by both men. After thirteen moves, Bobby resigned, shook hands with Spassky, and strode offstage as cheers and applause for Spassky filled the dome. Bobby seemed to think the applause was for him. Half turning as he left, he flashed the audience a big smile and a casual wave of acknowledgment.

Schmid left the playing hall in a pink snit. "Bobby should not have spoken to me like that!" he kept muttering, shaking his head. "We could have discussed the matter like gentlemen and the same result could have been achieved."

Half an hour in this vein drove Schmid to some ominous conclusions. "All right. He has gotten away with it this time. But I am not obliged to accept such insults and from now on I *will* not. I will simply go by the rules. If Bobby will break the rules, then so much the worse for him!"

That night a three-hour council of war was held in the Saga Hotel. Geller, Thorarinsson, Stein, Fox and a dozen others were there. All agreed, even the Russians, that not to have a film of the match would be calamitous.

For the next five hours, Stein, Cramer and Lombardy sat in Cramer's room at the Loftleidir knocking down coffee and shaping up schemes to shoot the match without disturbing Bobby. Every time a plan matured, they picked up the phone and tried it on the man in the presidential suite. Every plan was rejected.

At 2:30 A.M. Cramer told Bobby that if he refused to allow cameras in the hall Fox/Stein and I.C.F. would have the right to sue him for breach of contract and consequent damages.

"Sue *me!* I oughta sue *them!* I was promised I wouldn't even know the cameras were there!"

Cramer told him he ought to talk things over with Stein—after all, they were partners.

"Listen, Fred!" Bobby answered. "You're here to do what I say, not to give me advice, unnastan'?"

Finally Bobby said there was no way the cameras would not disturb him. "Just the *idea* of them being there is a distraction."

Soon after that, Bobby pulled his phone out of its jack. Stein wrote Bobby a letter incorporating his main proposals and at about 5 A.M. slumped off to bed. "I'm in too deep to pull out," Stein said bitterly. "If Bobby wants a fight, then believe me, that's what he's going to get."

13

The High Cost of Photophobia

On Thursday, July 13, at 7 A.M., a million needles of sunlight spattered the big white igloo in the Valley of the Hot Springs; off to the west, sparks of water blew across Reykjavik Bay. These natural wonders went unobserved by Stein. After less than four hours' sleep, trousers as rumpled as an elephant's legs, he took breakfast with Fox. "Everybody's kissing his ass," he told Fox. "They're crazy. Hold your hand out to Bobby, he'll eat your arm. This kid's a crocodile."

Stein's idea was to call Bobby's bluff. "He says either the cameras go or he goes. I say when he comes to the hall today, the cameras will be in position. If he decides not to play, it's *his* tookis."

Would Thorarinsson go along with the scheme? "He's got to," Stein said. "He can't take the cameras out of the hall without our consent!"

Stein and Fox rolled off to see Thorarinsson in a state of euphoria but found their partner stone sober. If Bobby refused to play, all Fox and Stein lost was money. Thorarinsson lost his political life. But Thorarinsson doubted that Bobby would be willing to lose the match in order to win a moral victory. "I think Bobby is committed now," he told Stein. "If he were ahead, he might break off the match. But his pride will not let him leave while he is losing."

With Thorarinsson in the bag, Stein and Fox put on a campaign to whip up sympathy for themselves and indignation against Bobby. All day long, all over Reykjavik, they collared newsmen and told their tale of woe, justifying in advance the confrontation they meant to force.

"You think I'm gonna sit here an' suck my thumb while this maniac steals the food out of my kid's mouth?" Fox demanded. "Ha!

Am I a man or am I a mouse? But don't get the idea I'm just doin' this for myself. It's a matter of principle. I'm doin' it for Iceland!"

At 2:40 Schmid turned up at the playing hall, saw the towers back in position and realized he was on the spot. The cameras were in or out, as he decided. But the Amsterdam Agreement and the match rules, rigged by Edmondson in Bobby's favor, were potholed with risks for the referee. Each player had the right to say that any camera was disturbing, and could order its removal from the hall. On the other hand, rule 21 specifically allowed "filming, video taping [and] television . . . in the playing room." Schmid concluded that the organizers could put the cameras in at the start of every game—and that Bobby could not order them out until he had noticed that they disturbed him. In practice, of course, Bobby simply had to show up at the playing hall and order them out.

When Schmid saw the towers back in place, he understood that Thorarinsson intended to force the issue. As chief arbiter he could do many things: order the cameras out or in, order them relocated, call a meeting of the principals, negotiate privately with both sides.

But Schmid, thoroughly disgusted with Bobby, closed his eyes to the towers. "It is a matter between the players and the organizers," he said primly. "If Bobby wants to destroy himself, that is his right."

When Thorarinsson saw the burlap hulks still in place, he instantly ordered them removed. When Fox yelped, he said, "We cannot give Bobby a slap in the face. We must find a way to bring back the cameras that will allow him to feel that he has won."

Somebody reminded Thorarinsson that one story above the stage were two rooms that housed the air-conditioning equipment for the hall. In each there was an alcove barely large enough to hold a camera and a cameraman.

The cameras were set up and aimed at the playing table through four-inch holes. Only the lenses could be seen from the stage, and not a whirr could be heard. For the first time the conditions that Bobby had been promised were met.

Schmid examined the setup and complimented Thorarinsson. "If Bobby will object to this," he said, "I will rule against him."

Bobby meanwhile was still sleeping. At 12:15, Cramer knocked at Bobby's door to tell him Marshall was on the line. Five minutes later

Bobby stumbled to the door. "Too tire'," he mumbled. "Wa'e me a' 4:30."

Hoping to avert the crunch he saw coming, Marshall dictated a letter to Schmid requesting that the Wednesday moratorium on filming be extended to cover the second game. "This would give us three days to discuss the matter fully, and hopefully solve it." About the same time, Edmondson called Schmid and warned him that Bobby had gone too far to give in. "You've got to give him a way out," Edmondson insisted. "Otherwise you'll lose the match."

Schmid agreed, but did nothing.

At 4 P.M. an American grandmaster made a grim prediction. "Up to now everybody wanted the match so much they'd put up with almost anything to get it. Now everybody's exhausted. This time they're going to let Bobby drown in his own shit."

At 4:30, Lombardy jimmied Bobby out of bed. Cramer called from the playing hall.

"Well," Bobby asked drowsily, "they got the cameras out?"

Cramer did his damnedest. "The towers are out," he answered cheerfully. "So is the camera backstage. And Bobby, they've found a marvelous new place for the cameras. Completely invisible and inaudible! All you see is—"

"I told you I want those cameras out!" Bobby yelled so loud that Cramer yanked the receiver away from his ear. "You saw what happened in the first game—I can't concentrate with those things watching me. Tell Thorarinsson I'm not leavin' this room until you swear to me that every camera and every person employed by Fox is *out of that hall!* Unnastan'?"

Thorarinsson asked Cramer to tell Bobby that he was very sorry the cameras had distracted him and that it would never happen again. "Tell him that I ask him to come to the hall today. If he still finds the cameras distracting, we will remove them."

Bobby's answer was an angry no.

At 4:50, Thorarinsson and Stein conferred backstage and decided to stick to their guns.

At 4:59, Spassky walked onstage. At 5:00 Schmid started the clock. Cramer had urged him to delay the game so the disputants could find a solution, but Schmid answered huffily that the rules would not permit—"and furthermore, it would not be fair to Boris, who is here."

An image of Bobby's clock was projected onto the closed-circuit screens. Since the second game gave Bobby the first move, it was his time that was wasting. If he wasted sixty minutes, he would be forfeited. Spassky sat quietly for about five minutes, then went backstage.

At 5:10, Thorarinsson phoned Bobby from a junk-filled passageway between the auditorium and the players' area. Thorarinsson fed arguments to Lombardy, who passed them on to Bobby, who was striding around in his underwear.

"I want the cameras out!" he insisted again and again, his eyes rolling.

At 5:15, Marshall got a call through to Schmid, who said stiffly that if Bobby did not come he would have to declare a forfeit.

At 5:20, Stein and Fox held another quick conference with Thorarinsson.

"We must not show the slightest weakness now," Thorarinsson said. "Our only chance to win is to convince Bobby that we will give up the match rather than give in."

Teeth clenched, Fox and Stein nodded.

"But between ourselves," Thorarinsson went on, "we must understand that if Bobby is crazy enough to hold out, we will have to give in first."

"What!" Stein gasped. "I'll never give in to this punk! Remember, Gudmundur, you signed a contract with us!"

"I have not forgotten my responsibility to you, Mr. Stein," Thorarinsson answered with a gray-blue stare. "Neither have I forgotten my responsibility to my country."

"Gudmundur," Stein said, "those cameras come out over my dead body!"

"If necessary," Thorarinsson answered, "the police will take them out."

About 5:30, Andrew Davis phoned Stein from New York. "Dick, you've got to help us," Davis said. "He's in a stubborn rage and we need at least a day to cool him down. If you can pull the cameras out for this game, I'll fly up tonight and do my goddamnedest to help you. Otherwise, it's all over. He won't accept a forfeit."

Stein agreed instantly—after what Thorarinsson had told him, he knew he had to. But by the time Stein got back to Thorarinsson, the Icelander had made his move. Convinced that Bobby really would wreck the match over the cameras, Thorarinsson told Lombardy that he was ordering the cameras out and sending a police escort to rush Bobby to the hall. Grandmaster Fridrik Olafsson, the only Icelander

Bobby had been heard to say he liked and respected, raced to the Loftleidir in another car.

Backstage there was an epidemic of relief. "For a minute there," Cramer was saying to Fox, "I thought you guys were as crazy as he is." Stein was screwing a large cigar into his uncertain smile. Thorarinsson was deciding he would never again slug it out with Bobby. "Slowly," he thought. "It will take time but I will get those cameras back in that hall."

Relief ceased abruptly. "Bobby says he'll come," Lombardy announced over the phone, "but only if his clock is set back to zero."

Thorarinsson's eyes went wide. "But that is impossible!"

"The chief arbiter had been warned *in writing*, many hours before the game was to start, that Bobby would not play unless the cameras were removed. Grandmaster Schmid refused to do this and started Bobby's clock instead. Bobby feels that the chief arbiter acted illegally and will not play unless his clock is restarted."

Thorarinsson was still fighting off shock. "Just a moment—I will speak with Mr. Schmid."

It was 5:39.

"*Impossible!*" Schmid was outraged. "If Mr. Fischer had come to the playing hall I could have helped him. But he did not come, and his protest was not valid. I had no choice but to start his clock. It cannot be set back."

Thorarinsson was blocked in all directions. Taking a deep breath, he went back to the phone and reported what Schmid had said.

"But please tell Mr. Fischer that the chief arbiter's ruling can be appealed to the Match Committee, which will meet tomorrow morning. The cameras are at this moment leaving the hall. I hope very much that Mr. Fischer will play the game today *under protest* and postpone the problem of the clock until tomorrow."

Bobby was charging back and forth across his room so fast that he seemed to meet himself coming when he was going. "Play under protest! What does he think I am, a *fool?* I knew it! I should never have come! Was it *my* fault the cameras were there? Was it *my* fault the clock was started illegally? Ha! You tell Thorarinsson if they forfeit me, that's it! I'm takin' the next plane back to the States!"

Olafsson arrived. Tall, fine-boned, frigid as an Ingmar Bergman pastor, he despised Bobby and had told friends privately he hoped the challenger would be disqualified for misbehavior. He had agreed to carry the olive branch out of a sense of obligation to Thorarinsson and now found himself holding a conference with a wild man in jockey shorts.

"Don't talk to me about the match!" Bobby stormed at him. "I lost interest in it six months ago!"

Steeling his smile, Olafsson said, "I come as your friend, Bobby, not as an organizer."

"I *hope* you're not involved with that bunch! It's a Communist front!"

It was impossible to conduct a rational discussion on such premises, but Olafsson tried. Bobby lapsed into a smoldering silence, turned on his shortwave radio and gnawed cold cuts.

At 5:47, Olafsson phoned Schmid and told him only he could save the match. "Speak to Boris. Ask him if he will agree to restart the clock."

"I cannot," Schmid replied in his flat, official voice. "Bobby has twelve minutes. I suggest you come."

When Schmid's reply was transmitted to Bobby, he yanked the phone cord out of the jack.

At 6 P.M. Schmid stepped to the playing table and stopped the clock.

"Ladies and gentlemen," he announced, "Mr. Fischer did not appear in the playing hall. According to Rule Number Five of the Amsterdam Agreement, if a player is one hour late, he loses the game by forfeit."

The crowd raised a dispirited cheer. Spassky hurried off. "It is a pity," he muttered backstage. "A very pity."

Back at the Saga, he cut loose. "This is *ridiculous!* What are we doing here? Is it a chess match or an insane asylum? Bobby is trying to destroy the match, F.I.D.E., Thorarinsson, me—everything! And he is succeeding! Now I will have to beat him by at least two points. Otherwise everyone will say I won because of the forfeit. And even if I beat him by five points, everyone will say the forfeit broke his spirit. Ech! Let us all go home!"

After Spassky left the hall, Schmid took the stage and answered reporters' questions for fifteen minutes, carefully justifying everything he had done. Stein then explained how he too had done everything humanly possible to bring Bobby to reason.

After the formal press conference, Fox held forth on the floor of the auditorium. "I'm glad he forfeited! He deserved it. Somebody had to break this person and that somebody turned out to be *me!*"

A British reporter asked Fox, "Does it disturb you that in destroying Fischer you are destroying yourself?"

"No!" Fox said instantly, looking noble. "There are bigger things than me."

Thorarinsson was in a rage with himself, with Bobby, with all the other self-important clowns who had created the mess they were all in. "After so many difficulties, the match had begun. I thought I had won. And then this! I was tempted to give up."

One thought stopped him.

"Bobby is a fighter. How could he quit with Spassky ahead?"

"I must most vigorously protest . . ."

From the first sentence it was obvious that the Bobby who on July 5 had kissed off a quarter of a million was not present on July 13. This Bobby was hard, clear, acute. He knew what he wanted and he went right after it. With Cramer's assistance he constructed the first draft of his letter to the Match Committee as solidly as a brief: complaint, evidence, summation, demand for redress. It followed a line of argument as clear as the theme of a Bobby Fischer chess game.

The letter was a cry from the heart, a grand soliloquy from the role he had memorized at his mother's unbending knee. He was Victim Invictus, Underdog Biting Back, Injured Innocence Rising Up to Beat a Bum Rap. "I was told these devices were completely silent and invisible and out of sight. Regretfully, nothing could have been farther from the facts . . . The bungling unknowns who claimed to be professional motion picture cameramen were clumsy, rude and deceitful. The only thing invisible, silent and out of sight was the fairness on the part of the organizers, who seemed far more eager to placate this intolerable movie-camera gang than to provide playing conditions worthy of the chess championship."

The body of the text, which ran more than 2000 words, was a passionate but rational recital of the history of the film operation from Bobby's point of view. Once again he had asked me to help him polish the text, and as I saw it unfold, I realized what a strong case Bobby had. Up to 5 P.M. on the day of the second game, Bobby had been more in the right than anybody else involved in the fracas.

Riding his righteousness like a big white horse, Bobby galloped into his second revision.

"But it's 11:30. Schmid needs the protest by 12:00 and we still have to type it up."

"Schmid," Bobby said, "can wait."

Schmid couldn't. He tapped on Cramer's door at 11:58, and told Bobby that according to the match rules he had to have the protest within six hours of the forfeit. "That leaves exactly two minutes."

Bobby scowled. "You can't have it, Lothar. I'm not done."

"Perhaps," Schmid said, "if you could read it to me in its present form . . ."

The scowl lifted. An audience was an audience, even if it was only Schmid. Tilting back on his chair, Bobby began to elocute. When he finished the first page, Schmid saw that there were half a dozen more.

"Uh—well—yes, Bobby," he broke in quickly, "perhaps it will be enough if I touch the letter. There! And now I can say that you gave me the letter in time and I gave it back to you—for typing. But please, I must have it before the morning."

Bobby looked irritated. Schmid had done him a terrible wrong and now he was trying to get off the hook by performing a trivial favor.

"Yeah, well, so long, Lothar," he said with a sneer. Schmid edged nervously out the door.

An hour later I was sitting behind the main desk in the Loftleidir lobby, pecking out a final draft. Bobby was pacing and dictating, leaning over my shoulder to make sure I got it right. We were still there at 6 A.M.

At 6:40, when we finished the Xeroxing, Bobby was rarin' to go. As we rose toward the eighth floor of the Esja Hotel, I asked him if it wasn't a bit early to wake Schmid.

Bobby chuckled wickedly. "Lothar? He doesn't sleep anyway. He just lays there and worries."

Bobby was not far wrong. Schmid had tossed most of the night. After seeing Bobby, he had gone to the Saga to tell the Russians what he had done about Bobby's letter. Spassky and his seconds, who were playing bridge when Schmid arrived, looked dubious. "That is not acceptable," said a Soviet Chess Federation official. "If the letter is still in Bobby's possession, it was not really delivered. It is therefore not a valid protest."

At 4:30 Schmid awoke, sobbing, from a nightmare in which he "destroyed a great genius."

At 6:50, Bobby hammered at his door.

Schmid's hair was combed with care, but there were ragged circles under his eyes.

"Good morning, Bobby," he said smoothly, as though Bobby hammered at his door every morning at 6:50. "Please to come in."

It was a large room. Bobby and I sat on a sofa with a coffee table in front of it. Schmid sat in a chair opposite.

"I want to tell you, Bobby," Schmid began, "about—" All at once he jumped up to get something and hit his head on a lamp that hung over the coffee table.

Bobby grinned. I gasped and asked Schmid if he was all right.

"Yes, thank you very much, Bobby," Schmid answered. "I am quite all right."

Many times since, Schmid has told friends how on the morning after he gave Bobby the forfeit, at a moment when resentment would have been natural, Bobby gasped in sympathy when Schmid bumped his head, and asked if he was all right. "Say what you like," he likes to say, "down underneath, Bobby is a good fellow."

Encouraged by this imaginary evidence that Bobby still liked him after all, Schmid told him he was afraid the Russians would not accept Bobby's protest letter.

Bobby cut him off. "Well, Lothar, that's *your* problem. Here's the letter. See ya." And he went tromping off.

After leaving copies for Spassky and Thorarinsson, Bobby moved on to the Loftleidir cafeteria for a breakfast that would have sedated a boa constrictor. On the way up to his room, he burst out laughing. "D'ja see that Lothar when he hit his head? Ha! Ha! Ha!"

Reading through Bobby's letter again that morning, I tried to guess his intentions. It was a fighting letter—what was he fighting for? To prove he was right? To beat Thorarinsson, Fox, Stein, Schmid? Yes, but he was fighting to erase the forfeit too. He wanted the match, for the first time I was sure of it. But did he want it enough to swallow the forfeit?

Tired but hopeful, I hurried to the front desk to see if Davis had checked in. He hadn't, but a room clerk called me aside and said two seats had been reserved on Sunday's 3 P.M. flight to New York. The seats were being held, he said, in the name of Fred Cramer.

14

A Judicial Assassination

The Match Committee met at 10 A.M. Friday to adjudicate three American protests—two by Cramer, one by Bobby—against Schmid's decision. Since awarding the forfeit, Schmid had spent every waking moment canvassing support for his decision. He saw the meeting as a chance to exonerate himself and lay the blame for ruining the match on Bobby. His idea was to keep the meeting small and get it over fast. But there was a noisy fly in the ointment: Andrew Davis.

Davis turned up in Reykjavik about 9 A.M. and demanded an opportunity to present his client's case before the assembled committee—otherwise, he said, he would instantly bring suit against all the parties involved.

"Well," Schmid said, "it is not allowed under the rules"—in fact, nothing in the rules prohibited the Match Committee from hearing evidence in a dispute—"but since Mr. Davis has come so far, I suppose we must hear what he has to say."

The mood on the American side was grim. If the forfeit were upheld, the match would be over. Cramer in any case was utterly sick of Bobby, determined to do his duty but at the same time disembrace the albatross as far as he decently could. Davis, whose feelings for Bobby were much stronger, arrived in a depression. "Well, how's Bobby?" he asked with a forced grin. "Feeling fine, I suppose. It takes a lot of energy to fuck things up this bad."

For the first time, Davis's mood diminished his performance on Bobby's behalf. Addressing the Match Committee, his tone was contemptuous, outraged. "My client has been abused and cheated of his rights!" he shouted, pounding the table with his fist. "The rules have been flagrantly violated by the organizers and my client has been punished for refusing to accept this gross mistreatment! We demand redress!"

As a shock tactic, the shouting might have been effective. But the shock wore off and Davis kept right on shouting. After eighteen minutes, Schmid cut him off so Geller could reply. With no further effort to seek out the facts of a very complicated matter, the committee then voted to support Schmid's forfeit and to overrule Bobby's protests about playing conditions in the first two games.

At the end of the meeting, flushed with vindication, Schmid couldn't resist kicking the man who was down. "For the second game," he said, "I ordered the first three rows of seats to be kept empty. I did this at Bobby's request, but it was not correct. For the third game these rows will be filled."

"Well, there goes the ball game," Lombardy said.

"Shit!" Davis agreed, and went back to his hotel room.

Cramer arrived and began to describe the end of the meeting excitedly.

"I refused to vote on the forfeit," he declared proudly. "I told 'em I'd reserve comment for a more fitting forum."

Davis sat up. "You mean that the vote on the forfeit was *three to nothing against Bobby*? That you were there as Bobby's representative and did not record a vote in Bobby's favor?"

"We've got to get rid of him!" Lombardy said as soon as Cramer left—but why bother? The match was finished.

Reporters rushed to make plane reservations. Americans were cursed openly in the streets. Hate calls for Bobby inundated the Loftleidir switchboard. Somebody on a Reykjavik talk show proposed that "Fischer and all the foreign reporters be given eight hours to get out of Iceland or be shot." Anti-Semitism reared its pointy head. Icelanders who had never seen a Jew—there was only one permanent Jewish resident in Iceland at the time—began snarling about the *"helvitis gydingar"* (goddamn Jews). What would they have said if they had known that the Icelandic police, tipped off that members of the Jewish Defense League had come to Iceland to bomb Spassky, had questioned two people and assisted them to leave the country?

The object of these frustrated attentions took off for Borgarfjord-hur in disgust. "I cannot catch Bobby," Spassky told his teammates. "Let us see if I can at least catch a salmon before I go home."

Several grandmasters began to organize an alternative tournament among the twelve grandmasters then in Reykjavik, all income to help defray I.C.F.'s expenses.

Schmid and Golombek were wondering what would happen next. According to the match rules, Spassky would have to show up for the third game and wait until an hour had ticked away on Bobby's clock before Schmid could award him the game by forfeit. Would the champion have to go through this sad little charade ten more times before Schmid could announce that he had won the match?

I.C.F. had more obdurate problems, most of them financial. If Bobby broke off the match, he would forfeit his right to a share of the purse. Spassky had promised Thorarinsson not to accept the prize money if Bobby failed to show up for the match—would his promise still hold? Even if it did, would Iceland's pride permit the champion to go away with empty hands? On the other hand, if the government paid the prize money out of the public revenues, would the voters accept the bill for Thorarinsson's Folly?

As for Fox and Stein, no doubt they would sue Bobby. Would they also sue I.C.F. for breach of contract, claiming that Thorarinsson had forced them to remove the cameras from the hall? Thorarinsson was ready. He had found a clause in the contract that released both parties in case of a strike—and any way you looked at it, Bobby was on strike!

Fox and Stein meanwhile were having trouble with each other. "If you hadn't been such a goddamn nickel-squeezer," Fox was heard to yell, "we coulda done this thing right and Bobby'da had nothin' to holler about!"

Stein shrugged and turned away. "Chester's mouth," he said, "is not his best feature."

There was also rancor in the suite with the gold knobs. Bobby woke about 5 P.M. and called Cramer wanting his mail and *The New York Times*.

"You gotta do somethin' about that Mercury they gave me!" he said. "I told 'em two weeks ago I wanted an *automatic Mercedes*, right? Now when am I gonna get one? Anyway, this Mercury's a 1970 or something." His eyes bulged. "Whatta they mean, givin' me a used car? And the rear-view mirror is missing. Wow! They tryin' to get me killed or something?"

After Cramer left, Lombardy dropped by with Bobby's former teacher, Jack Collins, and Jack's sister Ethel. The idea was to let Bobby relax in the company of old friends, come down to earth. Smiling like the bucket of a steam shovel, he jumped up to shake Jack's hand and let Ethel hug him. For a few minutes he listened while Jack rendered the latest chess gossip in his own wry way. But his eyes soon glazed and he drifted back to his chess table.

A little later, dinner for four was served in the room. Ethel put her plate on the edge of the table where Bobby had set up his chess board.

"No!" Bobby yelled. "Don't put your plate there! You could mess up the position!"

Ethel contritely put the plate on her lap and struggled through the meal without complaint.

About 10 P.M. Bobby yawned his visitors out the door, saying it was time to start his Sabbath. For the next twenty-four hours, there would be no way to get at Bobby, no way to tell which way he was leaning, no way to influence his decision.

In desperation, Davis decided to trump up a "spontaneous" barrage of telegrams urging Bobby to play. Friday night Cramer, Lombardy and I started calling the States. A high official of the Worldwide Church of God agreed to "see if there was any way the church might help." About three dozen chess lovers said they would send telegrams and tell their friends to do the same. Somebody tried to phone Agnew, but he was out of town.

15

"So Be Right—
and Be Ruined!"

Marshall arrived just after 6 P.M. Saturday and hit Reykjavik like a wagonload of smelling salts. By 8:40 he had bullied Schmid into recalling the committee for reconsideration of the forfeit. By 9:30 he had assembled fresh evidence from four witnesses and was dictating an appeal. Hoping to give Bobby an excuse to stay but still save the committee's face, Marshall proposed an ingenious compromise. "Why not reserve decision on the forfeit until the end of the match and, for the time being, call the next game the second." Marshall sensed that if the decision were postponed until after the match, Spassky would not want the forfeit. If Spassky won, he would hardly want his victory sullied by an unearned point; if he lost, he would hardly want people to say he couldn't beat Bobby even with a two-game head start.

Marshall met the committee in the Esja Conference Room at 10 A.M. Schmid opened the discussion. "The rules state, 'the Committee reaches a decision within twelve hours of the lodging of a complaint and its decisions are final.' "

"The decisions," Marshall came back, "are final in that there is no appeal, but this does not mean that a decision cannot be changed! New information has come to light and you have not made a decision based on *that*. Until all this information becomes available, we ask that you temporarily withhold the decision you have made."

Schmid sighed. "Mr. Marshall, we cannot give Bobby back the point. According to Rule Six, only illness or injury can cause a game to be postponed, not circumstances."

Lombardy objected sharply, instancing a game between Bronstein and Cardozo when the lights went out and the game was officially delayed. Bobby had already experienced the bad playing conditions—why should he put his "neck in the noose"? He had "every right not to appear," Lombardy insisted, "until these circumstances were cleared up."

Marshall cut in. "May I remind you that no game in a championship match has *ever* been forfeited? Fischer is eager to play, but something has happened in terms of chicanery that has so shaken him as to destroy his trust. You can't ask him to play on Sunday under conditions that have so gravely disturbed him."

Schmid threw up his hands. "But the filming contract is out of my jurisdiction!"

Marshall looked skeptical. "Are you telling me you can allow filming but you can't prevent it?"

Davis pointed out that although the Amsterdam Agreement gives the organizers the right to make film arrangements, it also insists that these arrangements shall not disturb the players. "And that *is* your responsibility."

"*I* do not see or hear the cameras," Schmid answered blandly.

The meeting ended in total rebuff.

Evening brought more bad news.

A sound engineer, called in by I.C.F. to measure camera noise, reported that with the cameras off or on the sound level in the hall was exactly the same: 55 decibels.

At 5:48 a wire arrived for Schmid.

IN CASE OF NON-APPEARANCE FISCHER IN THIRD GAME PRESIDENT FIDE DECIDES AS FOLLOWS STOP IF FISCHER FOR THE FOURTH GAME DOES NOT APPEAR MATCH WILL BE CONCLUDED AND SPASSKY PROCLAIMED WORLD CHAMPION EUWE

Bobby woke up in a belligerent mood. The cable campaign had produced twenty-eight messages so far, fifteen pro, thirteen con. He riffled through them hastily, without comment. Marshall was waiting to see him, but Bobby said, "No. Later. I'm hungry now."

Bobby decided to have his afternoon meal in a private dining room the hotel had put at his disposal ("Tell 'em to get that room ready," he told Cramer. "I'm comin' down in five minutes.") and to have it with a middle-aged woman hardly anybody in Reykjavik had heard of.

"What!" yelped Ward of UPI. "Bobby having dinner *alone with a woman!* Clear the wires!" In ten minutes more than thirty reporters were crammed into the little bar across from Bobby's dining room.

Lina Grumette considered herself Bobby's "California mother" because he had stayed in her house for months on end during his dark age in Los Angeles. Now in her fifties, she was still showily attractive with Shirley Temple eyes and a smile meant to get results. For years she had run a successful public-relations agency in Los Angeles, and now was in semiretirement. Chess was her hobby and Bobby her darling.

At last she had him to herself. "I gave him hell," she said later. "I told him if he walked out of the match he'd be washed up. He said, 'But I'm right!' And I said, 'So be right—and be ruined!' I told him it'd be worse than it was before, when he was down and out in Los Angeles, and I reminded him how awful he felt then. Now he'd be a dirty word everywhere chess was played. Oh, I really laid into him. He listened very seriously. He didn't say he'd play, but I shook him up and I think he was glad."

Bobby's cheeks were flushed as he left the dining room with Lina. Marshall had left word that he was available, but Bobby put him off again and toddled away to a private showing of an Icelandic travelogue. "Very good, very good!" he said happily as the lights went up. Then, smiling and waving, he took the elevator back up to his room "for a rest." Marshall by now was mottled with fury. "Okay, that's that," he said. "He wants me, he can come lookin'."

At 12:30, Bobby summoned Cramer to his room and announced he would take the 3:15 plane to New York the next day. "I want you to pick up those tickets tonight and bring 'em up here to me. Then I want you to figure out some plan to sneak me out to the plane. They might be gonna try to stop me, see, so it's gotta be *secret.*"

Cramer went to his room, locked the door and sat down. Should he do what Bobby was asking him to do? If he didn't, he could be accused of disloyalty. If he did, he could be accused of handing Bobby the gun that blew his head off.

Shortly after 1 A.M., Cramer put the reservations in Bobby's name, picked up the tickets and delivered them. Bobby inspected the tickets, then with tight-lipped satisfaction tucked them in the top of his plastic suitcase. Cramer outlined a plan of escape, which Bobby approved, and at about 1:30 Cramer fell asleep, leaving a call for 6 A.M.

Why had Cramer done as he was told? Cramer says he simply decided that his first duty was to obey Bobby. Marshall says Cramer hated Bobby so much he couldn't pass up the chance to ruin him. In any case, the drama must have been irresistible—at last, once and for all he could take over the inside track.

Bobby meanwhile went down to the pool. Sometime after 2 A.M., he put through a call to Marshall.

"Hi, Paul," he said in his innocent-little-boy voice. "I'm in the sauna. Wanna come down?"

"You're sure it's not too soon for you?" Marshall asked with steely politeness, then took the elevator down.

After both men had taken a sauna and swum a few lengths, they began to talk business. Marshall said he was sure the forfeit would be reversed when Euwe saw all the evidence and Edmondson started to lean on him. Meanwhile, he pointed out, Bobby had won the battle of the cameras: Thorarinsson had promised to keep them out of the hall until Bobby agreed to let them in.

"That's not enough," Bobby said almost carelessly. "I said I wouldn't play unless they lifted the forfeit, and I won't. You know me, I never change my mind. If you're leaving tomorrow, I want to go with you."

"Not a chance," Marshall shot back. "I'm here to help you to play, not to quit."

Bobby looked shocked. "You mean you're gonna leave me alone up here with all these crazy Icelanders? They might not let me out!"

"That's your problem." Marshall started to climb out of the pool. All the stored-up fury and frustration of the day were bulging to get out. "I'm not wasting any more time on a quitter!"

Bobby gasped. "Whaddya mean, a quitter!"

"What I said. You're a quitter. And you're a coward!"

Bobby went the color of the white tile on the wall. "That's a lie, Paul, and you know it!"

Marshall wrapped himself in a towel and said nothing. Bobby climbed on the opposite edge of the pool and sat shaking with anger.

"You got no right to call me a coward!" he burst out.

"You're afraid to play because you're afraid you're gonna lose," Marshall said calmly.

"Lose to that fish? Hah! Everybody *knows* I'm better than he is!"

"That's not what *I* hear," Marshall went on. "After the way you blew that first game, I'd say most people figure *he's* better."

Bobby was gripping the edge of the pool. "One game! That's nothing. Nobody who knows anything thinks he can beat me."

"He's beat you four times now. How many times have you beat him?"

"That's *old* games! That's different!"

"Then why don't you play?"

"Because I don't play if the conditions are wrong! You know that! What's the matter with you, Paul! Are you on their side?" Bobby shuddered, remembering his old fear that Marshall might be a silver-tongued exploiter. "Are you in on the *plot?*"

"Plot!" Marshall laughed. "Nobody needs to plot against you. You destroy yourself."

"Are you tryin' to tell me all this isn't a Russian plot? They're all in on it—Fox, Stein, Thorarinsson, Schmid. Maybe you're in on it too!"

"Listen, Bobby, that dumb the Russians aren't! For Christ's sake, can't you realize? That forfeit is the best thing ever happened to you! If you lose you got a perfect excuse. If you win, you're Superman! Either way, you smell like a rose. How do you think Spassky's feeling tonight? I'll tell you. He's feeling sick! Because there's no way now that he can win!"

The battle went on for another two hours. It was 5 A.M. when Marshall sank into the sack, and he still saw no sign that his assault had made an impression. By now he was too tired to care. Instead of angry or depressed he felt quietly absurd, like a man who had just spent four hours arguing with a turtle.

16

The Snake in
the Ping-pong Room

Bright-eyed and bushy-tailed, Cramer bounced out of bed at 6:00 and hustled downstairs to the cafeteria. He had slept a total of three hours, but being in charge had him gunning his engine. He needed a crew, and that was why he had scheduled a breakfast meeting with Kristjan Arngrimsson, the Icelandic guide who was working with the *Life* team.

"Listen, Kristjan," Cramer muttered, "I need your help, but you've got to promise not to tell Brad."

"My dear Fred," Kristjan answered, careful to promise nothing of the sort, "I understand the problem. There is a girl in your room, and she has threatened to scream unless you give her a thousand dollars. Naturally, I will be pleased to strangle her and take the body to my apartment, where I have a large collection of such things."

"You're right about one thing," Cramer said, chortling. "I'm trying to get a body out of here, but it isn't a girl's."

"Ah," said Arngrimsson. "You wish to get The Body out of the hotel and onto a plane—and you wish no one to know what is happening."

"Correct. Will you help me?"

"I am not sure I am ready to become a national hero. However, at what time do you wish The Body to be moved?"

"In time for the 3:15 plane."

Arngrimsson put together a neat scheme. At 1:30 P.M. Frank Skoff, president-elect of the U.S. Chess Federation, would drive the rearviewmirrorless Mercury to the side door of the hotel. Arngrimsson would filch a key from the front desk, open a hidden stairway and take Cramer and The Body down to the car, which would leave the hotel by a back road. Arngrimsson and the baggage would follow in my Volkswagen, pass the Mercury on the road to Keflavik and lead it to a small fishing village about two miles beyond the entrance to the airport. While the Mercury and its precious cargo sat in a side street, Arngrimsson and Skoff would drive to the airport, check the baggage aboard, make sure when the plane was leaving, shuttle back to the fishing village, pop Cramer and The Body into the Volkswagen and show up at the airport just in time for takeoff. No sweat, no reporters.

Cramer gave the go-ahead. Then he had a second thought—"This dramatic episode should be recorded for posterity." Two minutes later he rapped on Benson's door. "Listen, Harry. I need your help, but you've got to promise not to tell Brad."

Benson and Arngrimsson arrived in my room at almost the same instant. When we stopped laughing, we decided that Benson and Arngrimsson would go along with the plot. In the meantime I would sabotage it.

At 10 A.M. I woke Marshall and told him what was afoot.

"Why, that motherfucker!" he exploded. "Okay, I'll get on it."

Twenty minutes later he met Cramer in front of the hotel and asked him what in hell he thought he was doing.

Cramer announced defiantly, "My loyalty is to *him!*"

When Cramer held firm, Marshall approached several reporters and told them what was going down. In half an hour every newsman in Reykjavik knew about the escape. Dozens of reporters and photographers took off for the airport. Six or eight waited in cars along the Keflavik highway. Though journalists were not allowed to rent rooms in Bobby's corridor, some British correspondents rented one in the name of a South African chess buff and posted him there to sound the tocsin when Bobby made his run for it.

Thorarinsson got the story next. He said Iceland was a free country—Bobby was free to go, we were free to stop him from going. An aide to the manager of the hotel hid all the keys to the stairway that Cramer planned to use. A telephone call produced a local garageman, who obligingly made a mare's nest of the wiring under the Mercury's hood. "It will take two hours to get this thing started," he promised. A cab driver was hired to stand by so that Arngrimsson could call him when the Mercury refused to start. The cab driver had instructions to take a wrong turn on the way to the airport and have a breakdown on a back road to nowhere.

If all else failed, and Bobby reached the fishing village, Arngrimsson would simply tell him that the air terminal was awash with reporters and American soldiers, who were waiting for him in an ugly mood—and Arngrimsson would be telling the truth. A delegation of off-duty G.I.'s was planning to give Bobby a bon voyage party he wouldn't soon forget.

Cramer meanwhile went padding through the hotel corridors looking like a teddy bear that had just eaten his master. He bought a few things in the hotel gift shop and telephoned Milwaukee to tell his wife he'd be home late that night or the next day. After that he sat down and began his farewell message to the press. A stack of telegrams had arrived overnight, most of them urging Bobby to play. Cramer decided it was his duty to hand them over as soon as possible. At 1 P.M. he pounded on Bobby's door.

All down the corridor, doors flew open and heads popped out. One man watched the scene through field glasses.

Cramer disappeared inside. A few seconds later he came out again. He had told Bobby they should move right away, but Bobby had only yawned and answered, "Call me a little later, will ya?" So Cramer had handed him the telegrams and left.

At 1:15, Cramer pounded on the door again. Doors opened, heads popped out. This time Cramer didn't get in. "Call me a little later, Fred," Bobby hollered from bed.

At 2:00, Cramer insisted Bobby let him in. "If we don't leave in the next half hour," Cramer said urgently, "we'll miss that plane."

"When's the last flight?"

"Five-thirty."

"Put me on the last plane," Bobby ordered, and went back to sleep.

Cramer went back to his room. At 3:00, he knocked on Bobby's door again. Lombardy opened it! And Marshall was there too! The telegrams were scattered all over.

"I guess they'll really kill me if I don't go through with this, huh?" Bobby had asked Marshall after reading them.

"They really will."

"That two-game edge is gonna make it hard," Bobby said, looking downcast. Then his eyes glittered. "But I can still do it, y'know!" he said fiercely.

"I *know* you can, Bobby," Marshall answered quietly.

"All right," Bobby said, scowling. "But ya gotta get me in that back room!"

When Cramer arrived, Marshall was on the phone to Schmid, setting up an immediate meeting backstage at the playing hall. Cramer was stunned. All the careful arrangements he had made—for nothing! When Marshall and Lombardy rushed off, Bobby told Cramer to wake him in an hour, and went back to bed.

Marshall and Lombardy gunned toward the playing hall, laughing with relief at the lucky turn of events. What had changed Bobby's mind? Was it the mysterious influence of Lina? the set-to with Marshall? the impact of the telegrams? the money, his pride, his fear of what people would say? Was it the urge to be champion or simply the gut need to play chess?

It was probably all of these things, but Marshall and Lombardy suspected it was something else too. "Bobby had the same fear of leaving Iceland," Marshall said afterward, "as he had of coming to Iceland. When it came to a decision, he was less afraid of playing than he was of the unknown. But make no mistake, he was terrified of playing."

Bobby had decided to play, as Marshall carefully pointed out to Schmid and Thorarinsson, only if he could be in the "back room." Schmid, Thorarinsson, Marshall and Lombardy inspected the room, a thirty-by-sixty-foot rectangle with bare plaster walls on three sides and a row of large windows on the fourth. The janitor called it the ping-pong room and it was quite a comedown from the playing stage. The lighting was pure luncheonette, the air conditioner a grumbler, and through the window floated summer sounds of boys playing tag. Not a bad setting for a Cub Scout meeting, but hardly up to snuff for a World Chess Championship.

Marshall's opening statement set Schmid dithering.

"What? But that is impossible! The game cannot be moved to the back room unless there is a disturbance."

"There is a very grave disturbance to Mr. Fischer, I assure you," Marshall said.

"But the cameras have been removed from the hall!"

"What happened in the hall on Wednesday and Thursday," Marshall explained, "constitutes the disturbance, Lothar. Bobby feels that he was lied to and cheated, and the thought of returning to the scene of these events is still so upsetting to him that he could not possibly concentrate on the game."

Schmid was appalled. "First he is disturbed by the *idea* of the cameras. Now is disturbed by the *idea* of the hall! But the rules do not recognize this as a disturbance. I am sorry. He must play in the hall."

"Lothar, I don't think you understand the problem," Marshall went on. "Why do the rules exist? In order to regulate the match. But if there is no match, what good are the rules? Believe me, Lothar, ten minutes ago Bobby was on his way to the airport! Think it over. If you insist on one little rule, you alone will destroy the match. On the other hand, if you can find a way to avoid the rule, then you alone will save the match."

Schmid said he understood the seriousness of the situation. "But I would be acting *beyond* my authority! No, it could only be done with Spassky's approval."

Thorarinsson stepped closer, closing a ring around Schmid. "We cannot let a rule destroy the match. But I agree. We must have Spassky's approval."

Schmid looked wretched. "How can I ask Spassky *again* to break the rules for Bobby's sake?"

"I've got it!" Striding to the nearest wall, Marshall jerked a fire ax out of its socket and brandished it. "You need a disturbance? I'll give you a disturbance!"

Schmid stared at him aghast.

"I'm going down on stage right now and bust up that chess table! With the table wrecked, you couldn't play in the hall, right? You'd *have* to play up here. Gudmundur, how many days in jail for destroying private property? One day? Hell, it's worth it!"

Marshall moved for the door, ax in hand. Lombardy and Thorarinsson were grinning. Schmid was horrified.

"No! Wait!"

When Lombardy and Thorarinsson burst out laughing, Schmid tried a little laugh too.

"Ha, ha. That will not be necessary," he said. "I—I will call Mr. Spassky."

Three minutes later Schmid was back, blinking incredulously. Spassky had agreed!

"You did it, Lothar! You saved the match!" Marshall, Lombardy and Thorarinsson fell upon Schmid, slapping his back, pumping his hand.

Overwhelmed by his success, Schmid decided they were right. From that moment, he took full credit for the decision. "I took the responsibility to break the rules," he now says weightily, "for the reason to save the match."

At 4:45, as the hall began to fill, Thorarinsson stood watching the customers arrive with all the exquisite relief of a storekeeper who has just escaped bankruptcy. Bobby had won—but so had he. The match was still alive.

Spassky had waked up Sunday morning feeling out of sorts. The weekend in the country had not given him the pickup he needed. "What a mess!" he told Krogius. "This match has lost its charm to me. I will not be sorry if Bobby breaks it off."

Then came Schmid's call. Feeling it would be churlish not to give Bobby something in return for the free point, Spassky agreed quickly and carelessly to play in the ping-pong room "just this once." The instant he hung up, he was disgusted. He had promised himself (and Pavlov) that he would not give in to Bobby any more. "Ech!" he said. "I do not feel like playing today."

Geller gave him a pep talk, but when Spassky arrived at the playing hall just before 5:00 he looked shaken and upset.

The ping-pong room did nothing to lift his spirits. A wooden chess board had been set up on a plain table at one side of the room and on the wall above it hung a curious bundle of brown blankets trussed with parcel cord. Out of the bundle peered the lens of the TV monitor. Spassky circled the room like a nervous cat.

Out front, in the playing hall, another kind of pressure was building. Nine out of ten Icelanders now considered Bobby the worst thing that had happened to Iceland since the British fishing fleet. With the champion leading 2–0, they had told themselves the match was safe, but now they were twitchy. What if Bobby had just had an off day when he played the first game?

For the Americans the question was reversed: What if he hadn't? The odds against Bobby were now prohibitive. "It has never happened," grandmaster Svetozar Gligoric noted, "that a player who was two games behind in a world championship match came back to win the match." Even Byrne, Bobby's strongest partisan, was doubtful. "A two-game advantage in a chess match is like a ten-run lead at the end of the first inning of a baseball game."

Five o'clock. Bobby had not arrived. With a silent prayer, Schmid started the timer: 5:05 . . . 5:08 . . . Spassky was pacing slowly, his face drawn tight. For more than two weeks now he had been putting up with Bobby's insults and infractions. Now, less than two hours after he had rescued Bobby's challenge by agreeing to play in this absurd little room, Bobby was late again—an intolerable insult!

Bobby burst through the door. Spassky stopped short. Bobby's momentum carried him ten feet into the room before he saw anything. Then he veered toward Schmid and the chess table. His skin was gray-white, his cheeks sucked in.

Schmid came forward now and shook Bobby's hand. Gracious but a little stiff, Spassky shook hands too. Bobby's hand was limp.

"Hello, Bobby."

"Uh—hi, hi."

As Spassky hung his coat on the back of his chair, the closed-circuit television came alive. In the main hall more than a thousand people watched the screen above the playing stage. As Spassky was recognized, a cheer went up. About ten seconds later, Bobby rushed into camera-range and a cheer of similar volume arose, mixed with some boos.

Both players sat down. Spassky played Pawn to Queen Four. Bobby replied Knight to King's Bishop Three. Then the picture became confusing. Bobby began to point and gesticulate wildly. Then he ran off camera. Schmid followed him. Then Spassky disappeared too. A grumble went through the crowd—what was going on back there?

Plenty. After Bobby made his move, he looked up and saw the blanket bundle on the wall with the lens peering out of it.

"What's that camera doing there?"

Schmid explained that it was only the closed-circuit TV monitor.

"No! No!" Bobby yelled. "I said *no cameras!*" And he rushed out of camera range.

"Bobby! Be quiet! Please!" Schmid said. "The game is already started!"

Bobby spun around. "Shaddap, Lothar!"

Schmid jerked. "Excuse me, you will not speak to me in this way!"

Spassky stood staring, outraged. Then his face reddened and, lifting his chin proudly, he snatched up his coat and strode toward the door.

Schmid saw the movement and decided in a split second to stop Spassky's clock, a breach of the rules he had refused to make for Bobby. Then he ran to intercept the champion.

"Boris!"

Spassky spun around, quivering with anger. "I am sorry, Lothar. I am leaving. I prefer we will play in the large hall."

"But Boris! You *promised!* Will you break your promise?"

Spassky stared at him. Slowly he let out his breath. Then he gave a little shrug.

"Thank you, Boris!" Schmid murmured fervently, then hurried

back to Bobby, who had also been shaken by the sight of Spassky's back.

Schmid approached him soothingly. "Bobby, please be kind."

Bobby insisted on an explanation of "that camera."

"It is not a camera, it is a monitor and it *does not move*," Schmid reassured him. "It is the same thing you have allowed to be in the main hall. It shows the game to the people in the audience."

"We-ell," Bobby said. "You're *sure* it doesn't move?"

It was 5:12 (though the official records show 5:08) when Schmid restarted the clock. Bobby sat down looking surly and tense. For the next five minutes he objected to the size of the squares, the colors of the squares, the finish of the board, and so on. Finally Spassky duplicated his second move in game one and Bobby did the same. Was he urging a Nimzo again?

As in Game One, Spassky held out for the Queen's Indian.

Eyes fastened to the board, Bobby grabbed his chair, as if to pull it close to the table. But instead of pulling the chair with his hand, he jerked it forward with three strong strokes of his pelvis that seemed to be out of his control. As the audience watched, the spasms went rippling up Bobby's spine and released themselves in three convulsive lunges of the head that eerily resembled the movements of a striking snake.

The crowd tensed, sensing that something extraordinary was about to happen.

Reaching forward with a rapid slithering movement of his arm, Bobby moved.

Pawn to Bishop Four.

In the press room, grandmaster Byrne let out a whoop. "He's asking for the Benoni! He's gonna slug it out!" The Russians sat stiff and still. They knew their man was strained, depressed, unready. This was not his day to face Bobby Fischer in a game as mercurial as the Benoni.

Spassky agreed. He intended to move cautiously and make Bobby play catch-up chess, but at the moment of decision he was too angry to back down. After only brief reflection, he answered the challenge.

Pawn to Queen Five.

Bobby leaned even more sharply forward, his eyes cold and slitted. For five more moves the Benoni unfolded with deceptive placidity. "It's a walkdown," Byrne muttered. "A lot depends on who gets off the first shot." On the eleventh move, Spassky made a subtle shift of direction (Queen to Bishop Two), hoping to put Bobby off balance.

And then it happened. Just as he had in the first game, Bobby made a move that brought Spassky bolt upright and almost knocked the grandmasters out of their chairs.

Knight to Rook Four!?

"Oh, no!" Evans gasped. "Not *again!*" Lombardy went pale and covered his mouth—as Bobby's second, he didn't want the press to see and interpret what he was feeling.

Thorarinsson came rushing into the Western press room. "What has Bobby done?"

Byrne said softly, "He has just demolished the Pawn formation in front of his own King, thus violating one of the basic principles of the game, and he has saddled himself with the permanent weakness of a doubled pawn. All with no compensation that I can see in my present state of shock."

On the stage, Spassky was still staring at the position. Two major blunders in two successive games—had Bobby gone crazy? He flicked a glance across the board. Bobby looked a little crazy, all right, but there was nothing unusual in that.

"But if he isn't crazy," Spassky asked himself, "how *dare* he play like that against *me?*"

In thirty seconds Spassky realized that the blunder was not so simple as he had thought. In two minutes he understood that Bobby was inviting him into a prepared variation of unusual depth and peril. The gap Spassky could open in front of Bobby's King was a trap. Spassky put his head to the problem—his head felt slow and unlucky. For ten, fifteen, twenty-five minutes he pawed around without turning up what he was looking for. Taking the dare, he captured Bobby's Knight with his Bishop.

The American grandmasters groaned and Geller grinned—so far, only Spassky realized the seriousness of his situation. But the next set of moves brought consternation. A colossal breach had been opened in Spassky's Kingside defenses and six powerful units stood poised to crash through.

"My God!" Schonberg gasped, bouncing up and down in his chair. "It's a stroke of genius! When have you seen anything like this in chess?"

Two moves later, Bobby forced an exchange of Knights that straightened out his Pawn formation. Thirteen moves later, pressing all over the board, he forced exchanges that put him a Pawn up and left his Queen hanging over Spassky's head like a two-ton safe.

Close to defeat and knowing it, Spassky tried to steal a draw on the last move of the day. But he moved too quickly and blundered. Looking pained, he watched Bobby deliberate for five minutes and then reach for the envelope.

His move set down, Bobby leaped up, rushed out of the hall and jumped into the Mercury. "I sealed a crusher!" he crowed, smashing a fist into his palm. "I'm crushing him with brute force! Haaaaaa!"

Back at the hotel, Bobby skimmed through the game quickly with Lombardy and put himself into such a state of euphoria that he thanked Cramer for something he had done. After wolfing a couple of the admiral's steaks, Bobby and Lombardy headed for Keflavik, where they bowled seven games. Going out and coming back, Bobby laughed, joked, chattered and even sang snatches of ballads and rock songs. While they were bowling he kept asking Lombardy eagerly, "How was that one? Did I do it right?" Bobby bowls with the form of a waltzing ostrich but Lombardy didn't have the heart to rain on the winner's parade. Bobby beat him 6-1 and came back to the hotel in such a great mood that when he burst into Cramer's room and saw his assistant shortening a bottle of scotch with a few cronies he looked as if he wanted to join the party.

All over Reykjavik the booze was flowing as the chess crowd played the day's game over and over. By 11 P.M. Bobby's worst enemies had conceded the victory. By midnight the Bobby Lobby had decided that Game Three was "a classic example of power chess" and a portent of wonders to come. As Jack Collins put it, "From now on there's gonna be a lot of blood on the floor. Spassky's blood."

17

Thinking
As a Blood Sport

A chess match between grandmasters is psychological warfare waged at nerve-tearing intensity for as long as two months at a stretch. As a match grows older, the mental, physical and emotional strains shoot off the graph. Chess masters often sweat away five pounds during a single game. Even short matches have ended in nervous breakdown. At least two grandmasters have been fatally stricken at the board.

The Reykjavik match was the most violent in history. Fourteen of the twenty-one games were finish fights of total ferocity. For fifty days the two players battered each other, acquainting millions with the dark joys of thinking as a blood sport. By mid-August, Bobby was nearing nervous collapse; Spassky, that apparently most normal of men, was producing delusions that under other circumstances would have put him in the care of a psychiatrist.

The psychological battle took an unexpected turn in the fourth game. After his third-game victory, Bobby came up too confident and Spassky met him with a defense so ingenious it may have permanently wrecked one of Bobby's favorite lines, the Sozin Attack. Then something scary happened. In a few seconds, as if a plug had been pulled, the energy drained out of Spassky's head. One minute his mind was working perfectly; the next he couldn't think two thoughts in a row. Slowly the ideas returned, but now Spassky was in time trouble. Bobby hung on by his eyelashes and found a surprise stroke that broke the attack. Spassky, forced to split the point, left the hall in shock. Score: Spassky 2½, Bobby 1½.

At a council of war, Geller told Spassky he was playing like a man interested less in winning than in displaying his art. Spassky froze and, when Geller had left the room, said angrily, "I am simply not a variation player. I am a composer. I cannot play like Geller and I will not!"

Both players arrived for the fifth game looking frazzled. Bobby was several minutes late—he was late for every game in the match except one. A faint whine in an air duct and the whirring of a shoe-shine machine outside his suite had messed up his sleep. Spassky rapidly drove a pawn wedge into Bobby's center. Then once again, inexplicably, the ideas fell out of Spassky's head like dead birds out of the sky. Squeezed for time, the champion made the worst blunder of his career, turned white, and stopped his clock. Bobby swaggered offstage without a backward glance. The match was now tied 2½–2½. Bobby had won two and a half points out of the last three.

Under such hammering, Taimanov, Larsen and Petrosian had cracked like chicken bones. Would Spassky crack too? "I cannot allow a bad streak to frighten me," he told his seconds. They were not reassured.

Bobby allowed himself a small victory celebration after the fifth game—dinner in the Loftleidir's main dining room. About 9:30 a tipsy blonde with the kind of body the Vikings collected on their slave raids wriggled a well-rounded butt against his eating arm. "Would you like some company? Hmmm?" Mouth full of herring, eyes rolling in alarm, Bobby replied, "Huhlp!" A massive bouncer literally threw the blonde out of the room. Bobby watched with a look of shock that changed slowly to furtive appreciation. "Wow!" he said. "They really treat women rough up here, huh?"

Spassky got another jolt in the sixth game. Bobby, playing White, failed to open with Pawn to King Four. Incredibly, he began the game with Pawn to Queen's Bishop Four—a move he had used only twice in a career of more than 750 games! It was as if Tom Seaver, the finest right-hand pitcher of his generation, had strolled to the mound in a World Series and pitched with his left hand.

Bobby played his new opening to perfection. By move twenty-five he was closing for the kill, one deadly move after another. "This is horrible!" said a Yugoslav grandmaster. "It is like watching a python crush a sheep!" On the forty-second move, Spassky abased his King.

A masterpiece had been executed. Two thousand people rose and cheered. Smiling warmly, Spassky applauded too. Bobby stared at him—amazed, confused, embarrassed. Then he ducked his head and rushed offstage. As the car pulled away, he asked incredulously, "Did you see Spassky applaud? Wow! That shows he's a *true* sportsman!"

But that night, lolling in the hotel pool, Bobby listened eagerly to a review of Russian reactions, relishing every indication that Spassky was suffering. When I mentioned the remark about the python and the sheep he let go a roar of delight. "I'd like to crush *all* those Russians. Only most of 'em aren't sheep. They're pigs!"

The new opening and Bobby's masterly performance wrecked the Russians' match strategy. Alone, uncounseled, jouncing to rock music in a borscht-belt hotel, Bobby had outgeneraled the mighty Soviet chess establishment. For the first time the Russian team despaired.

Not Spassky. Thrilled by the beauty of Bobby's sixth game, he refreshed his resolve. But in the seventh game, Spassky sacrificed three Pawns and a Bishop for a luridly imaginative attack that collapsed. He was lucky to rescue a draw. In the eighth game, suddenly cautious, he pondered over one move for 54 minutes and 26 seconds. Exhausted, running out of clock, Spassky produced the mother and father of all blunders. A flash of pain crossed his impassive face. In the endgame, Bobby's Rooks beat his brains out. The score was now Bobby 5, Spassky 3.

Back at the Saga, Spassky was almost in shock. "My friends," he said, tears rising in his eyes. "I am sorry!" His seconds hugged him roughly and said the right things. "What kind of horseshit is this? You think you're the only turnip ever fell in the Volga?" The Western point of view was expressed by grandmaster Byrne: "After this, Spassky's got to ask himself if it's safe to go back to Russia."

Chess fever was now sweeping the world. "Things have gone wild," Marshall reported. "In England people are betting millions. In Russia Bobby's a secret national hero. In the States *a million people* are watching the play-by-play on TV in the New York area alone! He's gonna go home a goddamn Charles Lindbergh! I've got offers already that would net him two million dollars in the next year and a half!"

Marshall was playing the game for money now—"Bobby needs management. Why not me?" In Marshall's view, Bobby had to move fast if he meant to catch the gravy train. "And the first thing we've got to do is get those cameras back into the hall." To appease Bobby, Marshall persuaded Fox/Stein to yield operation of the cameras to ABC's "Wide World of Sports," but Bobby was still scared of being disturbed.

ABC was represented by Lorne Hassan, a hot-tempered young man who at 3 A.M. on the day of the eighth game had a twenty-five-minute conversation with Bobby that started a grotesque imbroglio. Hassan promised Bobby he would shoot without disturbing him. Bobby didn't believe it. Finally he said, "Talk to Paul Marshall." At 7 A.M. Hassan exultantly proclaimed, "We're in! Marshall said it's okay—if ABC buys out Fox and Stein. ABC's gonna do it!" But there was a careful look in Hassan's eyes that didn't match the sound of his voice.

At 1 P.M. Marshall, Hassan, Fox and Thorarinsson began a five-hour meeting that played like the last act of *Götterdämmerung*. Fox screamed and at one point yelled "Fuck you!" seven times in a row. But at 4:25 the contract was okayed and at 4:56 ABC's cameramen slipped into the darkened hall with their cameras under their coats. Why the hugger-mugger? If Bobby knew about the cameras, why shouldn't everybody else know?

The plot thickened when Bobby arrived and peered suspiciously for eight or ten seconds into the dim auditorium. He had never done this before. Did he know the cameras were in—or did he just suspect? Answers of a sort came later.

After the game Bobby relaxed with visitors from the States—his sister and brother-in-law, Joan and Russell Targ. At 11 P.M. he dialed a newscast and heard a report on his smashing victory. The game had been filmed, the newscast said, "with Fischer's permission."

"What!" Bobby yelled. "I never gave anybody permission to film!"

Two minutes later Bobby crashed into Cramer's room. "What's this I hear about the game bein' filmed? Who said I gave my permission?"

"Why—uh—Hassan told Marshall—"

"He's a *liar!* Get Marshall! I want that film, unnastan'? Otherwise the match is over!"

When Marshall called at last, Bobby demanded letters of apology from ABC, Schmid and I.C.F. From ABC Bobby got something more than he may have wanted—a polite notification that the network was no longer interested in filming the match. "He busted the project once too often," Marshall said. "Maybe it's just as well. Maybe mystery is better for Bobby's image."

After this dust-up, Bobby felt a sharp letdown. His team figured he was relaxing because he was ahead, but the real trouble was a nervous system that had been superstressed for almost a month.

Bobby's morale got a lift when Benson returned from a White House assignment with a personal message from President Nixon. "Wait! Wait!" Bobby told Benson. "I want to get ready." Then he sat well back on a couch, hooked his arms over the back, and stretched out his feet. "Okay, go ahead!"

Benson began. "The President said, 'Tell Bobby that I admire his fighting spirit. He's a fighter. I like that!' And then he said, 'Tell Bobby from me that when it's all over I want him to come down here and visit me, even if he loses.' "

Really bowled over, Bobby could only say in hushed tones, "Yeah? Yeah? That's very good."

But the lift did not last. Something was missing in Bobby's life. "He hasn't got all those people crawling to him about the film," said grandmaster Evans. "He's got to find some other way to get attention. And he will."

Spassky postponed the ninth game for two days. Physically, doctors could find no problem. Mentally, Spassky felt curiouser and curiouser. After the eighth game he no longer believed that nervous exhaustion explained his collapse at the board. Just before blundering, he had "sensed" that Bobby was hypnotizing him. He saw himself as a rabbit paralyzed by a snake, and the image gained strength in his mind. Finally, he talked with his teammates, who gave him a soothing and practical suggestion: "Play within your strength. A draw today will be very nice."

For the evil eye, Spassky's seconds came up with another piece of good advice. After every move he made in the ninth game, Spassky disappeared backstage. The instant Bobby moved, Spassky reappeared. The trick amounted to a public confession that Spassky could not sustain direct confrontation with Bobby, but it worked. Spassky played a good professional draw.

In the tenth game, nothing worked for Spassky. After an even opening, Bobby sprang a strong surprise attack. Spassky began patting his forehead lightly with a folded handkerchief. Bobby swung his chair from side to side and smiled. If he moved three games ahead, could Spassky play on? The crowd, disliking Bobby, admiring Spassky, did not want to see the blow fall but no one could look away. "There is a fascination in executions," Gligoric said. This one was slow but thorough. The score: Bobby 6½, Spassky 3½. The champion had not won since the first game and of the last eight points had only one and a half.

By the day of the eleventh game, Spassky had seen clearly that he was about to lose his title, his special privileges as a Soviet celebrity, maybe even a piece of his sanity. Badly scared, he dropped his lofty notions about the match and decided to drop Geller too. "He is too narrow, too sure he knows best." Nei and Krogius talked him out of that and focused his fears into a white-hot will to win.

Bobby, on the other hand, was in a shocking condition. Now that his cushion had thickened to three games, letdown had sprawled into collapse. After the tenth game, he holed up in his suburban house for two days and nights, shades drawn, windows shut tight, air heavy with essence of used underwear. At 6 A.M., eleven hours before the game, he was wakened by a "mysterious noise in the wall." A burglar? The heating system? Again and again the noise woke him. Finally he fell asleep on an understuffed sofa in the living room. When Palsson arrived, Bobby looked awful.

Spassky opened Pawn to King Four and Bobby led the action into the Poisoned Pawn Variation of the Sicilian Defense—a line so dangerous it is known as "kissing the cobra." Bobby had never lost the Black side of the PPV, but after the thirteenth move, Spassky was in full attack formation, and Bobby was three moves behind. After Spassky's twenty-third move, Bobby's Queen was a standing corpse. The game was over and both men knew it. But Bobby refused to admit defeat. Even after Spassky stood only one move from checkmate, Bobby sat with his mouth in a stubborn knot. Incredulous at first, then disgusted, Spassky walked backstage. As soon as the champion was out of sight, Bobby resigned and left the stage so quickly that he didn't have to shake Spassky's hand in front of the audience.

The score was now Bobby 6½, Spassky 4½. Since Spassky needed only twelve points to win the match (while Bobby needed twelve and a half), he was really only one and a half games behind. The match was a match again.

After the game, Jack Collins was uneasy. "That wasn't Bobby up there today," he said. "Something was wrong." Two Icelanders seconded the notion.

During the tenth game, two days earlier, three men who had been heard conversing in Russian entered the auditorium separately. One sat close to a side aisle. The second sat directly in back of the first. The third stood in the aisle with his back to the wall and a clear view in all directions.

Soon the first man took something out of his pocket and put it in his mouth. Then a thin rigid tube emerged between his lips and pointed toward the players. Whenever an Icelandic policeman strolled down the side aisle, the third man coughed, the second man coughed, the tube was instantly drawn back into the first man's mouth. When the policeman was gone, the tube reappeared.

This went on for some time and was observed by two Icelanders, a father and son. Then the third man noticed he was being watched and gave a signal. The three Russians left the hall quickly. The Icelanders followed them, got the license number, and told their story to the police.

The car belonged to the Russian embassy. Alarmed, the police secretly added six plainclothesmen to the force guarding the hall. When the Russians were identified as embassy employees, round-the-clock surveillance was ordered. Four days after the incident, the three men were recalled to Russia. The affair was hushed up.

The Icelandic police never found out what the Russian had aimed at the players. They speculated it was a whistle that emitted a sound of higher frequency than is normally audible to the human ear. "Everyone knows," said an Icelandic official, "that Bobby's ears are extremely sensitive. Perhaps these people were attempting to disturb his play by producing noises that only he could hear. Perhaps the device had another purpose. Perhaps," he added diplomatically, "the witnesses were mistaken."

The police were sure the three men had not been in the hall during the eleventh game. But there were hundreds of Russians on the island.

The thirteenth game, played Thursday, August 10, was the great human moment and emblematic battle of the summer. As the game began, Spassky forced a fight with Pawn to King Four. Bobby, playing Black, replied with the dodgy Alekhine's Defense. The play seesawed. On the seventh and eighth moves Spassky muddled up two variations and Bobby ripped off a pawn. Then Spassky improvised one of those coffeehouse attacks that like pastry appear with a flourish and vanish in two bites.

When the game adjourned, Bobby figured he was a dead cert to win. Twenty minutes later he was wrestling with an octopus. The Russians were wrestling too, and by 2 A.M., when Spassky turned in, they had roughed out a twenty-move continuation of insidious brilliance.

Bobby meanwhile was having a personnel problem. After six

weeks of trying to pull as a team, Bobby and Lombardy had developed halter sores. During dinner, Lombardy sneezed a few times; Bobby made a five-act drama of the incident. "You got a cold, Bill! You *know* I can't afford to catch a cold now!" Half an hour later, when Lombardy arrived in Bobby's suite to resume analysis, he found grandmaster Lubomir Kavalek across the board from Bobby.

"Bill, you go analyze somewhere else," Bobby said carelessly. "I want to work with Lubosh." As Lombardy left, Bobby sat looking after him. "You know," he said, "I think Bill is a vicious person."

Though only the inner circle was aware of it, Bobby worked with Kavalek from the thirteenth game forward more than he worked with Lombardy.

That night Bobby and his seconds spent nine hours threading the maze that remained of the thirteenth game. Most lines eased quickly into a win for Bobby, but on one spectacular continuation Spassky led a charmed life. After five hours' sleep and a final crash attack on the problem, Bobby arrived at the playing hall twenty-five minutes late. Spassky had discovered the line Bobby feared and sealed the best move. Wills locked like horns. Aura battered aura. On the fiftieth move, Spassky chopped Bobby's Bishop and brought the position dead even. Still sure he could win, Bobby launched the Black King on a long risky march toward victory. Deep in the clutch, Spassky had less than four minutes to make four moves.

On move sixty-nine, he made the second best decision and three moves later offered Bobby his hand. Bobby sat staring at the board like a child regretting the end of an enthralling story. Weaving a little, he left the stage. Spassky sat moving the pieces, a man alone with his ruins.

Both Bobby and Spassky came out of the thirteenth game worse than depleted—they were damaged.

In the fourteenth game, Spassky took the action away from Bobby and by the twenty-fifth move had a sure win. Then suddenly he was seized again by an eerie feeling that something was trying to get hold of his mind. The feeling was so strong he made a mistake a fairly smart chicken could have avoided. A draw was agreed. Match score: Bobby 8½, Spassky 5½.

Bobby knew that only Spassky's blunder had saved him from a loss—if he wasn't careful he could still blow the match. All his life he had called the Russians cowards because they played safe. Now, desperately tired, he decided not to play too hard for a win if it meant too much risk of a loss.

Spassky called a staff conference immediately after the fourteenth game. Pale, trembling, eyes glazed and strange, he announced, "An attempt is being made to control my mind!"

Horrified, Geller and Krogius decided to humor their man. With apparent earnestness they wondered aloud if Bobby might be practicing hypnotism on the champion.

"Sometimes I drink fruit juice backstage," Spassky said. "It could be drugged."

Krogius mentioned experiments that altered mental states by the release of chemicals in the atmosphere and by the use of electronic devices emitting vibrations.

"Why," Spassky asked in a mysterious voice, "did Bobby turn against the filming of the match? Why does he demand that the first seven rows of seats be removed? Is it because he does not wish to have his actions under surveillance?"

Spassky also wondered why Cramer always insisted that Bobby get the same chair. "Has something been placed inside my chair to affect my state of mind?"

Geller wondered if a device had been hidden in the lighting fixture over the playing table. Krogius recalled reports that Bobby's assistants were frequently in the hall at night—"What are they doing there?" Spassky suggested that the CIA might be involved and wondered who the agent might be—Fred Cramer?

The thing was out of control. When Spassky said he would demand an investigation, Nei decided it was time to take a stand. "But we have no evidence on which to base an accusation."

Spassky snorted. "Bobby has protested many times. Surely I am allowed to protest once!"

Nei pointed out that the accusation must be proved—otherwise people would say Spassky was reaching disgracfully far to find an excuse for his defeat.

Spassky glared at Nei. "But what am I to do? Simply sit and let this be done to me?"

The meeting ended in a compromise decision to get an outside opinion. The next morning, Krogius had a chat with Thorarinsson, whose reaction was emphatic. "You will be very foolish to say anything about this."

But in the fifteenth game Spassky felt the force coming after his mind again and was lucky to hold a draw. His last doubts out the window, he ordered Geller and Krogius to prepare the protest. Nei was not told the protest was being written until he was asked to sign it.

The statement was pure looniness. It charged Bobby with using "electronic devices and chemical substance ... to influence Mr. B. Spassky" and make him "lose his fighting spirit." The letter concluded with "an urgent request that the playing hall ... be examined with the assistance of competent experts."

Nei refused to sign Spassky's letter. "Is it loyal," he asked, "to encourage him to do something I believe is bad for him?"

Furious at Nei, Spassky brooded revenge. Geller obligingly suggested that Nei had been passing secret information to Westerners. Spassky ordered Nei home—implying that the trainer was in some way to blame for his defeat. Knowing what happens to scapegoats in the Soviet scheme of things, Spassky can hardly avoid the charge that he threw his friend to the wolves to help save his own skin.

Instead of delusions, Bobby had Saemundur Palsson. Whenever Bobby seemed on the verge of a freak-out, Palsson prescribed hydrotherapy—a soak in some "hot pots" of volcanic water. After parboiling for an hour and a half, Bobby was so relaxed he looked practically prenatal.

Bobby and Palsson were almost always together now—at the pool, at the bowling alley, on the indoor tennis court. Several nights a week they had dinner together. Once Bobby said wistfully to Palsson, "Would you believe it, I haven't worked a single day in my life?" And Palsson answered, "Oh, yes, Bobby, I can believe that. Because, you see, you have been a genius since very young, and you are still a genius, Bobby."

Day by day Palsson's power expanded. Cramer began using him as a go-between—once he dragged Palsson to Bobby's door, then knocked and ran away, leaving Palsson to raise a question he was afraid to discuss. Palsson's superiors in the Police Department were grateful. Prominent men thanked him in the name of Iceland. Reporters wrote stories about him. Beautiful girls pursued him.

But power had not translated into money. On leave from the police force in order to give full time to Bobby, Palsson was living on savings. When Bobby had his prize money, Palsson consoled himself, there would be a windfall. Meanwhile, he picked up change by selling his own autograph at 100 kronur ($1.15) a shot.

At home there was another problem. For weeks now Palsson had been giving everything to Bobby and nothing to his family. Finally his wife Asa gave him a choice: "It's me or Bobby!" Palsson talked her around but he knew that someday the decision might have to be made.

Lulled by Palsson, Bobby had almost no reaction to the Russian charges, but the rest of the chess community gulped in disbelief. "Is this a joke or something?" a wire-service correspondent asked Geller. "Statement is correct," Krogius answered bluntly. "No questions, please."

"Spassky's snapped!" gasped Schonberg of the *Times*. "Now they're *both* crazy!" Grandmaster Evans sang out that "the hall's been Bobby-trapped!" Laughter soon gave way to sadness. "Why did they do it? The whole world was rooting for Spassky. Now he's just another sore loser!" But Spassky's gallant image was so solidly established that in half an hour the press convinced itself he couldn't possibly have authorized such a vicious and stupid statement.

"This sort of thing just isn't Spassky's style," said Jim Ward of UPI. "These are criminal charges. If they're proven, Bobby could be prosecuted for conspiracy to defraud." Grandmaster Byrne agreed. "Moscow's preparing the Russian public for a defeat. They always think up some dirty excuse. Spassky must feel sick about this."

Two hours after the news broke, a tidal wave of sympathy for Spassky was rolling around the world. But sympathy revived a recurring rumor that Spassky was planning to defect. Millions were soon wondering which way Spassky would jump. Spassky had to believe the KGB was wondering too. It was one more problem for a man who already had too many.

Playing it straight, Thorarinsson ordered a scientific examination of the playing hall. Next day the stage looked like the scene of the crime in a murder movie. An assistant chief of police, a police reporter and two of the main suspects (Lombardy and Cramer) were there. So were Thorarinsson and three experts—a professor of chemistry, a lighting engineer, an X-ray technician. One of the chemist's assistants unfolded a gray plastic container about the size of a garbage bag and, striding across the stage, scooped the bag full of air. The bag was then sealed and labeled AIR FROM STAGE. The second assistant, using an absorbent cloth, wiped all the surfaces of Spassky's chair. With another cloth he wiped Bobby's chair. The cloths were then sealed in plastic bags and labeled. The evidence was transported to a laboratory and analyzed by centrifugal separation and gas chromatography.

Meanwhile a technician took X-ray pictures of each chair from eighteen different angles, and the lighting engineer took two rolls of photographs inside the overhead light fixture.

The chemist soon reported, as *The New York Times* put it, that "no alien or toxic chemicals were present in any body residue of either player." But the lighting engineer discovered foreign bodies in the fixture—two dead flies. Cramer instantly saw the possibilities. "Moscow will accuse us of conducting chemical warfare against Icelandic flies! I demand an autopsy!" The Case of the Two Dead Flies became the joke of the week. The capper was provided by Schonberg of the *Times,* who got thirsty one afternoon while he was backstage and failed to notice the two dead flies in the bottom of the glass he was drinking from. When he put the glass down, there was only one fly in it.

The X-ray technician's report posed a puzzle. "There seems to be a large metal object in the seat of Spassky's chair and there is nothing like it in Bobby's chair." Spassky's chair was ritually dismembered, but in ten hours the only anomaly discovered was a patch of artificial wood. Then the X-ray technician handed Thorarinsson a really staggering piece of news. In a second set of X rays, taken after the chair was reassembled, *the strange shape had not shown up!*

"But this means that last Friday there was something in the chair that was not there this morning!"

"I am afraid so."

Thorarinsson told the press a cock-and-bull story. Just before the match ended, he told Spassky the truth. By that time, the champion had other problems and no interest whatsoever in the Mystery of the Second Chair—which has never been solved.

Larisa Spassky, who had flown in from Moscow with the wives of Spassky's seconds on the evening of the thirteenth game, was in her early thirties, slender and shapely with straight dark hair, a large expressive mouth and big dark wide-apart eyes. For the first week Larisa and the other wives had slept in a hostelry near the Russian embassy—the team had agreed to maintain chastity until the sacred mission was accomplished. But after the break with Nei, Spassky went to live with his wife in a suburban villa.

She kept their relationship simple. In the morning, while Spassky worked at chess, she went shopping. At least once a day she cooked for him, often a Russian dish. No emotional demands. But Spassky's condition continued to worsen.

Even the public could see that there was something wrong during the eighteenth game. After pushing his first piece, Spassky sat back, turned his chair halfway toward the crowd, and stared into the darkness of the auditorium. The audience stared back. After a while Spassky seemed to focus on one face at the edge of the audience. Then, like an ape in a zoo studying the people studying him, he shifted his gaze to the next face in the row, and to the next. Three minutes later, when he got to the end of the row, he suddenly lost interest.

Bobby noticed another odd thing. "Spassky was humming and singing to himself all during the game," he told Palsson later. "Loud, y'know? He *never* does things like that. Ya think something's wrong with him?"

With the match all but won, Bobby's attention shifted from his struggle with Spassky to his struggle with Marshall. Marshall had been through a long and nerve-shredding summer. The steady commute to Reykjavik—he had made five round trips in less than two months—was enough to jounce the bolts out of a DC-8. Add to that the very heavy trip of dealing with a client who clung to him like an infant and feared him like the plague. But Marshall never gave up. He was bound to get Bobby signed to some deals before the match was over.

In Bobby, two impulses were fighting hard for mastery. One was an animal spirit that longed to take a big bite out of the world and swallow it whole. When Marshall detailed an offer of $1 million for a Fischer-Spassky return match in Las Vegas—"and you can have 100 per cent of the film and television rights too"—Bobby's eyes glowed darkly. "Not enough! I don't put my title on the line for a measly million . . . Whatever Muhammad Ali gets, I want more! I want ten million! Twenty million dollars!"

On the other hand Bobby had a shrinking spirit that made him terrified of the fame he longed for and the people who offered it. This spirit made Bobby narrow and intolerant but also fiercely pure in thought, word, deed and diet. His purity was not a virtue—it did not improve his character. It was a substitute for character, aiming his ambition and liberating his genius. He struggled to be pure because only if he was pure was he worthy to play chess. For Bobby, chess was the most blessed sacrament.

After the eighteenth game, Bobby began to emerge from the groggy lull of the hot-pot era. He had found two (count 'em) two gorgeous Icelandic girl friends.

"He is very shy," Palsson told me, "but I think a little romance is starting."

The girls were both seventeen years old. Inga was tall, slender and blond with long legs and a pleasant girlish figure. Anna was somewhat shorter and bustier. The romance had begun for the girls when they first saw Bobby's picture in the paper. "He's so handsome!" they had agreed. One day they waited several hours in the rain until Bobby arrived at the playing hall. Eventually they met Palsson and he suggested they come to the hot pots.

Both girls were wearing bikinis when they strolled into view and, according to Palsson, Bobby's eyes almost fell out of his head. After some awkward gulps, conversation began.

Bobby: "Do you play chess?"

Anna: "A little."

Bobby: "Did you see any of the games?"

Anna: "All of them."

Bobby: "Really? That's very nice."

The next time Bobby went to the pool, he asked Palsson eagerly, "Hey, Sammy, do you think those girls will be there again?" They were, and with Palsson's cooperation they turned up one night at a restaurant too. Bobby didn't let himself get too friendly. "Gotta be careful, you know, till the match is over!"

Would it ever be over? For hundreds, the match had become a way of life. Exhaustion was general. Cramer talked to himself like the little engine that could. "We'll make it! We gotta make it!" Even the burly Geller looked fifteen years older and fell asleep on his chair in the crowded lobby. Krogius sustained himself with a pile of skin magazines. Schmid was a rambling wreck.

Thorarinsson was horrified by the bills coming in. "The money we spend for food for Bobby alone would keep twenty Icelanders well nourished," he told me. "And the Russians are cheating on their expense accounts. Just like capitalists!"

Thorarinsson was even more shocked by Fox and Stein, who sued Bobby for $1.75 million and then threatened to attach his prize money. To avoid a national humiliation, Thorarinsson handed over I.C.F.'s interest in the film in return for a promise not to start legal action in Iceland.

Public insults to Bobby increased. "You fool! You fool!" a crowd shouted at him. Once a little girl ran up and spit at him. And one night Bobby's long-suffering waiter pulled a Dubinsky.

"That's enough!" the waiter snapped. "You will not address me in this way."

"Who do you think you are?" Bobby roared back.

"I am an Icelander," the man replied, "and as good as you are. Remember that!"

And then one day, after seven successive draws, the score stood Bobby 11½, Spassky 8½. For the first time Bobby could finish the match with a single victory. "He'll be gunning for this one," Byrne said. "He won't want to back into the title with another draw."

At 3 A.M. on Friday, September 1, 1972, Spassky lay in bed and stared into the drab reverse twilight of a northern dawn. In the twenty-first game, Bobby had fooled him in the opening and in irritation Spassky had sealed a move that left him less chance of drawing than Bobby had of winning. A careless fluff had cost him his last hope of leaving a stain on Bobby's triumph and a doubt in Bobby's mind. Now all he could do was go down fighting. And yet . . . did he really want to let that arrogant Bobby rip off his scalp on the stage of the playing hall while thousands cheered? Spassky decided that for his own sake and for the sake of his country he must make a more carefully managed exit.

At 1 P.M., Harry Benson dropped by the Saga. To his surprise he saw Spassky stride out of the elevator, Krogius at his heels. When he saw Benson, Spassky broke into a big smile and casually handed him the news beat of the summer.

"Hello, Hahrry! There is new world champion! I have just resigned."

Benson's face fell. "I'm sorry to hear that, Boris."

"Don't be sorry," Spassky said. "It is sporting event and"—he shrugged—"I lost. Bobby is new champion. So! Now I must have walk." And off he went.

Benson called Bobby. "Congratulations! You're the world champion."

"Yeeaah?" Bobby was pleased but suspicious. "How ya know?"

"Spassky resigned. He told me so himself."

"Ya sure?"

When Lombardy arrived, Bobby was still hunched over the analysis board, eyes blazing. "How do I know it's not a trick to make me stop workin' so *he'll* win? Tell Schmid I demand to see Spassky's resignation *in writing!*"

At 2:25, Schmid was beside himself. Almost half an hour after game time, Bobby had not shown up to claim his victory. Schmid had refused to make Spassky come to the playing hall and write the word "resigned" on his score sheet—was Bobby taking his revenge?

At 2:30, Bobby burst onstage, looking surly-shy.

"Ladies and gentlemen," Schmid announced in a sweat of relief, "Mr. Spassky has resigned it by telephone at 12:50 o'clock."

Loud applause. Bobby winced and half looked up from the score sheet he was signing.

"Mr. Fischer," Schmid continued, "has won this game . . . and he is therefore the winner of the match."

Thunderous ovation. Bobby scowled as if he wished they would all go away. The ovation faltered, then swelled into rhythmic clapping and stamping. Hastily, as if afraid all those people were coming after him, Bobby bolted through the curtain and was gone. Applause subsided into exclamations of incredulous exasperation. "You mean," an American visitor asked, "this is how it ends?"

This was how it began, the reign of King Bobby.

18

"<u>Now</u> *What Do I Do?*"

Spassky foretold the first year of Bobby's reign. "I do not know which is more bad," he said, "the match or after the match. In a long match a player shall go very deep into himself, like a diver. Then very fast he comes up. Every time, if I win or if I lose, I am so depressed I want to die. I cannot get back in touch with other people. I want the other chess player. I miss him. Only after a year the pain will go away. A year!

"I have played many long match. But this is first for Bobby. It will be for him a hard time. Now he feels like a god. He thinks all problems are over—he will have many friends, people will love him, history will obey him. But is not so. In these high places is very cold, very lonely. Soon will come depression. I like him, and I am afraid what will happen to him now."

As Bobby opened the stage door on the last day of the match, he saw hundreds of people churning between him and his transportation. A loud cheer went up, followed speedily by a loud boooooo! Asa Palsson stepped up and shook his hand. Bobby grinned and ducked into his car. On the way home he dropped his head back against the seat and let go a sigh. "Well," he said softly, "that's that."

All afternoon Bobby was as happy as a man who has just pushed a three-hundred-pound rock off his chest. He held open house for a few friends and after two months of exhausting chess all he wanted to do was play chess. "I'm surprised at Spassky," he said, "giving up that easy! There was still plenty of play in that position—these things should be played out!"

In the early evening, Bobby gave five-minute interviews to the major networks. Afterward we talked.

"Spassky's a gentleman," he said seriously. "I hated to sacrifice him but I *had* to beat the Soviet system. He's a very good player, very subtle. Lots of times I had to stop and admire some move he'd made." He looked worried. "Those Russians are *very* tough. Spassky had a real good team. Overnight they always found the best line. But now they're in trouble. Ha! Ha! This one thing, me winning the championship, did them more damage than everything they did to me in the last fourteen years. They're *demolished!*"

What did he think of Iceland? "It's a tremendous place," he said earnestly. "Nice weather, no pollution. Nice people, very friendly and honest. No prostitutes or anything. Just pretty girls. Healthy-looking. In fact, I'd really like to buy a house here."

What about Thorarinsson? "I got nothin' against him. He's probably a pretty good guy."

And playing conditions? "Very good. Considering the hall they had to work with, the Icelanders did a fantastic job."

When we talked about the future his expression clouded. "I wanna play a lot of chess. The Russians only put the title on the line once every three years. That's bad for chess. I'm gonna play every six months, maybe more often. Aside from that, I don't know. I never had this question of goals before. All my life I knew what I wanted. To be champion, right? Well, I made it." He shook his head irritably. *"Now what do I do?"*

Two days later, on Sunday September 3, I.C.F. held the prize ceremony in the playing hall. Icelanders said it was the island's biggest brawl since the Christian converts threw all the worshipers of Odin off a cliff. At eleven dollars a head, more than two thousand people attended. The menu featured wild Icelandic mountain lamb, spit-roasted and served by waiters wearing plastic Viking helmets, and a drink called Viking's blood (red wine, cognac, orange juice and Seven-Up served in a glass shaped like a mead horn).

Dinner was scheduled for 7 P.M. Bobby was keen to get there but first he had a photographic session with Benson and me. Then he heard that his sister and two of her children who had returned to Iceland specially to congratulate him, were at the hall for the prize ceremony.

"*What?* I didn't say she could go! Bill, you go over to the hall right away and *get her out of there!*"

Lombardy drove to the hall but managed to look for Joan where she wasn't.

At 7:45, Thorarinsson decided to start without the guest of honor. At 7:55, Bobby charged into the hall through the wrong entrance and stumbled through an obstacle course of charcoal pits and steam trays. He was wearing a new blue corduroy suit and for the second time that summer strode past Spassky without seeing him. Euwe gently indicated the ex-champion. "Oh, hi," Bobby said. They soon had their heads in Bobby's chess wallet.

"I sealed the wrong move," Spassky said.

"You'da lost," Bobby assured him, laughing, "no matter what you sealed."

Then came the coronation. Summoned to the stage, Bobby was handed a gold medal and a check for $78,125. He was also circled by a large wreath made of an ordinary life preserver to which some Icelandic bushes had been stapled. Lifting his horsey jaw and grinning toothily, Bobby looked like a prize colt at Aqueduct. When Euwe congratulated him, he giggled.

When Spassky was called to the stage to take his silver medal there were tears in his eyes. The crowd gave him a foot-stamping, name-chanting ovation twice as loud and long as their applause for Bobby. As soon as good manners permitted, Spassky left. "Goodbye, Bobby," were his last words. "Be good champ."

The speeches over, hundreds of boozy Icelanders rushed Bobby's table and demanded his autograph. A circle of the faithful formed around Bobby and for more than an hour a physical battle raged. Now and then Bobby gave a few palliative autographs. "Te'l 'em if they bother me any more, I'll go home!" he sulked.

Palsson brought Bobby's two seventeen-year-old girl friends to his table. While thousands gaped and the cameras rolled, Bobby showed them his trophies. Then at the first slow number, Bobby steered the tall blonde to the dance floor. A gasp swept the hall. "*Bobby er ad dansa!*" It was as if a cow had jumped over the moon.

Bobby and his party were the last guests to leave. On the way back to the hotel he took out his check and squinted at it under the streetlamps.

Bobby stayed two more weeks in Iceland. He was guest of honor at a party given by Iceland's president and sent Spassky a goodbye present—a thirty-five-dollar camera. One day, to Bobby's dismay, his mother arrived. He made frantic efforts to conceal her presence and identity. About the same time he took a notion that he might be the next target of the Palestinian terrorists who had attacked the Olympic Village. Davis demanded protection. There were twenty-three Arabs in Iceland at the time, and the Icelandic police put a tail on every one of them.

There was more news about Chester Fox. All through the match Fox and Stein had gloated privately over their ace in the hole: a secret videotape of the match captured from the closed-circuit TV system. But on the last day of the match, when Fox showed up to collect his tapes, the engineer who had made them said Fox could have them when he paid the bill. Fox blew his stack and in the hearing of hostile witnesses called the man a liar and a thief. The engineer swore that Fox would never get those tapes—which were worth at least $200,000 in potential rentals. They sit today in an Icelandic bank vault, a complete, high-quality film of the match that may never be shown.

Flightseeing, salmon-fishing, pony-riding, having dinner with Anna and Inga—Bobby and Palsson now spent every waking hour together. It was hard to tell which was the parasite, which the host. "Sammy's been a real help to me," Bobby told Iceland's president. "Without him I mighta lost the match!" He told Palsson he wanted him to come live in the States and be his bodyguard there. Palsson agreed to go back with Bobby, and persuaded Asa to come along and look the situation over.

Bobby left Iceland on September 15 at 7:35 in the evening. He kept the plane and more than a hundred passengers waiting on the runway for almost an hour and a half before takeoff.

Spassky stayed in Reykjavik a full week after the prize ceremony. Larisa took him shopping and by the end of the week had stacked her husband's new Range Rover to the roof with Western gadgets. Spassky spent the days in a funk. By the time he landed at Moscow's Vnukovo Airport, he was acutely depressed. No officials met him. He was driven home by friends. All summer long he had been attacked in the Soviet press, and after his return the attacks became virulent.

Vengeance was exacted in other ways. Spassky was refused permission to travel or play tournaments abroad. There were threats to subject his winnings to a confiscatory income tax, to cancel his foreign-credit account, to kick him out of his four-room flat, to send him on arduous chess tours of the provinces. He was publicly accused of goofing off when he should have been training and his charges of electrochemical neurosabotage were privately censured.

In the end, Spassky was not severely punished because the Soviet chess bosses believed he was still their only hope of knocking the American eagle off his perch. Spassky repaired his relation with Bondarevsky, and in June 1973, ten months after the match ended, he was at last permitted to play abroad. In a one-week tournament in West Germany, he finished in a three-way tie for first place.

I spent two days with him after the tournament ended. He was a picture of roaring health—fuller in face and chest, tanned all over, glowing like a beach boy. But the minute we spoke of Reykjavik, his fine eyes veiled. "It is very painful for me," he said, "to speak of this match. So many things happened to me that I do not understand. It is frightening to think of these things. For me it is not over yet. There is a closed door. I do not go into that room."

But the match had done more than damage Spassky. "In this terrible fire," a friend says, "I think he was refined. He is less self-indulgent now. He takes better care of himself and of his marriage." In my opinion Spassky was now living for one thing—revenge. On the wall of his apartment in Vyesnina Street hung a large photograph of Bobby Fischer. Often he stood and studied it. Sometimes he spoke to it. For the first time in his life he was totally involved in chess, and the involvement produced startling results.

In November 1973, he won the year's strongest tournament, the National Championship of the Soviet Union, by a wide margin. In January 1974, he trounced grandmaster Robert Byrne 3–0 in the first of three elimination matches in the 1975 World Championship cycle. "If he keeps on playing this well," said an American grandmaster, "there's a strong chance he'll be sitting across the table from Bobby in 1975."

But it was not to be. Overconfident, Spassky failed to prepare in sufficient depth for his second elimination match. He was drubbed, 4–1, by a 23-year-old economics student named Anatoly Karpov. Tiny and frail but with nerves like tendons, Karpov is the most formidable young grandmaster to appear since Bobby burst out of Brooklyn. Though his repertory is not yet complete, Karpov rarely makes even small mistakes and his chess ideas have astonishing depth and originality. "Karpov is developing at fantastic speed," says one of his grandmaster victims. "He is totally realistic and totally determined to win the championship—and the Russian establishment will spend millions of rubles to make sure he does." If Karpov gets past Victor Korchnoi in the third round, Bobby in 1975 will face the full power of the Soviet Union marshaled for revenge.

Thorarinsson had his problems too. Faced with the sad fact that the match did not make money because I.C.F.'s deal with Fox and Stein came a-cropper, Thorarinsson's colleagues found it convenient to blame him for the financial failure and to forget that without his strength and political ingenuity the match that put Iceland on the map would never have happened. After a year-long whispering campaign, the Icelandic electorate turned Thorarinsson out of office.

Back in the States, Bobby and the Palssons stayed with the Marshalls for six weeks. How did it go? "Let us say," Marshall observed, "that it was a mistake. Bobby is not your perfect guest."

Bobby declined Mayor Lindsay's offer of a tickertape parade ("I don't believe in hero worship"). Of the many honors offered him, New York City's medal of honor was the only one he accepted. After some hesitation, he decided to appear on the Bob Hope show in Los Angeles and at the last minute asked the Palssons to fly west with him. Asa made a stand. "I'm going back to Iceland. If you go with Bobby, don't expect me to be waiting for you. I've got four children and I want a man who puts his family first." Palsson decided to go with Bobby.

He headed for L.A. with high hopes. As Bobby's bodyguard he would meet Bob Hope, maybe appear on the show, maybe even get a chance to sing and dance! All his old dreams of a show-biz career came surging on—and then crashed. Before the show, Bobby neglected to tell Hope that Palsson was with him; after the show, Hope said, "Oh, too bad! If I'd known, we'd have used him!" Then Palsson was locked out of his hotel room because Bobby was late paying the bill. A little later, in San Francisco, he was attacked by three muggers. After a month of disappointments, Palsson told Bobby he had to go home. He was hoping Bobby would urge him to stay and offer him a salary. Instead, as payment for more than four months of devoted full-time service, Bobby gave Palsson a check for three hundred dollars.

Six weeks after winning the championship, Bobby vanished. The world lay at his feet. He was about to become "the first chess millionaire"—Marshall said he had $10 million worth of record deals, TV specials, book contracts and product endorsements in the offing. Then without warning or explanation, Bobby abandoned the game that had made him famous and went to ground in a closely guarded California compound operated by the extremist sect of his choice. "He's flipped again!" said Marshall, but Bobby didn't think so. He thought he was fooling all those people who wanted to exploit him.

Though Bobby is not a full church member, the Worldwide Church of God welcomed him as its most glamorous "co-worker." Bobby in return offered Herbert Armstrong a double tithe (20 per cent) of his $156,250 winnings. "Ah, my boy, that's just as God would have it!" Armstrong replied, and passed the word that Bobby was to be given VIP treatment.

For a starter, Armstrong offered Bobby the services of the church's own high-powered general counsel, Stanley Rader. A few days later Marshall received his reward for nine months of devoted effort—a notice that Rader was replacing him as Bobby's attorney. Marshall shrugged. "Why cry? I always knew he was a schmuck." But Rader had no better luck persuading Bobby to cash in on his celebrity. In the next eighteen months Bobby made only one major deal—with a record company—and that fell through. When a Las Vegas promoter offered him $1.4 million and all rights for a return match with Spassky, Bobby sniffed, "Ten million would be better." Meanwhile, friends said, he was living off the remains of his prize money—of which at least two-thirds was reportedly sopped up by tithes and taxes.

The church offered Bobby a pleasant three-bedroom apartment in a church-owned development. He was invited to use the gymnasium, squash court and swimming pool of the church's Ambassador College, and high officials of the Armstrong organization were told to make sure Bobby had plenty of dinner invitations. "The word went out," says a church member, "that Bobby should never be left alone." As Bobby's personal recreation director, the church assigned a weight lifter in the phys. ed. department whose manner was almost as obliging as Palsson's. The two of them played paddle tennis almost every day, and Bobby worked out with weights to build up his arms and torso.

The reason soon became clear. Bobby confessed to a high church official that he wanted to meet some girls. There is a rigid rule against dating between church members and nonmembers, but in Bobby's case the rule was suspended. What sort of girls did he like? Bobby said he liked "vivacious" girls with "big breasts." Later the official was heard anxiously asking a colleague, "Who have we got that's vivacious and has big breasts?" Most Ambassador College coeds dress and talk like the girl who lived next door to Andy Hardy, but a suitable young lady was found and Bobby began to date her frequently—chaperoned of course by the weight lifter and his wife. When Bobby's companion got too serious, another church member with appropriate attributes was brought forward. And another.

Dating was so much fun that for six months Bobby forgot almost everything else—even chess. He saw hardly any of his chess friends and for the first time in his life stopped studying the game. When a message came that Henry Kissinger wanted to have dinner with him, Bobby said, "Naa, I'm too busy." He was playing the big fish in a little pond, and not all the inhabitants of the pond were pleased when he was admitted to Bible classes strictly reserved for full church members, or when he was flown to Texas in the founder's jet. The weight lifter complained secretly that the expense of entertaining Bobby, who seldom picks up a check, had become intolerable. A church official said the champ should be encouraged to spend more time with people his own age who would not be impressed by his celebrity.

"People around here are too restricted in what they can say and do," Bobby suddenly objected, and took off to Denver with some disaffected church members. Was he leaving the Armstrongites and returning to chess? In October 1973, Bobby showed up at a major chess tournament in Manila as the personal guest of President Ferdinand Marcos—but he didn't play. He hardly put his head out of the Hyatt Regency's Presidential Suite, and when he did he was festooned with secret agents.

The prodigal was soon back in Pasadena, but now he saw hardly anyone but the weight lifter and his wife. Dating slowed to a stop. Bobby kept the shades in his apartment drawn, slept till late afternoon, stayed up all night, listened to shortwave radio, read *The New York Times* and an occasional skin magazine—and gradually, for the first time in more than a year, got back to studying chess.

Brooding alone, Bobby began to set traps for the man he will play for the championship in 1975. First, he fired off a telegram to the

International Chess Federation protesting that six victories were too few to decide a championship match. Ten, he said, would be more like it. "He's looking for insurance," said grandmaster Larry Evans. "In a short match a cold streak could beat him. In a long match Bobby figures his energy and talent will tell." Then Bobby set another trap. If the score reached 9–9, he said, the match should be called a draw and the champion allowed to retain the title. "What he's really saying," Evans pointed out, "is that the challenger would have to win by at least two points, 10–8."

Bobby made even more bizarre demands—about fifty of them. He wanted free inspection trips to proposed match sites, a gag rule prohibiting the match referee from speaking to reporters, a special pair of tiny pawns more easily palmed during the drawing ceremony, the right to eject the cameras whenever he pleased. Worried by the epidemic of political kidnapings, he demanded elaborate and expensive police protection.

Wheeling and dealing, Edmondson persuaded a F.I.D.E. congress to grant all but one of Bobby's major demands. When the delegates refused to lift the 36-game limit, Bobby abruptly resigned as champion. F.I.D.E. meekly asked him to reconsider.

"Whee!" said Marshall. "Here we go again." Chess officials were less amused.

"He's backed way off from reality again," said a man who spent time with him in the spring of 1974. "Seeing almost nobody, living in fantasies. Everywhere he looks he finds enemies. Lawyers are crooks, chess people want to use him. He doesn't trust the church any more. After dating all those goody-goody college girls, he's decided girls are a waste of time too. He's right back where he was when he was seventeen, daydreaming about automobiles."

I remembered a talk we once had.

"I'm gonna get a really good car, y'know?" he told me, leaning back dreamily. "Not one of these big American junk heaps, like a Cadillac or a Lincoln. I mean a *Mercedes* or *Rolls-Royce.*" He crooned the names. "You think maybe a Rolls-Royce is a little —uh—pretentious? Maybe people would think I was—like acting ritzy? Maybe I better *start out* with a Mercedes. One of those *big* Mercedes, y'know? Costs around ten, twelve thousand. Leather seats, mahogany, like, on the dashboard, automatic shift. And any time I felt like it I could throw my stuff in the back and take off, y'know, anywhere I wanted. A car really gives you freedom, right? Yeeaahh

... I could drive along..." He was dreaming up a storm now. "Did you ever drive along and see some girl standing at the side of the road, hitchhiking? Did you ever stop and pick one up? Do you think it's safe? I think it would be all right, don't you? I mean, you could meet a nice girl that way, right? And some of them are *beooodyful!* Ha! Ha!" His mouth gaped wide as he laughed. "I mean it would be adventurous, right?"

Acknowledgments

The summer of '72 was one of those moments when life imitated art. Sometimes it seemed that The Author of Us All—part Sophocles, part Mel Brooks—had decided to write, produce and direct the damnedest happening that ever happened. More often it seemed that Bobby Fischer was in full charge of everything and everybody.

I want to thank Bobby for this book—without him, nothing it describes would have happened.

I also want to thank everyone Bobby drew into the vortex of his demon—all the people who appear in the pages of this book and dozens who do not. They gave me hundreds of interviews that took up hundreds of hours. More essential, they gave me the chance to lean in close and watch them live.

I cannot thank them all here but I must expressly thank Gudmundur Thorarinsson, Fred Cramer, Paul Marshall, Andrew Davis, Ed Edmondson, Frank Skoff, Saemundur Palsson, Boris Spassky, Chester Fox, Richard Stein, Jack and Ethel Collins, Joan Targ, Bill Lombardy, Larry Evans, Robert Byrne, Lubomir Kavalek, Arthur Bisguier, Isaac Kashdan, Don Schultz, Frank Brady, Milunka Lazarevich, I. S. Turover, George Koltanowski, James Slater, David Frost, Leonard Barden, Nicholas Bethell, Hans Indridason, Tedd Hope, Bob Hallowell, Herb Hochstetter, Morris Dubinsky and the Saidy family.

I would like to thank Ralph Graves and Richard Stolley of *Life* for assigning me to the Bobby Fischer story and for supporting the project through many vicissitudes; Arthur Kretchmer and David Butler of *Playboy* for the courage of their convictions; Harry Benson for being a superb reporter as well as a great photographer; Kristjan

Arngrimsson for being an imaginative and tireless interpreter and facilitator; Sigridur Hallgrimsdottir for contributing valuable insights and a dozen important interviews; Grace Harrington for two years of ransacking newspapers and magazines for articles about chess; my agent, Dick Curtis, for his energetic persistence; my lawyers, Charles Rembar and Frank Curtis, for much practical wisdom; my publisher, Sol Stein, for his daring and imagination; my editor, Michaela Hamilton, for her strong sense of the whole book and her scrupulous loyalty to its best interests.

To my family I feel a special gratefulness. I suspect that most books are family productions; this one certainly was. My brother Robert, my oldest and closest friend, gave till it hurt to keep the project afloat. My wife and children, making do for months with half a husband and half a father, brought me tea, sympathy and on occasion, razzberries. I want especially to thank Jack and Betsy for all their help with Xeroxing and proofreading; without them we could never have got those jobs done on time. And finally, what can I say to the young woman who for months on end stalled creditors, called repairmen, made banquets out of leftovers, carted children to doctors, dentists, museums, music lessons and stamp dealers, drove 200 miles a week to college and ballet classes, wrote a novel, read and discussed every scene in this manuscript and typed it at least four times—for free. Thank you, Sue.